# REPRESSION AND MOBILIZATION

# Social Movements, Protest, and Contention

**Series Editor:** Bert Klandermans, Free University, Amsterdam

**Associate Editors:** Ron R. Aminzade, University of Minnesota
David S. Meyer, University of California, Irvine
Verta A. Taylor, University of California, Santa Barbara

*For more books in the series, see page 000.*

# REPRESSION AND MOBILIZATION

Christian Davenport,
Hank Johnston, and
Carol Mueller, Editors

Social Movements, Protest, and Contention
Volume 21

 University of Minnesota Press
Minneapolis • London

Published by the University of Minnesota Press
111 Third Avenue South, Suite 290
Minneapolis, MN 55401-2520
http://www.upress.umn.edu

# Contents

Introduction

# Repression and Mobilization: Insights from Political Science and Sociology

*Christian Davenport*

The events of September 11, 2001, raised numerous issues. It made us initially think about terrorism, terror, and loss; later, it made us think about revenge, strategic bombing, and Islam; later still, it made us think about protest policing, freedom, democracy, and recovery. Are we prepared for such thinking and policy formation/analysis? Are the interactions and complexities involved well enough comprehended to provide some basis for understanding—especially those relevant to state–dissident relations, the core of the whole issue?

In many respects, we are well prepared for this line of inquiry. For approximately thirty years scholars have been investigating the relationship between dissidents and dissent, on the one hand, and authorities and protest policing (or political repression), on the other. From this work, we have a general sense of what tactics will be used on both sides (e.g., violent as well as nonviolent activities), and a sense of what provokes violent behavior—again, on both sides (e.g., political opportunities, mobilizing structures and ideological frames); we have some insights into what aftereffects are most likely (e.g., escalation, adaptation/substitution, de-escalation, fear, paranoia, and community development); and we have some idea about where to look for information (e.g., the international, national, and local media).

In other respects, however, we are not at all well prepared. Most of the existing research on the subject ignores certain types of behavior (e.g., covert and less institutional activity); it has ignored the multidimensionality and temporal complexity in explaining contentious politics (addressing the fact that multiple things occur simultaneously across time and space);

it has ignored the bias and difficulties with obtaining information from a variety of frequently conflicting sources about what has taken place; and it has even ignored the role of this information in creating as well as sustaining conflict itself.

In the summer of 2001, approximately thirty political scientists and sociologists convened at the University of Maryland to assess what we knew collectively as a subfield about mobilization and repression and where we should go in the future to improve our understanding. The experience was simultaneously enlightening and frustrating. On the one hand, we had a tremendous amount of information and substantive knowledge available. A large number of studies had been conducted, which varied across time (from the late 1700s to the present), space (from Boston to Belarus), and methodology (from case studies to formal models), as well as substantive interest (from civil war and genocide to everyday resistance). On the other hand, there was a tremendous amount of variability in the empirical results from these analyses and the attention that was given to the subject was somewhat imbalanced across topic areas. For example, confronted with state repression, dissidents have been found to run away (e.g., White 1993), fight harder (e.g., Eckstein 1965; Feirabend and Feirabend 1972; Gurr and Duvall 1973; Ziegenhagen 1986; Koran 1990; Khawaja 1993; Francisco 1996), and alternatively run away or fight harder (e.g., Bwy 1968; Gurr 1969; Gupta and Venieris 1981; Lichbach and Gurr 1981; Weede 1987; Rasler 1996; Moore 1998)—varying according to political-economic context. Additionally, work has been found where there is no response whatsoever.[1] Moving in the opposite direction, from protest to repression, only one relationship has ever been identified: dissent increases the application of state coercion—again, varying according to political-economic context.[2]

Why have the findings varied within the former line of inquiry but not in the second? Are we really confused about the impact of repression on mobilization? Is there nothing that is unclear about why repressive behavior is applied? What should we focus on? Our initial impressions provided an interesting point of departure.

## We're Mad as Hell and We're Not Going to Take It Anymore: From Repression to Mobilization

In a recent survey of the literature, Johnston and Mueller (2001) maintain that historically

> the inconclusiveness of [the results concerning repression's impact on dissent stem] from a variety of factors: too heavy a reliance on the World

Handbook of Social and Political Indicators (Brockett 1992); measures of
repression that more appropriately reflect system characteristics such as police expenditures or size of the armed forces rather than state sponsorship
of repression (Koopmans 1997, 152–53); the failure to use longitudinal
measures (Hoover and Kowalewski (1992, 156); and the rarity of data sets
complex enough to test mathematical modeling of the repression-protest
relationship (Gupta et al. 1987; Hoover and Kowalewski 1992).

Scholars in the field have not ignored such criticisms. Within the last decade individuals have:

1. used alternative data sources (e.g., Francisco 1996, 1998; McCarthy,
   McPhail, and Smith 1996; Bond et al. 1997; Mueller 1997; Beissinger
   1998; Davenport 1998, 1999a; Moore 1998),
2. used more direct indicators of repressive activity (identifying specific
   rates/acts [e.g., Francisco 1996; Krain 1997; Moore 1998] as opposed
   to some measure of coercive capacity),
3. employed longitudinal data (e.g., Bond and Bond 1995; Francisco
   1996; Beissinger 1998),
4. applied more complex mathematical modeling techniques (e.g., Francisco and Lichbach 2001),
5. investigated the importance of diverse contextual factors (e.g., Gupta,
   Singh, and Sprague 1993; Davenport 1999b; Carey 2001),
6. explored the importance of lagged influences (e.g., Rasler 1996), and
7. competitively evaluated alternative hypotheses (e.g., Moore 1998).

These analyses have allowed us (very recently and very tentatively) to
make some important strides in our understanding about how state repression influences dissent.

For example, Moore (1998) has investigated three explanations for the
impact of repressive behavior on protest: Lichbach's (1987) argument that
challengers substitute violent for nonviolent activity, Gupta et al.'s (1993)
argument that regime type influences the relationship between repression
and mobilization, and Rasler's (1996) argument that repression has both
instantaneous and lagged effects. Within the analysis, Moore finds that empirical evidence supports the first hypothesis but not the others.[3] Dissidents
are thus more likely to alter their repertoire when confronted with repression, and those who do not disaggregate their measures of dissent will
likely find contradictory results. The "war on terrorism" and "Homeland
Security" may thus decrease suicide bombing but increase assassinations,
and if one does not consider the occurrence of bombings, assassinations,

hijackings, and other strategies simultaneously, then they will misunderstand the effectiveness of protest policing efforts in particular and what is taking place in general.

Despite such developments, however, questions still remain. Three in particular are worthy of mention.

First, certain types of protest and repression are still ignored by existing literature on mobilization. We are very much fixated on certain behaviors that take place in certain locales, ignoring the possibility that repressive behavior may ignite still other forms of mobilization that fall underneath our "radar screen." Specifically, we are generally interested in public, overt, large-scale manifestations of contentious politics (e.g., the World Trade Center attacks and subsequent mass detentions). In the public domain, we tend to ignore the less obvious forms of dissent such as "everyday resistance" (e.g., statements made by Al Qaeda before the crisis in informal, nonpublicized venues [e.g., Scott 1985]) and the less obvious forms of repression such as nonstate sanctions (e.g., the numerous instances where individual citizens in the United States attacked or insulted individuals who were believed to be of Arab descent both before and after the September 11 attacks). Indeed, as traditionally researched, these diverse actions would never be placed together in the same analysis (if they were studied at all).

Second, it is not clear how much confidence we should have with the existing empirical results. At present, there is a great need for the replication of analyses within diverse contexts (e.g., within the context of authoritarian regimes) and with diverse methodological approaches (e.g., case studies in conjunction with quantitative analyses). Most individuals analyze only one case or dataset, generally the one that they have studied for quite some time (frequently with one series of hypotheses) and one that they have compiled themselves. Such practices generate important insights (as they are most familiar with the strengths and weaknesses), but at the same time they move against the accumulation of knowledge. As a result, existing research does not inspire a tremendous amount of faith in the relationships identified as the importance of selection bias, and a host of other problems can never be explored (this is especially the case in a context where databases are not made publicly available and where no other scholar uses the relevant information).

Third, while there is an increased use of newspaper-generated data (e.g., Rummel 1964, 1996; Tilly, Tilly, and 1975; Tarrow 1989; Kriesi et al. 1992; Gurr 1993; Koopmans 1995; Tilly 1995; Beissinger 1998; Francisco 1998; Hocke 1998), there also has been a corresponding decrease in the faith of such information (e.g., Snyder and Kelly 1977; Jackman and Boyd 1979; Brockett 1992; McCarthy, McPhail, and Smith 1996; Mueller 1997; Hocke 1998; Oliver and Myers 1999; Davenport and Ball 2002). Unfortunately, little effort is made to better understand newspapers as they influence our comprehension of contentious political relations,[4] and little effort is made to identify or examine the effects of media coverage on mobilization itself; we tend to look at media coverage as a simplistic information-gathering and distribution process and as a by-product of contention and not the other way around.

### Threats and Consequences: From Mobilization to Repression

Our understanding of the repression–mobilization nexus is further complicated when one acknowledges that the impact of repression on mobilization represents only one-half of the relationship—albeit the more frequently studied component. When one reverses the causal arrow, one is confronted with another layer of the paradox: the stability of empirical findings. When confronted with protest behavior, government authorities have been shown consistently to apply some form of state repression—the magnitude of the application varying in accordance with the political-economic context involved (e.g., Hibbs 1973; Ziegenhagen 1986; Mitchell and McCormick 1988; Davis and Ward 1990; Poe and Tate 1994; Davenport 1995, 1999b; Krain 1997; Poe, Tate, and Keith 1999; Zanger 2000).[5] Subject to many of the same limitations as those identified by Johnston and Mueller (2001), within this context one is immediately led to ask: what accounts for the stability of the impact of mobilization on repression? Several answers exist.

First, one could maintain that historically there have been fewer data sources available for repressive behavior and thus investigations are similar because the same data was employed (e.g., Hibbs 1973; Ziegenhagen 1986; Davenport 1995; 1999b; and King 2000 all use the *World Handbook for Political and Social Indicators* [Taylor and Jodice 1983]).[6] This situation has changed over time with the development of other databases (e.g., Mitchell and McCormick 1988; Henderson 1991; Poe and Tate 1994; Fein 1995; Francisco 1998; Moore and Lindstrom 1998), which identify the same exact relationships and thus this cannot be the case. Second, one could maintain that there has been a greater amount of methodological conformity as many analyses have used OLS (Ordinary Least Squares) regression (e.g., Poe and Tate 1994; Davenport 1995). Again, numerous other methodological techniques have been used that confirm the same relationships (e.g., case studies [Goldstein 1978, 1983]; negative binomial regression [Krain 1997]; Vector Auto-regression [Zanger 2000]) and thus this cannot be the case either. Third, one could argue that there is simply greater stability in the government's decision-making process relative to social movement organizations, and, consequently, regardless of what time period and what context one observes, one is likely to find the same relationships. Given the fact that regime change is rare and that most political leaders stay in power for quite some time, this argument is perhaps the most defensible.

Upon reflection, the strengths of this work (stability and general uniformity) also turn out to be its greatest weaknesses. Similar to the previous discussion on dissent, certain aspects of repression are ignored: political and civil liberties as well as personal integrity violations are the only forms of coercion considered by the individuals in this area. The behavior of executives, National Guard personnel, the military, and police has been studied extensively, but no attention has been given to the secret service, militias, NGOs, or private citizens. In the context of democratic societies, which normally reduces the presence of overtly coercive organizations within society, this is especially problematic.

This line of inquiry is also limited because, although the community of scholars involved in the area is small, researchers do not address one another's work: for example, the quantitative and qualitative literature rarely consults the other and the interaction between sociologists and political scientists is minimal.[7] This becomes particularly detrimental for our overall understanding of what is taking place out in the world because in certain circumstances (as with the impact of democracy and democratization on state repression and dissent) the findings vary significantly across different research communities.[8]

Finally, the greatest criticism that can be leveled against literature concerning the impact of mobilization on repression (but also some of the work identified earlier) is the question of relevance or the "so what" question. What are the theoretical and/or practical implications of the relationship for democracy, state building, and freedom? How is the rest of social science, and society for that matter, impacted by the different findings identified here? On these questions, we have made very little progress (e.g., McCamant 1984).

Historically, the reasons for investigating the impact of mobilization on repression appeared to be clear: individuals subject to repression and civil war were dying (frequently in large numbers) and thus by definition the subject was important. Additionally, when individuals engage in protest they are engaging in one of the most direct forms of political expression, and therefore (again) by definition the subject was important. Unfortunately, this normative emphasis on the preservation of human life and freedom of expression has not been linked to other areas of research and, as a consequence, the implications of the repression–mobilization nexus for social science and society in general have been ignored—to the detriment of the subfield in terms of grants, publications, interesting graduate students, and educating a broader audience about why they need to understand such matters.[9]

Of course, all of this was before September 11. After these events, individuals understood the importance of examining the subject. As everyone now realizes, mobilization (below the threshold of civil war) can take lives at significant levels. It is also clear that when states look for "dissidents," they involve much of the population within their territorial jurisdiction as they attempt to figure out where the challengers are located, who they are, whom they interact with, who supports them, where they were engaged in dissent in the past, and where they might go in the future. In short, repression and mobilization have wide-ranging impacts on citizens lives, influencing multiple domains simultaneously.

## The Relationship: Components and Dynamics

Revisiting the repression–mobilization nexus, I wish to refocus as well as expand the parameters of the debate. I begin by first outlining what is believed to be the most fruitful way of conceptualizing the relationship between dissidents and state authorities. Following this, I identify how the Maryland conference has challenged, altered, and improved our understanding of the topic.

## Why Groups Rebel and Why States Coerce

The best place to begin is with an understanding of the underlying causal model utilized by scholars in the field (this is provided in Figure I.1). Because of the substantive interest in one form of behavior or another and the methodological sophistication required to study simultaneous relationships, few efforts have been extended to identify how the two are related to each other (e.g., Hibbs 1973; Eberwein 1983; Hoover and Kowalewski 1992). It is important to bring the two together, however, for there are just too may intersections to be ignored. When such an effort is conducted, one can clearly see where some of the earlier examinations have been deficient. Such a model begins within each respective domain (i.e., mobilization and repression), influenced by numerous aspects of the other part of the model (i.e., repression and mobilization—as well as other factors). Each is discussed in what follows.

As most researchers on mobilization have identified, dissent is largely a function of three factors: cultural frames, mobilizing structures, and political opportunity structure (e.g., McAdam, McCarthy, and Zald 1996). The

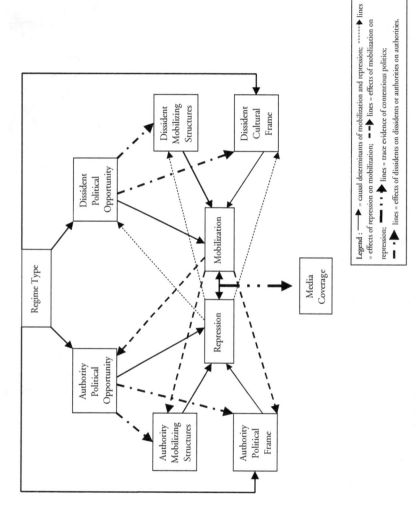

Figure I.1. The linkages between repression and mobilization—the basic story

first provides the ideological motivation for claims making, group identity, and group action; the second provides the means for taking action; and the third provides the "perceived" opportunity within which groups can engage in contentious politics (without much cost). As theorized, when these three conditions exist, sustained mobilization is likely to occur.

Although using different labels, many researchers within the field of state repression have identified similar factors and for the same reasons. It is through the combination of all these that one can understand why coercive actions take place. For example, instead of discussing "cultural frames," repressive scholars normally use government "ideology" as they attempt to pinpoint the motivation for group identity and action (e.g., Pion-Berlin 1989). Some even speak of the "ethos" of coercive institutions in their efforts to understand repressive behavior (e.g., Laswell 1941; Gurr 1986a, 1986b). Similarly, "mobilizing structures" are generally discussed within the context of very specific organizations: political institutions (e.g., Gibson 1988), military organizations (e.g., Stanley 1996), police squads (e.g, Donner 1990; Davenport 2001), and secret police/"intelligence" organizations (e.g., Churchill and Vander Wall 1990; Cunningham 2002). The third explanatory factor, political opportunity structure, is also discussed within the repression literature but with the label "political threat," which is defined as the perceived necessity for state repression in an effort to counter challengers who (left alone) could alter some form of the political-economic system. Opportunity thus is reframed as necessity; authorities act not because they can but because they must. Another variation of the political opportunity structure argument (more similar to the protest literature) is provided most clearly by literature on covert repressive action (e.g., Churchill and Vander Wall 1990; Donner 1990; Cunningham 2002); here, "opportunities" are moments of weakness within social movement organizations that must be exploited in order to bring about the end of the challenging organizations. In this case, authorities act because they can and because the costs are low.

## States and Dissidents

In this model, there are three ways in which repression and mobilization influence one another, each of which has received varied amounts of attention within the literature and also within the conference.

The first and most direct relationship concerns the interaction between repression and dissent itself. This concerns the relationship where agents of the state confront agents of claims making—for example, when police confront protesters at a rally, when guerrillas confront paramilitary forces during insurgency, and when the Secret Service raids a radical group's headquarters. Many analyses of repression and mobilization, especially those within the quantitative tradition, investigate this type of behavior as their studies are focused on the examination of overt group activity. Indeed, it is within this context that the repression–mobilization paradox was born.

One level removed from this relationship is the impact of repression and protest on the support system for the other behavior. Here, repression influences dissident mobilizing structures and cultural frames, which in turn influences dissent, or, alternatively, mobilization influences the authority's mobilizing structures and cultural frames, which in turn influences repressive behavior. In this work, there is less discussion about battles in the street. Rather, one would find discussion about the impact of specific behavior on organizational membership—changes in the morale of the organization, the willingness to act, defection to the other side, and so forth.[10]

Finally, one has the impact of contentious behavior undertaken by one actor on the political opportunity structure (POS) of the other. This relationship concerns the impact of repression and dissent on the perceived opportunity for dissidents and authorities, respectively. The category is separated from the previous one—despite the common practice of discussing opportunity structures with mobilizing structures and cultural frames—because of the temporal factor involved. For example, it is expected that political opportunity structure changes more slowly than mobilizing structures and that cultural frames would be located somewhere between the two. The impact on POS is important because it is clearly the case that repression and mobilization can influence external funding for relevant organizations, as well as the willingness of everyday citizens to assist the actors involved (either explicitly by enlisting or implicitly by not getting in the way).

The media is also an important topic for discussion within the context of repression and mobilization because it is frequently one of the main targets for mobilization and one of the main sources relied on by scholars to understand what is taking place when authorities and dissidents engage (e.g., McCarthy, McPhail, and Smith 1996; Wolfsfeld 1997; Hocke 1998; Davenport and Ball 2002). There are two ways that one could view the newspaper-contention interaction. In the first, the media conditions the activities of challengers and authorities by communicating to them what type of behavior is likely to be covered. Of course, the impact of this conditioning varies in accordance with what social movements and governments wish to achieve. If there is no consideration with the audience that newspapers reach, then relevant actors are more likely to do what they wish (this is especially the case if the dissidents have their own newspaper, as in the case of the Black Panther Party [Davenport 1998]). In the second, the media is merely a receptacle for what transpires in society, reporting events that occur out in the world for a particular audience. Of course, not all events are covered. Media coverage of contentious politics is influenced by several factors: for example, magnitude, violence, bizarre, prior announcement, and the size of the paper itself. With such information, researchers are able to identify and systematically investigate contentious politics: examining origins, dynamics, and the conditions of cessation.

## Searching for Answers (and a Little Clarity)

The Maryland conference was convened against the backdrop of the conceptual model (and research) identified earlier. This framework had been in part created by many of the participants within their previous work, and, at the same time, many of these individuals were involved with rigorously examining the model's components and in numerous situations dramatically challenging what had long been accepted.

The combination of research traditions (across political science and sociology, as well as across qualitative and quantitative methodologies) turned out to be extremely important because the degree of sophistication with which each community analyzed the topic significantly advanced the others' understanding of the larger field. As a result, states and social movements were discussed in a manner that was not easily visible within earlier work; cases were introduced that were generally not considered in the literature; and diverse methodological approaches were brought to bear on the same problem in a way that one would not find in any journal or manuscript on the topic. All benefited from the interaction and all desired that the interaction be "taken on the road" so that others could benefit as well. Several points in particular seemed worthy of mentioning; each of these topics represents a section in this volume.

## Under the Looking Glass:
## Toward a Better Understanding of Casual Relationships

One of the most important insights provided by the conference was that some seemingly well-understood truths about repression and mobilization are much more complex than we normally acknowledge, challenging and perhaps invalidating our research. For example, in the existing literature it is generally believed that political opportunity structure within democratic contexts is uniformly structured toward pacifistic protest policing. In these contexts, authorities are less inclined to engage in aggressive and violent repressive activity.

McPhail and McCarthy, in their essay in this volume, "Protest Mobilization, Protest Repression, and Their Interaction," challenge this claim. Through their analysis of state–dissident relations in the United States (over the last three decades), as well as an overview of the literature on contentious politics, they quickly identify that within a democratic regime repression likely varies by police jurisdiction and "in accordance with the extent of the agency's experience with policing public order in general and protest in particular"; simply, decentralized mobilizing structures within a single democratic political system facilitate diverse patterns of contention. The authors note that one should not expect random variation: repressive agents are influenced by not only their own history but also what takes place in areas around them; habit, diffusion, and contagion thus matter a great deal.

In the U.S. case, this latter issue becomes important because dueling training protocols exist, and to the degree that one begins to predominate over another, one will likely see similar protest policing strategies being adopted. This complicates the study of contentious politics because it becomes incumbent on researchers to avoid the assumption of independence across observations and cases. Quite the contrary, those interested in studying state–societal relations need to be on the lookout for causal linkages across both time and space and account for them within their investigations. To miss such relationships could be to misunderstand the different factors involved, attributing dynamics identified within one locale (e.g., time-space a) to factors present within that locale as opposed to those within another (e.g., time-space b).[11] Repression is not the only form of contention influenced by factors within democratic political systems; protest is influenced as well.

The McPhail and McCarthy study has important implications for the observation and study of mobilization. The authors argue that violent activity within collective action is generally overplayed within existing research—such actions are less frequent and less severe than normally thought. One could explain this misrepresentation by the fact that the political opportunity structure within a democracy, while being facilitative of protest, simultaneously limits the overall degree of hostility within such activities because of the same permissiveness. Political space thus both pacifies and alters the structure of contentious behavior. This differs significantly from the trace evidence normally found in print and visual media, which tend to pay attention to a high degree of drama and conflict. The reality, however, is quite different from the biased samples that we normally investigate.

Democratic political systems are not the only ones that current literature incorrectly depicts as uniformly structured in a particular manner. Much of the work on repression and mobilization in autocratic contexts suggests that state–societal relations are uniformly structured in such a way that states exercise large amounts of power (frequently of a violent nature) and that citizens are subject to these raw manifestations of coercion. Differing from this position significantly, however, others have highlighted the extremely tentative hold that autocratic political systems have over society (e.g., Scott 1985).

Continuing in this latter tradition, Vince Boudreau, in "Precarious Regimes and Matchup Problems in the Explanation of Repressive Policy," highlights the general sense of insecurity that exists within and across authoritarian regimes. Based on his extensive casework (in the Philippines), as well as on literature on contentious politics, Boudreau argues that because of the relatively tentative hold that this regime has over nation-states (both spatially and administratively), they are constantly on the search for "subversives" and they are willing to do whatever is necessary to eliminate them; that is, their guiding "frame" is one of perpetual battles with citizens in order to make the society "safe" for the polity.[12] But, how far will repression take them toward this end and how much repression is deemed too much in different locales?

In answering this question, Boudreau focuses on the capabilities of the state (mobilizing structure) relative to the capabilities of challengers across the relevant polity of interest (i.e., across the space contained within the territorial jurisdiction of the state). If the balance is equitable, he concludes that state repression (a discrete instance of state power) will not prove very effective—regardless of how much is applied. If the balance is inequitable (in favor of the authorities), however, then repressive activity can be very effective. Here, the very meaning of contention is altered, as individual events communicate seemingly nothing about state–dissident interactions in and of themselves. Instead, one must be cognizant of the actors involved, as well as the condition or structure of that relationship, in order to properly evaluate what is taking place (the when, how, and the why—what Tarrow [1998] refers to as "eventful" history). Only in this context will the stakes (the meaning) of repression and mobilization really be understood: in this case, state building, state maintenance, and political freedom itself.

The last chapter in this section addresses what is commonly referred to in the literature as the "conflict–repression nexus." In this volume, the relationship between repression and mobilization is studied by assessing the way in which individual repressive events influence the behavior of dissidents. This approach, while straightforward and easily comprehended, appears to miss an important aspect of the interaction, which (if ignored) could significantly bias empirical findings: all repressive events are not the same. It could be that by separating out particular types of repressive activity, one could gain a clearer understanding of what happens to social movements when they are coerced; Francisco undertakes just such an inquiry in "The Dictator's Dilemma."

Through an analysis of massacres across the twentieth century, Francisco finds that extreme levels of state violence generally provoke a "backlash" of mobilization (i.e., an increase). Against prior expectations, he observes that repression does not eliminate mobilizing structures through the decimation of leadership and that it does not provoke an alteration in the perceived opportunity structure through the increased restrictiveness of the political environment. Rather, he finds that within these contexts, leadership is sustained or replaced across members of a social movement family (this is similar to the argument of della Porta 1995). He also finds that dissidents do not perceive repression (specifically massacres) as an indication of state strength and thus as a deterrent, but rather as one of state weakness and thus an opportunity (Duvall and Stohl 1983). In the face of large-scale, state-sponsored violence, Francisco argues that dissidents alter their tactics during moments of repressive "backlash" (this is similar to McAdam's [1983] tactical innovation argument and Lichbach's [1987] substitution hypothesis). This suggests that researchers might have to investigate distinct segments of a conflict cycle, which alters the substantive understanding of the same type of behavior (e.g., repression as differentiated by magnitude), and, moreover, that they must examine the full repertoire of dissident action in their assessment of causal relationships so as to not mischaracterize strategic replacement with behavioral reduction.

## Moving Beyond, Moving Into: Developing New Insights

Whereas the chapters in Part I investigate issues that have been well discussed within the literature, subjecting them to innovative and thorough analysis, the three chapters in Part II depart significantly from these more established topic areas. Indeed, the research of Zwerman and Steinhoff, Johnston, and Ferree take us in directions seldom, if ever, explored.

For example, in "When Activists Ask for Trouble: State–Dissident Interactions and the New Left Cycle of Resistance in the United States and Japan," Zwerman and Steinhoff challenge the argument that repression is best thought of as a "cost" to social movement participants (influencing frames, mobilizing structures, and political opportunity structure) and argue that repression is frequently a "benefit" to dissidents (influencing the same three factors). They claim that state–dissident interactions are generally mischaracterized and misunderstood. Although similar to criticisms one finds in McPhail and McCarthy, the reasons for this mischaracterization and misunderstanding are quite distinct. Rather than pinpoint the trace evidence as being the problem, in an intriguing analysis of the United States and Japan, Zwerman and Steinhoff blame the rather conservative assessment of social movement actors and a limited conception of the temporal domain that is used to examine behavioral dynamics.

Regarding the first point, these authors argue that we have been looking in the wrong place, as well as looking in the wrong manner, for causal relationships between states and dissidents because we have been blinded by the fact that repression is believed to be a cost and something that dissidents wish to avoid. It is possible, they maintain, that certain activists seek out repression as a way of establishing their identity as "activists" and, as a result, do not attempt to hide or run from it. Here, repression influences dissidents and dissent, compelling a reinforcement of the frame that brought them to the point of contention in the first place. This line of inquiry is particularly important for it compels us to disaggregate social movement families, looking for those who might become radicalized by repression and those who might run away from it. Indeed, if Zwerman and Steinhoff are correct, then in our effort to understand contentious politics we must embrace a larger part of the social movement family, as well as the civil society, in order to understand the actions of authorities taken against a part of that movement/society. This is a much different approach than the single-movement or single-event focus practiced within much of the literature, and it is different from the large-N quantitative analyses as well, for it suggests that not all time periods are equivalent.

Regarding the second point, Zwerman and Steinhoff make the case that the dynamic interaction between repression and mobilization is important because it allows us (indeed, forces us) to understand trajectories of contention—that is, state–dissident interactions across time otherwise referred to as a "conflict cycle." They argue that one cannot understand the radical movements of the late 1960s (e.g., the Weathermen and the Black Panther Party) without meticulously documenting the development of the New Left of the late 1950s and 1960s that (in turn) was largely a function of prior repression and mobilization of the Old Left of the 1940s and early 1950s. In this view, state–dissident interactions in each period influence subsequent mobilization (and repression). The experiences at each stage foreclose particular life options for dissidents, which later constrain other individuals who come into the social movement. There are, of course, choices that can be made; what we see here might be a form of weak-path dependence. Regardless, the point remains clear: the present is largely influenced by the past, and to understand the former, the actors, actions, and sequences within the latter must be thoroughly interrogated.

Similar to Zwerman and Steinhoff, Johnston's "Talking the Walk: Speech Acts and Resistance in Authoritarian Regimes" puts forward an argument that repression and highly restrictive governing systems have been largely misunderstood and incorrectly studied. Differing from Boudreau and Francisco, he argues that one should not evaluate contentious politics within closed political systems through the analysis of overt manifestations of contention. Rather, drawing on cases in Estonia, Spain, and Poland (as well as the work of Scott [1985] and Kelley [1994]), he maintains that we should look for less obvious manifestations of resistance as repression sends individuals "underground" (away from more public, restricted spaces toward more private, "free" spaces) or, alternatively, into themselves (away from more overt, collective forms of resistance and toward more covert, individualistic forms of resistance).

Within the Johnston framework, repression influences dissidents and dissent because it compels a rethinking of the frame that brought them (or might bring them) to the point of contentious activity. The process of this rethinking is not one of "Should I give up resistance?" which has led numerous individuals to conclude that repression eliminates mobilization because of a reduction in overt behavior. Rather, Johnston argues that the process of this rethinking results in a different question: "How can I continue to resist in the current restrictive situation?" This conceptualization leads to the same empirical finding as that identified earlier in that a specific form of mobilization no longer occurs, but the difference in meaning is extremely important: within the one, mobilization is ended; within the other, mobilization is transformed.

Johnston's reframing is important for it compels one to look for mobilization and resistance in realms that are not frequently considered in existing research: for example, the Boy Scouts, neighborhood associations, barbershops, parties, comic books, and periodicals. These spaces are not just interesting in and of themselves, but they also create a context for subsequent mobilization: the gains of the previous time period set the stage for the next one and so forth. Johnston deviates from even Scott (1985) and invokes a little more of Kelley (1994) as he also pushes us to look for resistance within the realm of pro-government institutions. Specifically, he suggests that individuals in a seemingly nonconfrontational fashion use semiofficial and official organs of the state in an effort to bring about some form of resistance activity. This significantly changes how we go about studying contentious politics, for it increases the scope of locales within which one would need to look for mobilization.

Continuing in the direction set forth by Johnston, Ferree, in "Soft Repression: Ridicule, Stigma, and Silencing in Gender-Based Movements," moves still further along the path of unexplored domains. Correctly noting that much recent scholarship on so-called new social movements does not concern itself with "the state" at all, she asks: within the context of newer social movements, is our idea of state repression and the repression–mobilization nexus obsolete? Using the case of women's social movements in the United States and Germany to explore the issue, she definitively argues that yes, they are.

Ferree observes that with the new targets selected and the new organizations that engage in this "soft" mobilization (i.e., behavior not directed against political authorities), individuals and groups who seek to neutralize and eliminate challenges—similar to the role played by the state in context of more traditional social movements—use what she refers to as "soft" repression. This type of action refers to mobilization of institutions within civil society to eradicate opposition through ridicule (microlevel activity), stigma (mesolevel), and silencing (macrolevel)—each type signifying different units of analysis, as well as different degrees of institutionalization. These strategies may lack some of the "oomph" and flash that more traditional forms of repression possess, but they are nonetheless effective at diminishing challenges and they are likely more consistently present within democratic regimes that attempt to constrain the presence of overt state activity while facilitating nonstate behavior. The media specifically emerges as one important agent of soft repression (and not as a passive recipient of information that can be used as data), for it provides either voice or silence to mobilizers and thus either facilitates or represses mobilization itself. Ferree's analysis proves a formidable challenge to existing research because it opens up a large domain of behavior that has been ignored by literature on mobilization and repression—that concerning nonstate actors and actions.

## The Media Is the Message: Contention, Trace Evidence, and Social-Science Research

Most scholars interested in contentious politics consult the mass media for information (e.g., newspapers, news wires, magazines, radio, and television).[13] As designed, researchers consult the text, they systematically move through content (reconstructing events and/or coding information), and they compile relevant data into a spreadsheet before they investigate it with some form of rigorous analytic technique (e.g., graphical analysis, correlation or regression). The third theme at the Maryland conference directly questioned this process. Although many authors raised issues relevant to this point, two in particular addressed the problem in some detail, and each in a different way. Koopmans grapples with the problem of properly understanding the role played by the media within the process of contentious politics itself. Ball grapples with the problem of how individuals extract information from other members of society and how researchers should place this information into some structure for rigorous examination. Both ask researchers to reconsider what it means to have information covered in newspapers.

In "On the Quantification of Horror: Notes from the Field," Ball confronts the issue of media reporting and multiple observers. He uses data on Guatamalan state terror from 1960 to 1996, compiled from the news media, human rights organizations, and eyewitnesses in an effort to analyze the subject of data validity. As he correctly notes, all individuals in the study of contentious politics (and other aspects of the social sciences, for that matter) attempt to get as close to what really happened as possible, but we all realize that not all events are covered in the sources that we consult. What is missed by different sources (i.e., what is censored)? What is found and how much of what is identified is shared across observers (i.e., what is the reporting "density")? These are the questions that Ball addresses.

Ball argues that if we can understand these questions through a technique referred to as "capture-recapture" (that identifies changes in the relationship between what happens and what is reported), then we can fix our data—even when we have full coverage from only one source and partial coverage from others over the same time period. With multiple sources, the key lies in the overlapping (the reporting density). When density is identified, we can ascertain what is generally missed by different sources, as well as what is generally identified.

From a comparison of media-generated data, human rights documents, and interviews with victims and eyewitnesses, Ball also finds that when conflict was extremely violent in Guatemala, the press did not report much of anything relevant to contentious politics, whereas other sources did provide information about what was taking place. He finds that when human rights violations were taking place within rural communities, involving actions that did not produce evidence—such as a disappearance—newspapers were less likely to cover events than were other sources.

All is not lost, however. Ball suggests that after capture-recapture one could reweigh the data. He suggests that one can validly use newspaper data in a case where contentious politics was more visible and when the degree of publicity involved was something that was intricately connected with the conflict itself. Invariably, however, one must read Ball's essay as something of a wake-up call: *stop focusing on newspapers*; other data sources exist (human rights documents and eyewitness accounts)! These alternative sources may not be as neatly indexed as newspapers, but they do allow us to penetrate many sociopolitical conflicts (especially in developmentally "challenged" parts of the globe and those where authoritarianism and high levels of violence are present) that we will not be able to study or understand otherwise.

Koopmans moves in a slightly different direction from Ball in "Repression and the Public Sphere: Discursive Opportunities for Repression against the Extreme Right in Germany in the 1990s." While questioning the validity of newspaper-generated data, he does not question the collection of this data. Rather, he suggests that we have been reversing the causal order entirely when we discuss the media and contention. Koopmans argues that media coverage of state–dissident behavior should not be viewed as the output of contention (that we use to document, analyze, and understand what is taking place). Instead, he maintains that we should view the media as an input into contentious politics. Examining the use of repression against rightist organizations in Germany, he finds that repressive behavior is strongly influenced by reactions and evaluations of repression within the public (in the media) as well as by discussion about the targets of repression and the victims of extreme right violence (immigrants). He goes so far as to suggest that there are discursive political "opportunities" that, similar to more institutional or behavioral "opportunities," send cues to governing authorities that the environment is supportive of their efforts (or, alternatively, that the environment is not supportive).

The implications of Koopmans's work for the study of contentious politics are far-reaching, for they reveal that, simultaneously with "real" battles between states and dissidents, "virtual" battles are being waged in the realm of public discourse in the short, medium, and long term that are just as significant. This becomes an important contribution because it suggests that when individuals are interested in studying contentious politics, they cannot simplistically use information contained in the public sphere as if it where an accurate portrayal of the underlying battle. Quite the contrary, Koopmans's research reveals that the public sphere and the real battle have distinctive lives, each of which may or may not interact with the other.

## A New Look at Repression and Mobilization

What emerges from the research presented at the Maryland conference is a fundamentally different model of state-dissident interactions. Within this framework, numerous issues have been identified: new actions ("hard" and "soft" repression and mobilization), new conditions that influence the occurrence of repression and mobilization (discursive opportunities, non-authority as well as nondissident mobilizing structures), temporal dynamics (the lagged impact of political opportunity on mobilizing structures and framing processes), multiple sources for data regarding what has taken place (varying across ideology, place, and desired audience), and the importance of regime type (i.e., democratic and authoritarian contexts). All have been shown to alter state–dissident interactions significantly—suggesting that the conceptual model should be completely modified.

Rather than work through each element of the model in Figure I.2 (recapitulating what has been discussed in the review of the chapters in this volume), I would like to take a different approach and explore the dynamics present within the model through the examination of contentious politics within the United States (and abroad) after the September 11 attacks. This returns us to the subject with which this introduction opened, as well as the one that has been occupying so many who are concerned with contentious politics and human freedom (e.g., Johnston and Von Natta 2001; Sikkink 2001). Such an exercise not only will reveal how our understanding of contentious politics has been altered by the conceptual framework offered by the Maryland conference, but it also points us in the direction of new areas that require investigation; indeed, I would go so far as to suggest that it identifies a completely new research agenda.

## Moving beyond the Usual Suspects: Opportunities, Mobilizing Structures, and Frames

The model illustrated in Figure I.2 influences our understanding of what took place on September 11 and what is taking place now. One could understand the initial attack by Al Qaeda operatives at the Pentagon and World Trade Center to be a function of dissident political opportunity (the United States is a democracy and thus less secure than a more restrictive society), mobilizing structure (a complex, well-trained, but minimalistic network of cells throughout the globe possessed enough resources to procure identification passes, flight training, and so forth), cultural frames (a seething hatred for the United States and a belief that through violent collective action, movement toward some objective might follow, if the act in and of

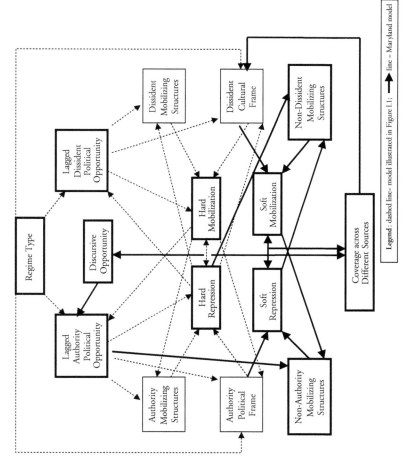

Legend: dashed line= model illustrated in Figure I.1; ──▶ line = Maryland model

*Figure I.2. The linkages between repression and mobilization—revisited and modified*

itself did not convey some benefit to the terror network). The response of U.S. authorities can also be addressed within the context of this model. Confronted with a domestic threat (the attacks of September 11), political opportunity for state sanctions within the United States were perceived and individuals were arrested or detained; locations that were potentially threatened (e.g., government buildings, monuments, and airports) were basically placed under martial law; and, legislation granting power to relevant coercive institutions was passed without much (if any) opposition. To bring this about, existing mobilizing structures were utilized (the executive, the military, the Secret Service, the Federal Bureau of Investigation, the National Guard, and the police) and the existing political frame for maintaining "law and order" was invoked. Finally, much of what took place came to us through the media—principally television, but those who wanted greater detail about the specifics consulted newspapers, news magazines, and the World Wide Web as well.

If one were to employ the traditional model to understand repression and mobilization, however, one would conclude that basically the story was complete: after the bombing, repression was applied and there has been no subsequent, visible mobilization of state opponents. One could argue that mobilizing structures and cultural frames of challengers are probably being readjusted and that assessments of political opportunity are being reevaluated within the context of militarized airports and strategic bombing of training facilities (which, by the way, should be viewed as international protest policing efforts and not interstate). Anyone that has been paying attention to the situation would disagree with this end-of-the-story narrative. Herein lies some of the relevance of the Maryland conference.

## Eden Is on Fire: An Example That Context Matters

The first insight that could be drawn from the Maryland model is that as different countries throughout the world engage in counterterroristic activities, they are likely to experience diverse conflictual dynamics. Within democratic political systems, for example, one will probably see an increase in the political opportunity structure for authorities to apply repression with the introduction of antiterrorism legislation (which grants increased powers to intelligence and police organizations). Indeed, many forms of legislation have been put forward (several had existed in some form already but were held back for fear that they would not be well responded to). Correspondingly, there will likely be an increased amount of discussion about the legitimacy of restricting the rights of those challenging political authorities and all others within the public domain (Koopmans), albeit varying somewhat across sources and audiences.

An increase in repressive activity should result within democracies themselves, varying somewhat across jurisdictions: one should see more restrictions within places like New York City and Los Angeles, California, relative to Lawrence, Kansas, and Dayton, Ohio (McPhail and McCarthy). One will likely see a decrease in the political opportunity structure for a wide variety of dissidents (including Al Qaeda and others), a reduction in support for different organizations involved with challenging authority— regardless of topic area—as well as a reduction in cultural frames, which advocate challenging authority. The transformation of the antiglobaliza- tion event a few weeks after September 11 in Washington, DC (which was planned to be rather large, diverse, and antagonistic), into an antiwar event (which was much smaller, less diverse and less antagonistic) was an interest- ing example of this process. Alternatively, one may see the cultural frame of Al Qaeda members become stronger as the repression that is applied against them increases their conviction that they are doing the right thing (Zwerman and Steinhoff).

In more authoritarian systems, we should also see an increase in po- litical opportunity for authorities, as well as an increased emphasis on bolstering mobilizing structures for repression and the political frame that supports such activity (Boudreau). Already challenged with a restrictive en- vironment, such enhancements should provoke specific types of responses within the populace: exit/migration from these countries, continued dis- engagement from mainstream political activity, and reinforced activities of local/underground resistance (Johnston). Within these contexts, therefore, we will need to look at different locations, and in different ways, for in- formation about what states are doing. Unfortunately, most of the media will probably be following events at the forefront of the "war on terrorism" and, as a result, many of these political systems will be able to do whatever they wish—what would they possibly do to become newsworthy in this context (Ball)?

## "Us" versus "Them" (but Not "them")

One of the more interesting aftereffects of the September 11 attacks con- cerns the activity of nonstate actors (Ferree). After the attacks, many in- stances of "soft" repression were identified that directly resulted from the cultural understanding that "outsiders" were among "us" who could poten- tially serve as vehicles for terrorist activity. "We" were seemingly defined relative to "them" as people who were not light-skinned (i.e., who were white, black, Asian, etc.), who spoke languages that were not from the Arab world (e.g., Spanish, Ebonics, English, Chinese), who did not wear clothing that veiled our bodies, who did not wear much facial hair, and who are not extremely patriotic. The precision here has not been laser-like: individuals from Puerto Rico as well as from India have been physically threatened, as individuals speaking Hebrew as well as Arabic have been removed from airplanes. The general parameters are probably right on the mark. The mechanisms by which this information was distributed were quite subtle: pictures were circulated about the perpetrators, discussion was undertaken regarding who was involved, and all of this took place against the backdrop of an American society that has been repeatedly inundated with negative images of people from the Arab world.

The changes in the American sociopolitical landscape prompted by this "soft" repression are also worthy of attention. First, it appears that African-Americans may be perceived to be less threatening to the average American than individuals from the Middle East, and the stigma applied to the former community might be lowered (albeit only temporarily). Whether or not this persists is subject to some debate. Second, there has been something of a countermovement within the Arab-American community linked with groups that have historically maintained an interest in human rights (e.g., the American Civil Liberties Union) in an effort to confront the stigma attached to individuals within their community and the numerous nonstate sanctions that have been and are being applied against them (e.g., beating, derogatory comments and graffiti). Third, there is starting to be policing of all discussion about the political legitimacy of the U.S. government and its actions, largely undertaken by nongovernment actors, but also by individuals within the Bush administration itself. University professors have been targeted as being unsupportive, political cartoonists have had their comics pulled, and Web pages have been closed for "questionable" content.

Another topic that prompts observation and discussion is the fact that a natural ally for the Arab community (African-Americans) does not appear to be assisting them. Blacks are probably somewhat hesitant to be seen as "un-American" in their support of a community with which they have had minimal interaction historically. Furthermore, as an aftereffect of subsequent mobilization, repression, and accommodation (Zwerman and Steinhoff), it is not clear that an African-American "community" exists to interact with the new victims of American repression and xenophobia. Over the last two decades, many civil rights organizations have been declining in membership and cultural importance (e.g., the NAACP and the National Urban League), and the connection between many political organizations of African-Americans and their constituents are tentative at best (e.g., the Congressional Black Caucus). Not all of the difficulty can be found on one side of the relationship. Arab-Americans are probably somewhat hesitant to interact with blacks because the historical stigma applied to African-Americans may still cloud their perception of who would be useful to them and what an alliance with this community would mean to the Arab community and as Americans. The aftereffects of social repression function here as well.

## Anthrax, Computer Viruses, and the Rise of the Disenchanted

Another aftereffect anticipated in the Maryland conference but ignored within the more traditional conceptions of state–dissident interactions is the importance of contentious copycats and spin-offs. It is possible that the destruction of the World Trade Center and the partial destruction of the Pentagon will communicate to challengers of the U.S. government that such institutions are vulnerable to attack. As a result, many individuals who had previously foreseen immense costs with challenging this government may discount some of this, especially if they move against targets that are less obvious than the Statue of Liberty, city hall, or the local police station. At the same time, it would be clear that in the context of increased repressive activity, as well as support for repressive activity in the public domain, not all forms of mobilization would be likely to emerge. Indeed, one would expect low-key, bizarre, and small-scale activities to take place as individuals and groups come to realize that these types of events communicate dissatisfaction (Francisco) and that they are less likely to illicit a coercive response from the authorities because they are otherwise occupied (Johnston). In a sense, similar to the argument of Boudreau, it is understood that the U.S. capacity for repression and counterinsurgency might be at its limits and, in this context, it is somewhat vulnerable—at least at the fringe (in the mail and in computers).

Interestingly, one would not come away from the September 11 events with a clear understanding that the costs of dissent in the United States are high. Although all of the hijackers died (a major cost to those who might wish to engage in protest), more attention has been given to Osama bin Laden and Al Qaeda in the media (Koopmans). Indeed, their resonance in public discourse may communicate just the opposite of what is intended: "challenge now and you will surely get some attention."

## Data Smog and Other Impediments to Knowledge

My final point is a personal one. After the attacks, we all sat still for about three days to three weeks staring at the images of the Twin Towers collapsing (well, at least in my house; I'm from the Lower East Side of New York). At first the image and information were pretty basic, but almost immediately it was multiplied as different angles were found (one from a tourist on the west side of town, another from some doctor toward the east). Amid speculation about who was involved and what took place, more images and more information came to the fore. Following this, there was a veritable explosion of information about possible perpetrators, prior terrorist activities in the United States and abroad, efforts to rescue victims, discussions about air traffic, discussions about what other foreign powers might be involved, reflections about the historical background of different actors as well as the history of the Middle East and Islam itself—endlessly, the spiral of discussion and causality seemed to move upward. At a certain point, I was just unable to take in additional information—my mind just froze. Discussion with others seemed to confirm that they were undergoing a similar process.

As I have attempted to reconstitute my life, parsing off the stream of information into the categories that are most salient to my interests, I became acutely aware about the discarding of information (Ball) and the potential silencing of history (Ferree). The American media seemed to be going out of its way to appear to be balanced in its coverage, but it was clear that something was being missed; that something was a mystery, and the mystery lay behind all of our attempts to reconstruct what happened as well as what was happening. What were the silences? This I could only address by assembling a list: there are dissidents and their supporters, there are government authorities and their supporters, there are third parties in, as well as across, territorial jurisdictions that exist who have varied amounts of interest in different aspects of contention as well as the political-economic context that lies behind these interactions. It is clear that each of these actors might have a different take on what was occurring—all are relevant for truly understanding 9/11 in particular and contentious politics in general. Unfortunately, not all will be identified or find resonance within the broader discursive community (Koopmans).

For example, in one African-American newspaper I saw mention of the fact that one aftereffect of the bombing was that the discussion about reparations to African-Americans that took place in Durban, South Africa, at the racism conference only days before the bombing had been completely ignored and that the growing income gap between blacks and whites would continue to grow without any substantive discussion whatsoever. The situation was not completely dire, however. The newspaper also noted that as all people in the United States (especially all people of color) would likely now be treated like black people, in all likelihood there would be a greater opportunity for forming alliances in the future to fight racial profiling, police harassment, and racist media characterizations (a grand meta-frame). Of course, the same articles speculated about the appropriateness of such discussion—wondering whether or not it was "unpatriotic" to address such issues. To even venture to ask the question, though, is to identify the salience of Ferree's point—silences are imposed in interesting ways, but our awareness of them is usually conscious at some level. Indeed, I myself was hesitant to write these words so as to not deleteriously impact the likelihood of publication. Even within the privacy of my own home, therefore, the salience of the repression–mobilization nexus is apparent. Retreating to the manuscript, I seek a way out; indirectly, inconspicuously, and (most assuredly) ineffectively.

Perhaps appropriately, the authors of this more nuanced and complex understanding of contention are not afforded the last word. On the contrary, the book is concluded with the observations of two of the most prominent theorists within conflict studies: Charles Tilly and Mark Lichbach. Observing the developments in the conference and reading the final manuscripts provided within this volume, each attempted to situate the puzzles of the conflict–repression nexus as well as the contributions of the authors into a broader theoretical context. Although seemingly quite different at first read, both Tilly and Lichbach are similar in what they recommend.

Tilly, in a chapter titled "Repression, Mobilization and Explanation," maintains that the key to understanding the complexity represented in the chapters and summarized in Figure I.2 is to focus on "mechanisms"—"a delimited class of events that change relations among specified sets of elements in identical or closely similar ways over a variety of situations." In a sense, he advocates moving into and illuminating what resides within the causal arrows of the figure. This is done in order to ascertain exactly what elements exist within specific forms of contention (e.g., brokerage, certification, and object shift), driving relationships to escalation or de-escalation. Toward this end, Tilly outlines the basic components of his research program—"Dynamics of Contention" or DOC, which he developed with Sidney Tarrow and Doug McAdam:

1. identification of the episodes' problematic and distinctive features;
2. comparison with other episodes for similarities and differences in those regards;
3. identification of processes that produce those problematic and distinctive features;
4. decomposition of those processes into component mechanisms;
5. development of account concerning how the relevant mechanisms combine, interact, and produce their aggregate effects given specified initial conditions.

His conclusion is straightforward: research into repression and mobilization would benefit from disaggregating conflict behavior. The same mechanisms might be involved with all forms of contention, but as we attempt to understand why specific forms of mobilization are influenced by specific forms of repression (and vice versa), we need to recognize that mechanisms might function in different ways within each dyad; this leads to diverse outcomes (e.g., escalation, de-escalation, tactical variation, inaction, and conciliation). Research should look for clusters of mechanisms and examine clusters of behavior for similarities and differences. Only in this manner will the diverse findings of the volume be comprehensible and only in this manner will our understanding of contention advance.

Confronted with the same puzzles and developments, Lichbach's solution (in a chapter titled "How to Organize Your Mechanisms: Research Programs, Stylized Facts, and Historical Narratives") is also directed toward the illumination of what resides within the causal arrows and identifying the causal mechanisms. He agrees with Tilly that our understanding of contention would benefit from some serious rethinking and retooling.

Rather than list mechanisms (exhaustively), however, Lichbach directs researchers to "embed" them within distinct research programs: for example, rationalism, structuralism, and culturalism. As he states,

> [g]enerating mechanisms . . . is easy; locating the mechanisms—factors and forces linking repression or accommodation with [contention]—is an interminable make-work project; and the breathless search for mechanisms substitutes an endless positivist list of hypotheses with an endless postpositivist inventory of mechanisms.

He continues:

> to mechanisms in larger and more organized structures of knowledge so as to deepen our understanding of interesting and important causal processes.

Whereas Tilly thus guides us to identify mechanisms and illustrate how they function, Lichbach guides us to identify and competitively evaluate concatenations of mechanisms to assess the usefulness of diverse research programs. Both lead us in the direction of getting a better handle on what the various chapters within this volume reveal: a deeply nuanced and complex interaction between authorities and dissidents that takes place seemingly everywhere at some point in time (within democracies, autocracies as well as transitional societies and on every continent of the globe), across almost all issues and with many individuals.

## Notes

1. Here, context matters to some extent (e.g., some have argued that the degree of democracy influences the challengers' response [Gupta, Singh, and Sprague 1993]), but in many respects this factor has been less rigorously investigated than the specific relationship between protest and repression itself.

2. This is especially the case with regard to violent behavior (e.g., Hibbs 1973; Poe and Tate 1994) or that which exceeds prior expectations (e.g., Davenport 1995).

3. Moore's investigation was conducted on a select group of countries with a sequential analysis.

4. Some advocate giving up the enterprise entirely (Brockett 1992).

5. For example: democracy, economic development, military influence, British colonial experience, and population size.

6. These individuals were not the only ones; See Jodice, Taylor, and Deutsch (1980) for discussion of general use of the database, which has been quite extensive to say the least.

7. Comparatively, the scholarship on social movements does tend to be more integrated, albeit somewhat one-sided in favor of political scientists reading the work of sociologists.

8. For example, quantitative literature generally finds that procedural democracy tends to decrease human rights violations, whereas much qualitative literature finds no relationship whatsoever.

9. With regard to protest and repression (but especially the latter), one can count the number of pieces in major political science journals on one hand. Sociology is slightly better (especially with the study of dissent), but not by much.

10. Frequently one will find that although individuals focus on behavior, when they attempt to figure out what is going on, more direct linkages tend to be downplayed.

11. One simply cannot assume randomness below the nation-state level (e.g., across states or cities).

12. See Faucher and Fitzgibbons (1989) for a similar discussion in the Latin American context.

13. Generally, print media is favored because it provides more information than other forms of media.

## Works Cited

Beissinger, Mark. 1998. "Event Analysis in Transitional Societies: Protest Mobilization in the Former Soviet Union." In *Acts of Dissent: New Developments in the Study of Protest,* ed. Dieter Rucht, Ruud Koopmans, and Friedhelm Neidhardt. Berlin: Wissenschaftszentrum Berlin für Sozialforschung.

Bond, Doug, and Joe Bond. 1995. "Protocol for the Assessment of Nonviolent Direct Action (Panda) Codebook for the P24 Data Set." Manuscript, Harvard University.

Bond, Doug, J. Craig Jenkins, Charles Taylor, and Kurt Schock. 1997. "Mapping Mass Political Conflict and Civil Society: The Automated Development of Event Data." *Journal of Conflict Resolution* 41, no. 4: 553–79.

Brockett, Charles. 1992. "Measuring Political Violence and Land Inequality in Central America." *American Political Science Review* 86, no.1: 169–76.

Bwy, Douglas. 1968. "Political Instability in Latin America: The Cross-Structural Test of a Causal Model." *Latin American Research Review* 3: 17–66.

Carey, Sabine. 2001. "A Comparative Time-Series Analysis of Domestic Political Conflict." Paper presented at the 2001 Annual Meeting of the American Political Science Association. San Francisco.

Churchill, Ward, and Jim Vander Wall. 1990. *Agents of Repression: The FBI's Secret Wars against the Black Panther Party and the American Indian Movement.* Boston: South End Press.

Cunningham, David. 2002. *Welcome to the Machine: The FBI's Repression of the Radical Right and Left.* Berkeley: University of California Press.

Davenport, Christian. 1995. "Multi-Dimensional Threat Perception and State Repression: An Inquiry into Why States Apply Negative Sanctions." *American Journal of Political Science* 39, no. 3: 683–713.

———. 1998. "Tsuris in the Soul: Inter-Ethnic Politics and the Black-Jewish Question." *National Science Foundation* (SBR-9731382).

———. 1999a. "Filling the Gap in Contentious Understanding: The Republic of New Africa and the Influence of Political Repression." *National Science Foundation* (SBR-9819274).

———. 1999b. "Human Rights and the Democratic Proposition." *Journal of Conflict Resolution* 43, no. 1: 92–116.

———. 2001. "Understanding Covert Repressive Action." DC Area Workshop on Contentious Politics. http://www.bsos.umd.edu/cidcm/dcawcp/ schedule.html. December 5.

Davenport, Christian, and Patrick Ball. 2002. "Views to a Kill: Exploring the Implications of Source Selection in the Case of Guatemalan State Terror, 1977–1995." *Journal of Conflict Resolution*: pages unavailable.

Davis, David, and Michael Ward. 1990. "They Dance Alone: Deaths and the Disappeared in Contemporary Chile." *Journal of Conflict Resolution* 34: 449–75.

della Porta, Donatella 1995. *Social Movements, Political Violence and the State: A Comparative Analysis of Italy and Germany.* New York: Cambridge University Press.

Donner, Frank. 1990. *Protectors of Privilege: Red Squads and Police Repression in Urban America.* Los Angeles: University of California Press.

Duvall, Raymond, and Michael Stohl. 1983. "Governance by Terror." In *Politics of Terrorism,* ed. Michael Stohl. 3d ed. New York: Marcel Dekker.

Eberwein, Wolf-Deiter. 1983. "Domestic Political Processes." In *The Globus Model: Computer Simulation of Worldwide Political and Developments,* ed. Stuart Bremer. Boulder, CO: Westview Press.

Eckstein, Harry. 1965. "On the Etiology of Internal Wars." *History and Theory* 4: 133–63.

Faucher, Philippe, and Kevin Fitzgibbons. 1989. "Dissent and the State in Latin America." In *Dissent and the State,* ed. C. E. S. Franks New York: Oxford University Press.

Fein, Helen 1995. "More Murder in the Middle: Life-Integrity, Violations and Democracy in the World" *Human Rights Quarterly* 17: 170–91.

Feirabend, Ivo, and Rosalind Feirabend. 1972. "Systemic Conditions of Political Aggression: An Application of Frustration-Aggression Theory." In *Anger, Violence and Politics: Theories and Research,* ed. Ivo Feirabend, Hugh Graham, and Ted Gurr. New York: Signet.

Francisco, Ron. 1996. "Coercion and Protest: An Empirical Test in Two Democratic States." *American Journal of Political Science* 40, no. 4: 1179–1204.

———. 1998. *European Protest and Coercion Data—Codebook.* University of Kansas. http://lark.cc.ukans.edu/~ronfran/data/index.html.

Francisco, Ron, and Mark Lichbach. 2001. Choice or Chance? Micro-rationality and Macro-randomness in Polish Conflict, 1980–1995." Paper presented at the 2001 Annual Meeting of the American Political Science Association. San Francisco.

Gibson, James. 1988. "Political Intolerance and Political Repression during the McCarthy Red Scare." *American Political Science Review* 82, no. 2: 511–29.

Goldstein, Robert. 1978. *Political Repression in Modern America: From 1870 to the Present.* Boston: Schennckman/G. K. Hall.

———. *Political Repression in 19th Century Europe.* Totowa, NJ: Barnes and Noble Books.

Gupta, Dipak, Harinder Singh, and Tom Sprague. 1993. "Government Coercion of Dissidents: Deterrence or Provocation?" *Journal of Conflict Resolution* 37, no. 2: 301–39.

Gupta, Dipak, and Y. P. Venieris. 1981. "Introducing New Dimensions in Macro Models: The Socio-Political Environment." *Political Psychology* 13: 379–406.

Gurr, Ted. 1969. "A Comparative Study of Civil Strife." In *Violence in America,* ed. Hugh Graham and Ted Gurr. New York: Praeger.

———. 1986a. "Persisting Patterns of Repression and Rebellion: Foundations for a General Theory of Political Coercion." In *Persistent Patterns and Emergent Structures in a Waning Century,* ed. Margaret Karns. New York: Praeger.

———. 1986b. "The Political Origins of State Violence and Terror: A Theoretical Analysis." In *Government Violence and Repression: An Agenda for Research,* ed. Michael Stohl and George Lopez. New York: Greenwood Press.

———. 1993. *Minorities at Risk: A Global View of Ethnopolitical Conflicts.* Washington, DC: U.S. Institute of Peace.

Gurr, Ted, and Robert Duvall. 1973. "Introduction to a Formal Theory of Conflict within Social Systems." In *The Uses of Controversy in Sociology,* ed. Lewis Coser and O. N. Larsen. New York: Free Press.

Henderson, Conway. 1991. "Conditions Affecting the Use of Political Repression." *Journal of Conflict Resolution* 35: 120–42.

Hibbs, Douglas. 1973. *Mass Political Violence.* New York: Wiley.

Hocke, Peter. 1998. "Determining the Selection Bias in Local and National Newspaper Reports on Protest Events." In *Acts of Dissent: New Developments in the Study of Protest,* ed. Dieter Rucht, Ruud Koopmans, and Friedhelm Neidhardt. Berlin: Wissenschaftszentrum Berlin für Sozialforschung.

Hoover, Dean, and David Kowalewski. 1992. "Dynamic Models of Dissent and Repression." *Journal of Conflict Resolution* 36, no. 1: 150–82.

Jackman, Robert W., and William A. Boyd. 1979. "Multiple Sources in the Collection of Data on Political Conflict." *American Journal of Political Science* 23: 434–45.

Jodice, David, Charles L. Taylor, and Karl W. Deutsch. 1980. *Cumulation in Social Science Data Archiving.* Verlog Ahton Hain: Konigsten.

Johnston, David, and Don Von Natta. 2001. "Liberty and Security: Ashcroft Seeking to Free F.B.I. to Spy on Groups." *New York Times,* December 1.

Johnston, Hank, and Carol Mueller. 2001. "Unobtrusive Practices of Contention in Leninist Regimes." *Sociological Perspectives* 44: 351–75.

Kelley, Robin. 1994. *Race Rebels: Culture, Politics, and the Black Working Class.* New York: Free Press.

Khawaja, Marwan. 1993. "Repression and Popular Collective Action: Evidence from the West Bank." *Sociological Forum* 8: 47-71.

King, John. 2000. "Exploring the Ameliorating Effects of Democracy on Political Repression: Cross-National Evidence." In *Paths to State Repression: Human Rights Violations and Contentious Politics,* ed. Christian Davenport. Boulder, CO: Rowman and Littlefield.

Koopmans, Ruud. 1995. *Democracy from Below: New Social Movements and the Political System in West Germany.* Boulder, CO: Westview Press.

Koran, T. 1990. "Sparks and Prairie Fires: A Theory of Unanticipated Political Revolution." *Public Choice* 61: 41–74.

Krain, Mathew. 1997. "State-Sponsored Mass Murder: A Study of the Onset and Severity of Genocides and Politicides." *Journal of Conflict Resolution* 41, no. 3: 331–60.

Kriesi, H., Ruud Koopmans, J. W. Duyvendak, and M. Giugni. 1992. "New Social Movements and Political Opportunities in Western Europe." *European Journal of Political Research* 22: 219–44.

Laswell, Harold. 1941. "The Garrison State and Specialists on Violence." *American Journal of Sociology* 46: 455–68.

Lichbach, Mark. 1987. "Deterrence or Escalation? The Puzzle of Aggregate Studies of Repression and Dissent." *Journal of Conflict Resolution* 31: 266–97.

Lichbach, Mark, and Ted Gurr. 1981. "The Conflict Process: A Formal Model." *Journal of Conflict Resolution* 25: 3–29.

McAdam, Douglas. 1983. *Political Process and the Development of Black Insurgency, 1930–1970.* Chicago: University of Chicago Press.

McAdam, Douglas, John McCarthy, and Mayer Zald, eds. 1996. *Comparative Perspectives on Social Movements: Political Opportunities, Mobilizing Structures and Cultural Framings.* New York: Cambridge University Press.

McCamant, John. 1984. "Governance Without Blood: Social Sciences Antiseptic View of Rule; or, The Neglect of Political Repression." In *The State as Terrorist: The Dynamics of Governmental Violence and Repression,* ed. Michael Stohl and George Lopez. Westport, CT: Greenwood Press.

McCarthy, John, Clark McPhail, and Jackie Smith. 1996. "Images of Protest: Dimensions of Selection Bias in Media Coverage of Washington Demonstrations, 1982, 1991." *American Sociological Review* 61: 468–99.

Mitchell, Neil, and John McCormick. 1988. "Economic and Political Explanations of Human Rights Violations." *World Politics* 40, no. 4: 476–98.

Moore, Will. 1998. "Repression and Dissent: Substitution, Context and Timing." *American Journal of Political Science* 42: 851–73.

Moore, Will, and Ronny Lindstrom. 1998. *The Violent Intranational Conflict Data Project* (Codebook for dataset—available from http://garnet.acns.fsu/edu/~whmoore/).

Mueller, Carol. 1997. "International Press Coverage of East German Protest Events, 1989." *American Sociological Review* 69: 820–32.

Oliver, Pam, and Daniel Myers. 1999. "How Events Enter the Public Sphere: Conflict, Location, and Sponsorship in Local Newspaper Coverage of Public Events." *American Journal of Sociology* 105, no. 1: 38–87.

Pion-Berlin, David. 1989. *The Ideology of State Terror: Economic Doctrine and Political Repression in Argentina and Peru.* Boulder, CO: Lynne Rienner.

Poe, Steven, and Neal Tate. 1994. "Repression of Human Rights to Personal Integrity in the 1980s: A Global Analysis." *American Political Science Review* 88: 853–72.

Poe, Steven, C. Neal Tate, and Linda Camp Keith. 1999. "Repression of the Human Right to Personal Integrity Revisited: A Global Cross-National Study Covering the Years 1976–1993." *International Studies Quarterly* 43: 291–313.

Rasler, Karen. 1996. "Concessions, Repression, and Political Protest." *American Sociological Review* 61, no. 1: 132–52.

Rucht, Dieter, Ruud Koopmans, and Friedhelm Neidhardt, eds. 1998. *Acts of Dissent: New Developments in the Study of Protest.* Berlin: Wissenschaftszentrum Berlin für Sozialforschung.

Rummel, Rudolph J. 1964. "Dimensions of Conflict Behavior within and between Nations." In *General Systems: Yearbook of the Society for General Systems Research,* ed. L. Von Bertalanffy and A. Rapoport. Ann Arbor: Society for General Systems Research.

———. 1996. *Death by Government.* New Brunswick, NJ: Transaction Publishers.

Scott, James. 1985. *Weapons of the Weak: Everyday Forms of Peasant Resistance.* New Haven: Yale University Press.

———. 1998. *Seeing Like a State: How Certain Schemes to Improve the Human Condition Have Failed.* New Haven: Yale University Press.

Sikkink, Kathryn. 2001. "Terrorism and Democratic Virtures: A Human Rights Approach to September 11th. After September 11th: Perspectives from the Social Sciences." Social Science Research Council: http://www.ssrc.org/sept11/essays/sikkink.htm.

Snyder, David, and William R. Kelly. 1977. "Conflict Intensity, Media Sensitivity and the Validity of Newspaper Data." *American Sociological Review* 42: 1105–17.

Stanley, William. 1996. *The Protection Racket State: Elite Politics, Military Extortion, and Civil War in El Salvador.* Philadelphia: Temple University Press.

Tarrow, Sidney. 1989. *Democracy and Disorder: Protest and Politics in Italy, 1965–1975*. Oxford: Clarendon Press.

———. 1998. "Studying Contentious Politics: From Eventful History to Cycles of Collective Action." In *Acts of Dissent: New Developments in the Study of Protest,* ed. Dieter Rucht, Ruud Koopmans, and Friedhelm Neidhardt. Berlin: Wissenschaftszentrum Berlin für Sozialforschung.

Taylor, Charles L., and David A. Jodice. 1983. *World Handbook of Political and Social Indicators*. Vol. 3. New Haven: Yale University Press.

Tilly, Charles. 1995. *Popular Contention in Great Britain 1758–1834*. Cambridge: Harvard University Press.

Tilly, Charles, Louise Tilly, and R. Tilly. 1975. *Rebellious Century, 1830–1930*. Cambridge: Harvard University Press.

Weede, Erich. 1987. "Some New Evidence on Correlates of Political Violence: Income Inequality, Regime Repressiveness, and Economic Development." *European Sociological Review* 3: 97–108.

White, Robert. 1993. "On Measuring Political Violence: Northern Ireland, 1969–1980." *American Sociological Review* 58 (August): 575–85.

Wolfsfeld, Gadi. 1997. *Media and Political Conflict: News from the Middle East*. New York: Cambridge University Press.

Zanger, Sabine. 2000. "A Global Analysis of the Effect of Political Regime Changes on Life Intergrity Violations." *Journal of Peace Research* 37, no. 2: 213–33.

Ziegenhagen, Eduard. 1986. *The Regulation of Political Conflict*. New York: Praeger.

# Part I
# Under the Looking Glass:
# Toward a Better Understanding
# of Causal Dynamics

1

# Protest Mobilization, Protest Repression, and Their Interaction

## Clark McPhail and John D. McCarthy

We offer some observations, reflections, and proposals about protest mobilization actors and protest repression actors and their interactions. Our
primary focus will be the United States during the last three decades. We
will attend mainly, on the protest side, to mobilization for protest events
rather than longer-term movement institution building. And on the repression side, we mainly attend to shorter-term obstacle creation by state actors
surrounding specific protest events or sequences of events rather than on
longer-term efforts at creating obstacles to movement institution building.

We begin with repression, then turn to mobilization and finally to the
interaction of the actors and actions in mobilization and repression. In the
first two sections we address four questions. What is it? What do we know
about it? What about it seems to be changing? What more do we need to
know about it? We will illustrate some of our points with ongoing and recent observations and analysis of the interaction of challengers and agents
of social control. In the third section we suggest an approach for thinking
about the interaction between protesters and the police.

## Repression

### What Is It?

Paraphrasing Tilly (1995, 136), we view repression as obstacles by the state
(or its agents) to individual and collective actions by challengers. The flip
side of repression is facilitation of, or the provision of opportunities for, individual and collective actions by challengers.

Repression must be considered along a continuum. The use of deadly direct force marks the most severe end of the repression continuum, illustrated by the 1967 attacks on Chicago Black Panther headquarters, the 1968 shooting of students at South Carolina State (in Orangeburg), at Jackson State (Mississippi), and at Kent State (Ohio) in 1970. None of these compare to Tiananmen Square in Beijing in 1989 with respect to the number of protester causalities. Less-than-deadly direct force during protest events has ranged from baton charges and tear gas in Chicago at the 1968 Democratic convention, sometimes accompanied by the beating of protesters, to the use of rubber bullets and pepper spray in more recent protests. Next along the continuum is the use of restraint in the form of cordons and barricades, then apprehension of challengers before or during protest events, followed by arrest, arraignment, and incarceration.[1]

Two other categories of repression should be noted. The first is preemptive strikes prior to protest events. These may involve invading and then closing organizing centers, confiscating various organizing resources (puppets, placard and banner standards), arresting and incarcerating organizers as well as large numbers of rank-and-file challengers only to release them without further penalty as soon as the protest event is concluded. Last, but especially important, repression can take the form of police surveillance from the outside or police infiltration of challenger ranks, which sometimes extends to the use of agents provocateurs (Marx 1974).

### What Do We Know?

The United States has a checkered history of protest policing over the past four decades (McPhail, Schweingruber, and McCarthy 1998). During the 1960s and 1970s, some civil rights and the antiwar protesters were shot and killed and many were injured. More recently, in the antiglobalization protests in 1999, 2000, and 2001, no one was killed in the United States, a few were shot and injured with rubber bullets; others were injured by police batons. Table 1.1 provides a brief comparison of the differences between these two eras of policing policy and practice.

### Escalated Force

Traditionally the police have justified their actions as upholding their sworn responsibilities to maintain law and order by protecting the property and person of the targets of protest.[2] At the same time, they have generally ignored their sworn responsibilities to protect the First Amendment guarantees of the protesters. They have kept protest organizers and protesters at a distance, neither encouraging nor accommodating contact and interaction before, during, or following protest events except to apprehend, handcuff, arrest, arraign, and confine. The Escalated Force doctrine places challeng-

## Table 1.1. A comparison of U.S. protest policing styles, 1960s versus 1990s

| Dimensions of comparison | 1960s escalated force | 1990s negotiated management |
|---|---|---|
| First amendment guarantees | ignored | protected |
| Tolerance for community disruption | none to low | moderate to high |
| Police–protester communication | undercover and exploitative | open, extensive, continuing |
| Use of force | initial show of force and progressive escalation | minimum necessary force |
| Extent and manner of arrest | frequent and forceful | infrequent and civil |

*Source:* McCarthy and McPhail 1999. Reprinted with permission.

ers at an obvious disadvantage, ranging from the violation of their First Amendment rights to serious injury and even death. This doctrine also poses formidable obstacles to protest mobilizing. But there can be negative consequences for police as well, among them mass media coverage of civilian injuries and deaths. Such coverage has both external and internal political consequences for police (Waddington 1994).

### Negotiated Management

Police agencies in selected U.S. cities (e.g., Washington, DC, New York City, San Francisco) and throughout Europe (della Porta and Reiter 1998) that must deal with protest on a recurring basis have moved in the direction of concern for protecting protesters' First Amendment and human rights. These concerns supplement the traditional ones of protecting the person and property of protest targets, including onlookers (McCarthy and McPhail 1998). This has been accomplished through the legal requirement that protest organizers give notice of their intent to demonstrate or obtain a permit to protest. In each case, an opportunity is created, if not required, for contact, interaction, and negotiation between police and protest organizers regarding the purpose, the time, place, and manner of protest.[3]

This policy can and frequently does allow the police to state their own responsibilities to the law, including the guarantee of protesters' rights to free assembly, speech, and petition. It can, and frequently does, allow the police to draw the figurative "line in the sand" so that protest organizers will know which protest actions will and which will not be tolerated by the police, when, and where. In turn, protest organizers are invited, encouraged, and cajoled to state their objectives and the means by which they intend to realize those objectives.

The advantage of this policy to both sides is that there is often sufficient openness in the reciprocal statements of ends and means that both parties can negotiate a mutually agreed-upon game plan—the protest permit—such that each will be "reading from the same page." Of course, both sides may not be completely forthcoming.[4] Organizers may plan to engage in civil disobedience in places and at times when they can exploit departures from the permit to their mass media advantage. And the police clearly use the "time, place, and manner" limitations to situate venues and routes to their own advantage. These problems aside, negotiated management policy and practice have yielded a dramatic reduction in disorder, damage, and death for challengers and a significant reduction in media, political, and bureaucratic problems for the police.

We do not, however, wish to paint a glowing picture of the current status of protest policing in the United States. Not all police agencies sympathize with, nor do they bend over backwards to accommodate, the efforts of protest organizers to stage successful protest events. First, the negotiated management policy and practice is not widespread in U.S. communities. Unlike England and other European nations, there is no national police in the United States and therefore no national public-order policy and practice. Second, there are some protest organizers who will not communicate, let alone negotiate with, the police. Third, large protest events are increasingly composed of diverse coalitions of groups and organizations, what we call "mixed-motive" challengers. Fourth, as we have noted elsewhere (McCarthy and McPhail 1998; Titarenko, McPhail, and McCarthy 1999), the police remain "agents of the state." Therefore, in established as well as emerging democracies, police agencies that might ordinarily practice negotiated management are always subject to the directives of the power holders for whom they work. And clearly, the negotiated management policy provides the opportunity for unscrupulous police to co-opt as well as repress protesters.[5]

Finally, it can be argued that the routinization of protest has yielded protest events that are boring if not ineffectual in achieving anything more than a short-term "feel-good solidarity" on the part of protesters who have rallied, marched, chanted, and sung together. (This is an example of useful rather than useless Durkheim; see Tilly 1981). The "time, place, and manner" limitations make it increasingly difficult for protesters to sufficiently disturb, disrupt, or discombobulate targeted decision makers, thereby creating a "power-dependency relationship" (Emerson 1962; Gamson 1975) that brings both parties to the bargaining table to negotiate challenger grievances (Alinsky 1972). This perceived ineffectuality of protest may have something to do with the recent increase in the number of challengers who will have no part of applying for permits, let alone negotiating or even talking with the police. We will return to this point later.

### What's Changing?

We have called attention to some changes in public-order and protest policing that have reduced disorder and death. There has been another change in police practices, however, that risks reversal of that trend. We refer here to the expanding role of SWAT teams in public-order policing. SWAT is an acronym for Special Weapons and Tactics.[6] SWAT teams were created in the early stages of the war on drugs in the 1980s and 1990s (Kraska and Kappeler 1997; Kraska and Paulsen 1997; Kraska, 1999; Waddington 1999). These specialized units were initially funded, trained, equipped, and deployed to enforce "no-knock" entry warrants against armed drug dealers. They were subsequently, and continue to be, used in hostage, terrorist, and other barricaded situations, as well as those in which armed civilians are threatening harm to themselves or to others.

Community-level SWAT teams are increasingly called into service for public-order policing. Television coverage filled screens with images of groups of black-suited "Darth Vader" police confronting the protesters during the World Bank/International Monetary Fund meetings in Seattle, Washington, DC, and Quebec City, the 2000 Republican and Democratic national conventions in Philadelphia and Los Angeles, respectively, as well as the 2001 presidential inauguration in Washington, DC.[7] With increasing frequency, police departments deploy their SWAT teams to deal with sport victory celebrations, campus beer riots, and other mixed-motive events.

SWAT teams in many communities are being trained in "crowd control" by such entrepreneurial organizations as the Miami Field Force (MFF), which is composed of former Dade County, Florida, police officers. The training consists essentially of teaching officers who are accustomed to working alone or with a partner to work collectively as part of a larger group of officers to form cordon lines and wedge formations and to retrieve or rescue officers who have been injured.[8] Anyone familiar with the crowd-control training manuals of the U.S. Army or Marine Corps would recognize the elementary training in collective policing formations and actions that Miami Field Force teaches.

Given the emphasis on coordinated action, SWAT teams that have undergone the MFF training will be better trained and equipped to act collectively if and when called upon to do so. That includes maintaining discipline in the face of taunts and harassment and forgoing any response to protesters until ordered to respond. Such training should, therefore, reduce unintended repression by police. However, in the training the first author has observed, no distinction was made between a common understanding of a protest event and what most observers would characterize as a riot. The trainers repeatedly slipped into the police jargon of distinguishing between "the good guys" (i.e., the police) and "the bad guys" (i.e., "the rioters" or "the protesters"). The trainers made neither any mention of protesters' First Amendment rights nor the importance of negotiating with organizers before, during, or after the protest event. And the emphasis in the training was on the eventual necessity of using force to restrain protest movements or to compel protest dispersal. That emphasis implies that the members of the "crowd" in question have diminished ability to control themselves and must therefore be forcefully controlled or restrained if and when they refuse to do the bidding of the police (cf. Schweingruber 2000).

## So What?

Increasingly larger protest events at local, state, and national levels require authorities to form coalitions of multiple law enforcement agencies whose personnel come to events with diverse training, equipment, and experience. Many officers pressed into service in such situations have almost no prior experience in policing protest events. This increases problems of coordination and control. A significant risk of that inexperience is that officers are frightened of injury from what many of them perceive as "the madding crowd" (but see McPhail 1991). Police have the tools, the strength, and the experience to retaliate against verbal or physical attackers with considerable force. In addition, inexperienced officers under the command of inexperienced superordinates may indiscriminately strike out at a gathering of protesters containing only one or a handful of persons who have thrown a missile or a punch at an officer or otherwise broken the law. Such impetuous responses to protesters are almost certain to yield a barrage of disapproving curses and may increase the number of missiles thrown at the police.

## What Do We Need to Know?

We need to know the range of public-order policing problems faced by police agencies across the United States, with particular attention to agencies in college and university communities, as well as in state capitol cities, two types of locations where protest events are more likely to occur. We need to know the public-order policing policies of those agencies, as well as what training, equipment, personnel, and related resources are available to them. At present we have very little systematic information about any of these features of police agencies around the United States.

## Mobilization

### What Is It?

Mobilization must be discussed at two levels. The first problem is one of assembling people at some specified location(s) as well as marshaling whatever additional resources and preparations are necessary for collective action by those people. The second problem is one of coordinating and adjusting what those people do collectively once they have assembled.

### What Do We Know?

We have learned a great deal about the mobilization of participation in protests (as well as celebrations that become riotous). We know that social networks are the means by which most people learn where, when, and sometimes why they should converge on a particular location, and what they should expect to find or what they are expected to do there upon arrival. Students of these phenomena have paid more attention to the "why" than to the "what" and "how" of mobilization (but see Gerhards and Rucht 1992). The frequently cited research of Klandermans and Oegema (1987) documents that singular attention to the potential or inclination of people to participate is insufficient to predict participation. Oliver and Marwell (1992) call attention to the nuts and bolts of on-the-ground mobilization. They emphasize that organizers must "solicit" participation; they must ask people to participate, not merely tell them when, where, and why they should participate. McPhail and Miller (1973) report that the more frequently people were solicited or invited to participate in a sport victory celebration (which turned riotous), the more likely they were to do so, provided that they were available (that is, they had no prior obligations or competing demands at the same time) and had access (that is, some means of transporting themselves) to the site of the event in question.

In the past, social scientists have tended to give limited credit to the role of mass media in mobilizing people for participation. The media have been viewed as tangential in mobilization. The recent research of Walgrave and Manssens (2000) documents one case in which hundreds of thousands of people participated in a massive procession through the streets of Brussels in the absence of any discernible mobilization effort by social movement organizations, churches, labor unions, political parties, or other traditional mobilizing agents. Walgrave and Manssens make a convincing case that the print media in Belgium essentially provided the necessary ingredients to produce the mobilization without benefit of traditional social movement organization infrastructures and related social networks.[9] The print media reported the disparity between public perception of the state's response to the murder of several children and what the public believed should have been done regarding those murders, and the media repeatedly emphasized that gap. When a call was issued for a mass demonstration in the capital city of Brussels, the print media reiterated that call. The media subsequently reported, repeatedly, what would take place, when, and where. Newspapers described how easily citizens could participate and went to great lengths to counter common excuses for not participating. The result was the largest protest event in Belgium's history.

A final but important social fact about mobilization must be reiterated here. Individuals seldom assemble alone; rather, they assemble in the company of one or more companions—friends, family members, colleagues, or acquaintances. This is true even when assembling as members of larger affinity groups, or other neighborhood, labor, religious, educational, or political collectivities. This yields at least three levels of social organization in a typical protest event: (1) companion clusters (family, friends, acquaintances), (2) some of whom are within larger units of social organization (affinity groups, churches, neighborhood associations, unions, etc.); and (3) some or all of whom may be part of a coalition mobilized by a coordinating committee or consortium of representatives from different sponsoring organizations and affiliates.

### What's Changing?

The Internet has significantly altered the means by which "the call" and "the message" are disseminated, the size and diversity of the monitoring audience, and the potential "mix" of mobilizers and the mobilized. It also provides a means of feedback by which "the calls" and "the messages" themselves can be altered. The Internet does not change the essential features of call and message—the what, when, where, the solicitation, and the why. Nor does it replace the importance of coalition formation among a variety of groups with overlapping objectives and preferences for similar means of achieving those objectives (Gerhards and Rucht 1992).

The Internet amplifies but does not replace the "two-step" flow of the call and the message from mass media into informal social networks that massage, or reflexively interpret, the message (Thompson 1995). It does increase the ease, the speed, and the scope of communications to mobilize participation in any single protest event. It makes possible the mobilization of multiple organizers to issue their own calls and messages in their own communities for simultaneous protest events in communities nationwide (Exley 2000). The Internet provides access to e-mail alert lists; to calendars of planning sessions, marshal training sessions, poster- and puppet-making sessions; to training manuals; to flyers and petitions for downloading, local reproduction, and distribution; to useful medical information about protection against and recovery from tear gas and pepper spray; and to essential legal information about rights of assembly, speech, and petition, as well as risks of arrest, arraignment, fines, and incarceration.

The Internet provides a means of electronic civil disobedience by using e-mail for "virtual sit-ins" that disable corporate servers or by flooding corporate fax machines. The Internet allows the use of encryption software to send secure messages about extralegal and illegal activities, as well as the time and place of those activities, all of which significantly reduce the possibility of surveillance by the police, as well as other opponents.

## Who Is Mobilized?

The Internet allows a greater diversity of groups to create their own Web sites and Listserv discussion sites on a wide range of issues and thereby to mobilize participation in local, state, regional, national, and international protest events and campaigns.[10] Within the last decade, Washington, DC, has been the site of several well-known protest events mobilized in large measure with the Internet: the Million Man March rally; the Promise Keepers Stand-in-the Gap rally; the annual March for Life rallies and processions; the annual gay pride rally and march; the Million Mom March against Handguns; the annual MIA/POW Rolling Thunder motorcycle procession and rally; the Trucker Convoy against High Fuel Prices; and the 2001 presidential inauguration protests. The most massive and complex international mobilizations have been those in protest against the World Bank and the International Monetary Fund in London (June 1999), Seattle (November 1999), Washington (April 2000), Prague (October 2000), Davos (January 2001), and Quebec City (April 2001). Mobilization for participation in all of these is facilitated by the Internet's reciprocal communication features between organizers and the organized.

Some challengers are collectively distinguished by the banners beneath which they march, the slogans they chant, the goals they seek, and the ideology that justifies the tactics they employ to realize those goals. One such set of challengers visible in European protests as early as the 1970s, but only recently on the U.S. protest scene, is the Black Bloc. The name seems to derive from a color associated with the ideology the protesters profess (anarchism) and the color of the clothing that has become their signature, as well as their preference for moving collectively through the streets in relatively tight formations.

In the United States, the Black Bloc is self-described as anticapitalist, antistate and antiimperialist. Its activists claim to model themselves on the German "Autonomen" (and the Italian "Atonomia"). The Black Bloc is at least as committed to resistance as to protest inasmuch as resistance entails disobedience, direct action, and noncooperation with the state. The Black Bloc will have nothing to do with the state or its agents of social control (except to attack them when and where opportunities present themselves). The Black Bloc in North America appear to be organized along the same lines noted in della Porta's (1995) analysis of the Autonomen and Atonomia in Germany and Italy. It stresses decentralized "leadership." It is organized in moderately sized (ten to twenty-five member) "affinity groups" who collaborate with one another only in terms of "loosely structured coordination committees" composed of group representatives who meet in "general assemblies."[11]

### Coordination Technology

There are two additional technologies used by both Black Bloc and many other segments of the contemporary antiglobalization challengers to coordinate their actions during protest events and to document their actions and interactions with the police. Mobile scouts on bicycles engage in continuous reconnaissance regarding the locations and strength in numbers of the police. Cell phones allow them to communicate instantaneously to an apparent central coordinator who in turn relays the information to cellphone holders in multiple affinity groups who can then relocate quickly to exploit opportunities for their repertoire of individual and collective actions.

Every affinity group is advised to have at least one designated videocam operator, who is responsible for recording every action in the presence of, directed toward, or received from the police. This has made possible the creation of an alternative and independent audiovisual record of protest actions and interactions that can be (1) reviewed and critiqued in preparation for subsequent protest event planning; (2) broadcast worldwide on the Internet as an alternative mass media report; (3) edited into documentary videotapes that are used to propagandize; (4) sold to pay for production costs; and (5) provide affinity groups with their own record of contact and interaction with the police should they have to defend themselves in court.

One other change should be noted. Della Porta and Rucht (1995, 253) note that the emergence of the Automonen movement—"the so-called Black Bloc"—followed a period of protest normalization in Germany. The recent routinization of protest in the United States, to which we have referred, is perhaps now being followed by the emergence of a movement of young, anticapitalist, antistate, antiglobalization anarchists in the United States and Canada. They made their first dramatic entrance in Seattle in 1999, followed by repeat performances in Washington in April 2000, with smaller presences at the 2000 Republican and Democratic conventions in Philadelphia and Los Angeles, but significant participation in Washington in January 2001 and Quebec City in April 2001. Police response to "Black Bloc" performances in North America has varied significantly by the experience and sophistication of public-order policing in the jurisdictions in question. It was very oppressive in Seattle and in Quebec City, but much more sophisticated in Washington (as it was in London). We will return to this point.

### What Do We Need to Know?

We have long been aware of the "two-step flow" of mass media messages into social networks (Katz and Lazarsfeld 1955) of family, friends, colleagues, and acquaintances. In the course of the daily rounds of contacts and interactions that constitute those networks, media messages are interpreted and massaged. We need to investigate the changing multistep flow of information from the Internet into and through a monitoring audience who can not only massage the message in face-to-face and electronic communications among themselves, but also provide feedback on the Internet and thereby reconstruct the messages that appear there. This is a powerful new arena for what Shibutani (1968) calls "improvised news."

### What Are the Implications of the Internet for How Mobilization Takes Place, as Well as Who Is Mobilized?

What is the diversity of "messages"—the whys that accompany the whats, whens, wheres, and solicitations that compose "the call to participate"— that shape the expectations and plans of those individuals and groups about what they might find (and expect or plan to do) upon arrival at the protest event? Further, are people mobilized through the Internet more likely to assemble alone than with companions? With mere acquaintances versus family, friends, and colleagues? In short, what are the implications of Internet mobilization for both the "mixed motives" of the participants and the social relationships among them during the protest event itself?

## Actors, Actions, and Interactions

### Our Assumptions

In our previous work on protest and repression we have assumed that both challengers and the state (or its agents) are purposive actors operating in dynamic environments that present their plans and their actions with variable opportunities and constraints. Purposive actors must adjust to those changes in their environment if they are to realize their purposes. Just as actors can make adjustments to exploit opportune openings, they can also make adjustments to disturbance, obstacles, and constraints.

The sources of random disturbances may be the weather, the terrain, the physical constraints of the setting; or it may be the unanticipated consequences of actions taken by other actors. Competing or opposing actors can engage in deliberate disturbances ranging from harassing to disrupting and thwarting, or ultimately to eliminating their competition or opposition. Civil disobedience and violence against person and property are examples of challenger constraints. The use of tear gas, baton charges, rubber bullets, arrests, and incarceration are variable examples of deliberate state constraint, as are surveillance and the use of agents provocateurs.

We also assume that purposive actors draw on past experiences in order to define the situation they are confronting, to answer to the question "What's happening?" or what Snow and Benford (1988; Benford and Snow 2000) call "diagnostic framing." Purposive actors also draw on their past experiences (individual memories or shared repertoires) for the objectives (goals and targets) in that situation, thereby engaging in what Snow and Benford call "prognostic framing" or "What should be happening?"

They compare what they see and hear taking place with their objectives, goals, or targets. If there are discrepancies (and there frequently are), they make adjustments in their actions such that the their answer to the question "What's happening?" matches or approximates their answer to the question "What should be happening?"[12]

The actions taken to achieve those goals are seldom taken in a stable, routinized environment, particularly if other actors are present. Instead, those actions are very likely to encounter both random and deliberate disturbances. Thus purposive actors must continually monitor and compare "What's happening?" against "What should be happening?" and they may be required to make continuing adjustments in order to deal with the obstacles as well as the opportunities with which they are confronted.

### The Complexity of Interaction

We are not the first to call attention to the importance of interaction between challengers and the state. Tilly's earliest discussion of repertoires (1979, 135) acknowledged the dynamic "interplay between authorities and other actors [that] significantly affects the collective-action repertoire." His more recent work takes this line of analysis a significant step further. In one of his many recent monographs, Tilly writes (1995, 39):

> [My] most contentious claim [is] that the prior path of collective claim-making constrains its subsequent forms, influencing the very issues, actors, settings, and outcomes of popular struggle. The particular path of contention has an important impact, I argue, because each shared effort to press claims lays down a settlement among parties to the transaction, a memory of the interaction, new information about the likely outcomes of different sorts of interactions, and a changed web of relations within and among the participating sets of people.

Nor is Tilly the first to call attention to the complexity of such interaction. Koopmans writes (1993, 637) that the "dynamic processes of interaction are difficult to grasp theoretically and analyze empirically. This is already the case for relatively simple interactions, involving a few, clearly circumscribed actors, which suggests that analyses of the dynamics of [admittedly more complex] protest [events] face formidable difficulties." The complexity of interaction dynamics increases with the diversity of collective actors involved in an event, their objectives, their tactics, and their alliances.

Therefore, what we have said to this point neither solves nor simplifies the problems of complexity, nor those of interaction; if anything, it renders them more complex. Among the various groups that are a part of the coalition that mobilizes any large protest event, there typically have been a diversity of means to mutually agreed-upon ends among the various contingents of protesters (McPhail 1985; Gerhards and Rucht 1992). The Internet appears to be increasing both the diversity of protester segments and their numbers.

There may have been more of a mix among the styles of protest policing in the past than we have assumed or documented, but the appearance of the negotiated management method was sufficiently different from traditional methods to make it stand out. That was and is the basis of our fascination with negotiated management.[13] The increased proclivity in the United States to train and deploy the ubiquitous SWAT teams for public-order policing further complicates the softening trend in negotiated management protest policing that we have identified (McCarthy and McPhail 1998). Our final comments will no doubt further complicate the picture. We think it is prudent to recognize the complexity of the phenomena to be explained before leaping to conclusions about the most useful explanations currently available.

### Outcome versus Intentional Violence

One of Tilly's early contributions (Tilly, Tilly, and Tilly 1975) documented the low incidence of violence in the century of European protest between 1830 and 1930 and hypothesized the sequence in which the majority of those protest-related incidents of violence might have developed. He suggested the following hypothetical sequence. First, one group engages in actions that directly or indirectly state a claim for some right, resource, or redress of grievance. A second group, or its representative, then resists the claim of the first group or states a counterclaim. Frequently, both claims and resistance are repeated, yielding a spiraling struggle between opponents that results in violence to the members of one or both groups. The important point is that neither party's initial actions are violent, nor is a violent outcome their initial intent. But the outcome produced by their interaction is a violent one because each set of actors is pursuing its own (nonviolent) interests and thus defending them against, or resisting, disturbances or threats presented by the other party.

Tilly's analysis is useful for the development of most violent incidents in large protest gatherings. However, McPhail (1994) has called attention to a second pattern of violence in European sport gatherings in which a subset of football fans—self-described "hooligans"—claim a "thrill to violence" and openly boast of their intentions to engage in violence toward, and repeatedly do engage in violence against, the person and property of the fans of rival football clubs, the police, and anyone else who may object or interfere. In recent years, American college and university campuses and communities have witnessed increasingly frequent incidents of disorderly exuberance in the course of sport victory celebrations, illustrating that intentional violence in large gatherings is not restricted to English hooligans or to European and American anarchists. In events like these, missiles are thrown at police, store windows are broken, trash cans are torched and become the centerpiece of bonfires that grow in size when park benches and "abandoned" furniture accumulate as fuel for the flames. Automobiles are overturned and stores are looted.[14]

It is important to recognize that whether the violence is intended from the outset or is the outcome of interaction between actors who resist disturbances to the realization of their nonviolent objectives, violence is still the exception rather than the rule in all temporary gatherings for which evidence is available.

### Variability in Individual and Collective Actions and Adaptation

Protest events not only entail variation in protester objectives and tactics and in protest policing policies and practices, they also entail considerable variation in the individual and collective actions of which they are composed.[15] McPhail and Schweingruber (1998; Schweingruber and McPhail 1999) have devised a taxonomy and a method for the systematic on-site observation and recording of collective action in protest events and other large temporary gatherings. They report that the most characteristic feature of the actions that occur in a large protest event (the annual March for Life) is alternation between and variation in individual and collective actions. Collective action is never continuous and seldom approaches mutual inclusiveness (unanimity) of action among all members of protest gatherings.

McPhail et al. (2000) used the same taxonomy and method to code videotape records of interaction between protesters and police in several protest events in London, including one of the largest British riots in the last quarter century: the 1991 Poll Tax Riot in and around Trafalgar Square. Adapting the methodology to videotape analysis has been tedious and slow (but otherwise successful) and there is reason to believe it will become easier and quicker with more repetitions. It is too early to offer even preliminary quantitative summaries and it would be premature to report that any one or few categories of action by protesters or by police consistently precedes violent actions by the other. There are, however, some clear impressions that are relevant to this discussion and the general problem with which this volume is concerned.

1. Violent actions by either protesters or police are comparatively infrequent, even rare.
2. When police observers who were on-site during the riot reviewed the videotape record, they were stunned by the disparity between their recollections and impressions that violence was widespread and more or less continuous, and the videotape evidence demonstrating that it was not.

3. The sequences of violent actions by protesters or police that do occur are short-lived and discontinuous.
4. The violent actions are almost always engaged in by no more than a handful of all the police or protesters visible in the gathering.
5. The majority of persons in the gatherings in which the violence occurs are spectators, albeit more often than not partisan spectators cheering on "their gladiators."

It is no exaggeration to assert that in this riot (as well as, for example, in videotape footage of the South Central Los Angeles riot of 1992 examined by the first author) violence by civilians or by police officers is the exception rather than the rule. This is not, of course, the impression left by the print and electronic media, who consistently report violence against person and property, if and when it occurs, to the exclusion of the more frequent, prosaic, and nonviolent actions by the majority of the actors in the riot area.

### Variable Police Adaptation

Our observations lead us to the tentative conclusion that most police will intervene when there are blatant violations of the law, whether they involve civil disobedience or violence against property and person. However, we suspect that police intervention in situations of perceived disparity between "What is happening?" and "What should be happening?" varies from one police agency to another as a function of the particulars of the situation, as well as of agency policy and experience with similar situations.

Table 1.2 provides a rough picture of police responses to encounters involving civil disobedience during protest events mobilized by four different social movement organizations (SMOs) during the early 1990s (McCarthy and McPhail 1998). These several SMOs specialized in one form or another of civil disobedience as their signature tactic and often violated any agreements previously negotiated with the authorities about the "manner" of their protest. The outcome of their encounters with the police, however, provides a useful portrait of the consequences of negotiated management policing even in the face of noncooperating protest groups. Negotiated management police prefer the inconvenience of minimizing the force required to effect arrests to the bad publicity created by media coverage of forceful arrests, not to mention the paperwork they must complete when injuries or complaints occur during arrest procedures or when panels of inquiry investigate such incidents.

## Table 1.2. Policing civil disobedience in protest encounters with four social movement organizations, 1991–95

| | Social movement organization | | | |
| Encounter features | Queer Nation | ACT-UP | Justice For Janitors | Operation Rescue |
|---|---|---|---|---|
| Civil disobedience (%) | 71 | 74 | 93 | 99 |
| Police presence (%) | 96 | 100 | 100 | 100 |
| Events with arrests (%) | 50 | 77 | 73 | 99 |
| Arrests per event[a] | 8.5 | 16.0 | 33.4 | 58.8 |
| Total number of arrests | 102 | 862 | 401 | 5,996 |
| Police use force (%)[b] | 4 | 20 | 13 | 5 |
| Total number of events | 24 | 70 | 16 | 106 |

*Source:* McCarthy and McPhail 1999. Reprinted with permission.

*Note:* Based on a Nexus-Lexus search

[a] For those protest events with arrests.

[b] Coded "present" if any hint of force by police in confronting and/or arresting demonstrators (including reports of resisting arrest) in the original report of protest or thereafter in other press reports.

These four SMOs engaged in extensive confrontational protest over the five-year period in question, resulting in many arrests. Nonetheless, the arrests, typical of negotiated management policing, usually were carried out in very orderly ways in spite of the passive resistance typical of the ACT-UP and Operation Rescue protesters.[16] Even those disorderly protest groups chose to conclude their attention-getting disorderliness by cooperating in ritually enacted arrests.

Police are more likely to use force against protester violence than against protester civil disobedience (Koopmans 1993). However, even police agencies with a history of violent response to armed protesters can change their policy and practice in the direction of negotiating standoff encounters with armed protest organizations (McCarthy and McPhail 1999). Table 1.3 portrays key features of U.S. federal police agency responses to three notorious stand-offs between authorities and armed challengers at Ruby Ridge, Idaho, Waco, Texas, and Jordan, Montana. The widespread criticisms and legal challenges to police use of deadly force at Ruby Ridge and Waco led to a reassessment by the U.S. Justice Department and the issuance of new guidelines for the policing of such events. Consistent with those guidelines, the negotiated surrender of the Freemen at Jordan, Montana, was distinguished by practices that more closely resembled negotiated management than those previously used at Ruby Ridge and Waco (McCarthy and McPhail 1999).

Koopmans reports (1993, 647) that his examination of several thousand protest events in West Germany between 1965 and 1989 established that about 75 percent of violent protest events were repressed by the police as compared with 20 percent of legal and nonviolent marches and rallies. Confrontational or civil disobedience protest events were less frequently repressed at the beginning of the period he examined, but repression increased to higher levels toward the end.[17]

In the United States, we suspect that repression varies by police jurisdiction and agency in accordance with the extent of the agency's experience with policing public order in general and protest in particular.[18] Black Bloc violence against property and persons was policed with indiscriminate use of force in Seattle in November 1999 and it spilled over to the policing of protest groups. Arguably, indiscriminate violence also characterized the policing in Quebec City in April 2001. Black Bloc violence against property and persons was policed selectively and proportionately in Washington, DC in April 2000 and January 2001.

Prior to the November 1999 protests against the meeting of the World Bank (WB) and the International Monetary Fund (IMF), the Seattle Police Department (SPD) had relatively little experience with protest policing at any level in the chain of command. This was evident to outside police observers and to social scientists. As a consequence, for example, the SPD had no "mutual aid" pacts with neighboring community police agencies.

**Table 1.3. Federal policing of armed encounters with three militant protest organizations, 1991, 1993, 1996**

| Policing dimensions | Aryan Nation 1991 Ruby Ridge, ID | Branch Davidians 1993 Waco, TX | Freemen 1996 Jordan, MT |
|---|---|---|---|
| Tolerance of defiance | Low | Low | High |
| Contact and interaction | Low and low | High and low | High and high |
| Negotiation strategy | Hard and manipulative | Hard and manipulative | Conciliatory and entrusting |
| Show of force | Ostentatious | Ostentatious | Subdued |
| Use of force | Lethal | Lethal | Restrained |

*Source:* McCarthy and McPhail 1999. Reprinted with permission.

In addition, it had little protective equipment for its officers; had done little logistical planning to support the officers with food, equipment, and relief; had depended on inadequate communications between superordinate and rank-and-file officers during the protest event; and had previously developed no effective mass arrest plan. Consequently, it was overwhelmed by the number and diversity of protesters, by the ingenuity of protest tactics, and by its dual obligations of simultaneously protecting WB/IMF delegates and policing the protesters (Gilham and Marx 2000; Smith 2000). The police responded inadequately and repressively; it is surprising but fortunate that no one was killed during the event.

In Washington, DC, there are between fifteen hundred and two thousand protest events every year McCarthy, McPhail, and Smith 1996). Each of the three major police agencies has officers up and down the chain of command with extensive experience in policing protest events, and each agency has a specialized public-order policing division. The U.S. Park Police probably confront more protests, and, therefore, may have more experience with negotiated management, than the Metropolitan Police of the District of Columbia or the U.S. Capitol Police. Nevertheless, all three agencies are well trained, well equipped, and generally well coordinated compared to most other U.S. police agencies when they confront protesters. Arguably, these agencies in Washington, DC, responded in restrained ways to the April 2000 World Bank/International Monetary Fund protests and to the January 2001 inauguration protests. There were, however, three exceptions. The first was the preemptive arrest and detention of several hundred protesters who were demonstrating in the streets one or two days prior to the opening sessions of the WB/IMF meeting when the main protests were scheduled to occur. A second was the raid and seizure of protest accoutrements at a protest command center. The third was that the larger events in that series of protests involved a greater number of protesters than the three local agencies could handle on their own. Of necessity, therefore, they had to bring in officers from several other police jurisdictions. This creates greater diversity in training and experience among the combined force and increases the likelihood that an inexperienced and frightened officer might break ranks and strike back when taunted by an aggressive protester.

Our impression is that Canadians have had considerably less experience than Americans with public-order policing. For example, when the Asian Pacific Economic Cooperation (APEC) summit was held in November 1997 at the University of British Columbia in Vancouver to celebrate the imminent globalization of "free and open trade and investment," several groups announced their intention to protest. The Canadian government and Vancouver and University of British Columbia officials were initially favorable toward "protest under suitable conditions" (Ericson and Doyle 1999, 592). But several Asian countries, Indonesia in particular, pressured the Canadian government to insulate their leaders and senior officials from visual exposure to the protesters. The Canadian government capitulated to that pressure and the principles of "negotiated management" were scuttled in favor of "more pressing political concerns" (Ericson and Doyle 1999, 595). There were preemptive, preventative arrests of protest organizers, and there was also censorship of protest banners and posters on and near the campus. A Canadian aboriginal speaker scheduled to address the opening session of APEC leaders was abruptly deleted from the program. When protests eventually occurred, police used pepper spray to dislodge protesters who were scaling a fence. Threats of force preceded the coercive dispersal of protesters engaged in a roadway "sit-in." And police bicycles were used as battering rams in an attempt to disperse demonstrators, resulting in the injury of dozens of protesters and several journalists.

We were not in Quebec City in April 2001 for the protests against the Free Trade Association of the Americas (FTAA) summit. Therefore, our observations are based on print and electronic media accounts and the reports of one veteran observer in personal correspondence with the first author.[19] By the time the protesters arrived in Quebec City, the summit organizers had erected a formidable obstacle to those who sought to disturb or shut down the meetings of heads of state. The obstacle was a two-and-one-half-mile-long chain-link fence bolstered by concrete barricades that formed a defensive perimeter around the summit meeting.

According to all observers, including demonstrators, the wall was both a real and a symbolic obstacle. One organizer stated, "This is a symbol of the struggle to have a discussion behind the wall." The veteran observer reports that from a distance of three hundred meters from the fence, "people of virtually every description [were observed] walking past the police with virtually no animosity evident by either party. The mood changed as the people neared the fence. They suddenly became more focused and much more vocal in their expressions of anger or dislike for what the fence represented or kept them from approaching. Away from the fence, even after contact with the police, there was almost an air of calm that was very interesting."

On the afternoon of April 20, the first day of major protests, several thousand demonstrators marched nearly five miles from Laval University to the fence. Upon arrival, some hurled bottles and other missiles at the riot police stationed on the other side of the fence. Many were chanting "So-So-

Solidarity." Some pushed against the fence; others scaled and rocked it until a section gave way to the cheers of the onlooking protesters. The police responded by hurling canisters of tear gas in the direction of the protesters, who replied by picking up the canisters and hurling them back at the police. On this day, the wind was blowing away from the protesters toward police, but they were protected with hi-tech tear-gas masks.

Eventually, the protesters retreated behind the fence line, but, according to the *Washington Post* (April 21, 2001, A16), they claimed a minor victory in downing the fence, while chanting "We are the champions." Police continued to throw canister after canister of tear gas and the protesters continued to throw them back along with other missiles. The same story in the *Post* states that "some reporters saw [anarchists] hurl a few firebombs as well." As the evening wore on, police eventually used bullhorns to call on the protesters to disperse. This resulted in protesters laughing at and taunting the police rather than leaving. Police then moved into the gathering of protesters and commenced apprehending, cuffing, searching, and arresting selected individuals.

Very much the same scenario was repeated on Quebec City's second day of confrontations and exchanges of tear gas between protesters and police, with the exception that the wind now favored the police blowing toward the protesters, who had only lo-tech, vinegar-soaked bandanas for protection against the gas. The protesters were a mixed-motive assemblage: some wanted peaceful demonstrations, others were determined to stop the FTAA meetings by any means possible. The *Washington Post* reports that on the second day, some "Demonstrators set fires, [and] police answered with water cannons, rubber bullets and clouds of tear gas" (*Washington Post*, April 22, 2001, A18). The veteran observer reported that the police selectively fired baton rounds only at specific individuals who were throwing rocks, bottles, and Molotov cocktails, and if a missile posed no immediate threat, no shot was taken. The other interesting comment by this observer was that "the majority of the crowd [of five to ten thousand] was watching a [smaller] number, perhaps several hundred, engaged in a variety of lawless behaviors, including throwing missiles, destroying public property, attempting to scale the perimeter fence."

In the final analysis, both sides claimed victory. The protesters did succeed in delaying or canceling some meetings; they did demolish a small section of the two-and-one-half-mile fence; and they even received what some of them considered a policy concession from President George W. Bush, who pledged to seek protection of the environment and to improve the conditions of workers. By the end of the protest event, the police had arrested more than 150 demonstrators. Eighty-five protesters and thirty-four police were reported to have received minor injuries in the course of the confrontations.

### Variable Protester Adaptation

Several studies of protest and repression (Lichbach 1987; Gupta, Singh, and Sprague 1993; Francisco 1995, 1996) establish very clearly that protesters in nondemocratic as well as democratic societies adapt their tactics in response to variable police repression. Our study of Minsk, Belarus, during the transition from communism (Titarenko et al. 2001) illustrates such adaptability. In the face of escalating repression by the state, Minsk challenging groups (who were otherwise organizationally strong) increasingly adopted simpler and less contentious protest tactics in order to avoid arrest.

Opp and Roehl (1990) surveyed antinuclear protesters previously repressed by the police over their intentions for subsequent protest participation. The protesters reported that previous police repression would not deter them from taking part in future demonstrations and that they would advise a previously arrested friend to participate in less risky actions; that they would encourage the friend to continue his or her involvement in subsequent protests; and that they would go with that friend to the next demonstration. Further, they reported that they felt more obliged than ever to take action against nuclear power, and to a greater extent than prior to police repression. They reported that they would participate in protests more than before and would encourage others to do the same in order to demonstrate that repressive police actions were unacceptable. (See Table 1.4.)

### Limits to Adaptation?

The only certain way to prevent human beings from adapting to the disturbances and obstacles in their environment is to kill them. Short of that, incarceration is an effective means of taking protesters out of play. In nondemocratic regimes, there are other ways that discourage adaptation; the state can take away jobs, housing, opportunities for education, and other avenues of occupational and educational mobility.

There are limits to police adaptation as well. We have already mentioned the difficulty police have in adapting to innovative protest tactics, to variability, mobility, and any other variable that reduces the capacity of the police to predict where, when, how, and under what circumstances the protesters will choose to confront them. This is precisely what happened in the spring 1964 civil rights campaign in Birmingham Alabama (Morris

## Table 1.4. Respondents' reactions to recent police actions in West Germany

| Items | % Agree | % Disagree |
|---|---|---|
| *Questions referring to a deterring effect* | | |
| 1. The police actions deterred me from taking part in demonstrations. | 33.1 | *52.1*[a] |
| 2. I'm downright afraid now to take part in a demonstration. | 28.1 | *50.4* |
| 3. I would advise him to take part in less dangerous actions.[b] | 47.9 | *24.8* |
| *Questions about the deterring effect of police actions* | | |
| 5. After these police actions, I have supported others to become active now more than ever. | *47.1* | 36.4 |
| 6. I will participate in demonstrations now more than ever to demonstrate that I won't just accept such police actions. | *43.0* | 31.4 |
| 7. I would go with him to the next demonstration.[b] | *40.5* | 17.4 |
| 8. I would encourage him to keep up his involvement.[b] | *75.2* | 0.0 |

*Source:* Opp and Roehl 1990. Copyright © University of North Carolina Press

*Note:* All questions refer to "hard police actions" in antinuclear power protests in West Germany in 1987. Respondents were arrested and detained for more than thirteen hours for what was subsequently declared a legal protest. We agree with Opp and Roehl's assessment that, with the exception of the response to statement 3, police actions had more of a radicalizing than a deterring effect. (Italicized numbers are our emphases.)

[a] The difference to 100 percent corresponds to a response of "undecided."

[b] These three questions were prefaced with the following statement: "Let's assume one of your friends is arrested in the course of such a police action. How would you react?"

1993). A more recent protest tactic that discombobulated the Seattle police occurred when protesters snap-linked their wrists together inside PVC tubes in such a manner that police were unable to quickly and safely cut through the tubes, disconnect the linkages, and apprehend the protesters, let alone transport them to jail. That tactic was not as widely used during the Washington, DC, April 2000 demonstrations against meetings of the World Bank and International Monetary Fund because the police made a concerted and successful pre-protest event effort to confiscate the extensive paraphernalia necessary to implement the tactic. Finally, the power of numbers can also impair police adaptation. In mid-June 2001, in Göteborg, Sweden, twenty-five thousand protesters literally overwhelmed a thousand police, who temporarily had to abandon the town center.

## Summary and Conclusion

We have attempted, first, to draw together diverse theoretical and empirical materials, including some of our own work, in order to think through more carefully what we mean by protest repression and mobilization. In doing so, we have tried to highlight what we see as the most salient recent trends in both repression and mobilization in the United States. Accomplishing the first task was necessary before we could address the second task: how do protest actors and repressive actors—challengers and police—interact with one another through time and space? Our interpretation of this process relies heavily on McPhail's (forthcoming) formulation of a negative feed-back model of purposive action, which provides a useful lens for analyzing how purposive individual and collective actors adapt their behaviors to one another as they interact through time. That model informs our assessment of how changes in mobilization and repression in recent years might affect such interactions in the future.

## Notes

1. Economic means of repression range from fines, and, more typically in nondemocratic nations, to the loss of employment and the loss of state-controlled housing.

2. For an assessment of how early social and behavioral science analysis of crowd phenomena provided police with a justification for a policy and practice of escalated force, see Schweingruber (2000).

3. The development of the negotiated management policy and practice has been facilitated, and sometimes directed, by court decisions establishing a body of First Amendment law, as well as by state funding for training, equipping, and deploying police officers in a variety of "public-order" circumstances (McCarthy and McPhail 1998). For early and recent views of such policies and practices from the vantage point of social-control personnel, see O'Malley and Lund (1970) and Beasley, Graham, and Holmberg (2000).

4. Police routinely inquire about the intentions of protesters beyond the details negotiated in a permit to engage in civil disobedience, specifically, whether or not they intend to cooperate, resist, or go limp when arrested. They also sometimes provide organizers with "prearrest" forms to be filled out in advance by demonstrators who plan to be arrested.

5. We have documented one case (Titarenko et al. 2001) in which a negotiated management policy was introduced during the post-perestroika "democratic opening" in Belarus but was then exploited and corrupted by a democratically elected populist-turned-tyrant in order to repress public protest.

6. Other acronymic innovations in specialized policing units include CERT (Corrections Emergency Response Team) and SORT (Special Operations Response Team).

7. "The standard attire worn by SWAT teams throughout the western world is a black or dark blue hooded coverall with elasticized wrists and ankles, worn with external body armor and a ballistic helmet, and a respirator if necessary" (Waddington 1999, 136).

8. The first author observed a Miami Field Force training session for policy agencies in Urbana and Champaign, Illinois.

9. Walgrave and Manssens (2000) fail to mention the likelihood that all the people who read newspapers are also members of informal social networks that result from their daily rounds of contacts and interactions. In the course of those rounds, individuals discuss many things, not least of which is what they see on television, hear on the radio, and read in the newspapers. Thus, there may well have been a "two-step process" of relaying and massaging the messages disseminated by the mass media through interpersonal networks (cf. Katz and Lazarsfeld 1955).

10. Examples at the state level include the march in 2000 from Charleston to Columbia, South Carolina, in protest against flying the Confederate flag over the state capitol; at the national level, they include the 2000 postpresidential election protest rallies in dozens of cities through the United States.

11. However, what is claimed and what is practiced are not always the same. Della Porta (1995, 105–6) provides an interesting report from one such representative: "Yes, [our general assemblies] were public, and then we went to a Bierhaus and, in a small group, solved in half an hour what we couldn't solve [in general assembly] in five hours. This was necessary, we couldn't do anything else, we couldn't leave everything up to spontaneity. Basically it was quite cynical behavior at the same time to propagandize about spontaneity and to do exactly the opposite."

12. This perspective is best described as a negative feedback model of purposive action. Individual actors operate as closed-loop negative feedback systems; groups operate as open-loop negative feedback systems. The explicit or implicit use of such models can be found in both micro- and macro-sociological theorizing and research by Shibutani (1968), Goffman (1974), Burke (1991, 1997), McClelland (1994), McPhail and Tucker (1990), McPhail (1991, 1994, and forthcoming), and Tilly (1996).

13. We have no "Pollyannaish" delusions of a utopian form of protester–police interaction mode that would answer Rodney King's plaintive question: "Can't we all just get along?"

14. The recent appearance of the Black Bloc in the United States may be more worrisome to some observers inasmuch as the violence in which its members engage has not been, perhaps cannot be, attributed to their overindulgent consumption of

in alcohol. Nevertheless, the escalating occurrence of campus community disorders has raised concerns about public disorders at the U.S. Justice Department (Beasley, Graham, and Holmberg 2000).

15. Individual actions involve visible movements of (or audible sounds from) one or more sections of their bodies: facing, body position/locomotion, voicing, manipulating. Collective action involves two or more individuals engaging in one or more of those actions judged to be parallel or differentiated in direction, tempo, form, or substantive content. We have identified more than forty elementary forms of collective action that occur in prosaic, religious, sport, and political gatherings. For details and data, see McPhail and Schweingruber (1998), Schweingruber and McPhail (1999), McPhail, Schweingruber, and Ceobanu (2003).

16. The majority of force present in ACT-UP arrests came at the hands of the New York City and Los Angeles police early in the period under consideration. Subsequently, large civil awards from both cities to protesters for their mistreatment by police were followed by sharp declines in the use of force in those cities.

17. Violent events included both light violence (breaking windows, throwing stones at police during demonstrations) and heavy violence (arson, bombing, sabotage) against property and the kidnapping or murder of persons. Demonstrative protest events consisted of legal and nonviolent marches and rallies and petition campaigns. Confrontational protest events involved civil disobedience in the form of blockades, occupations, illegal demonstrations, and the disruption of meetings (Koopmans 1993, 640).

18. For example, the Los Angeles County Sheriff's Department has a vast amount of experience with public-order and protest policing and has adopted a style that is very similar to the negotiated management policy and practice with which we are familiar in Washington, DC. The city of Los Angeles Police Department has less experience and continues to police in a manner that more closely corresponds to the escalated force policy we have described. LAPD had the primary responsibility for policing the 2000 Democratic National Convention in Los Angeles.

19. The observer was a recently retired senior command officer from a large police agency with two decades of experience in public-order policing in a large metropolitan area. He was retained by the Quebec City police as an observer/consultant during the event in question.

## Works Cited

Alinsky, S. 1972. *Rules for Radicals: A Pragmatic Primer* New York: Random House.
Beasley, N., T. Graham, and C. Holmberg. 2000. "Justice Department's Civil Disorder Initiative Addresses Police Training Gap." *Police Chief* (October): 113–22.

Benford, R., and D. Snow. 2000. "Framing Processes and Social Movements." *Annual Review of Sociology* 26: 611–39.

Burke, P. 1991. "Identity Processes and Social Stress." *American Sociological Review* 56: 836–49.

———. 1997. "An Identity Model for Network Exchange." *American Sociological Review* 62: 134–50.

della Porta, D. 1995. *Social Movements, Political Violence and the State: A Comparative Analysis of Italy and Germany.* Cambridge: Cambridge University Press.

della Porta, D., and H. Reiter, eds. 1998. *Policing Protest: The Control of Mass Demonstrations in Western Democracies.* Minneapolis: University of Minnesota Press.

della Porta, D., and D. Rucht. 1995. "Left-Libertarian Movements in Context: A Comparison of Italy and West Germany, 1965–1990." In J. C. Jenkins and B. Klandermans, eds., *The Politics of Social Protest: Comparative Perspectives on States and Social Movements,* 299–72. Minneapolis: University of Minnesota Press.

Emerson, R. M. 1962. "Power Dependence Relations." *American Sociological Review* 27: 31–41.

Ericson, R., and A. Doyle. 1999. "Globalization and the Policing of Protest: The Case of APEC 1997." *British Journal of Sociology* 50: 589–608.

Exley, Z. 2000. "Organizing Online: How a Former Union Organizer Accidentally Sparked a Nationwide Election Protest Movement via the Internet." *Mother Jones* (December 9).

Francisco, R. A. 1995. "The Relationship between Coercion and Protest." *Journal of Conflict Resolution* 39: 263–82.

———. 1996. "Coercion and Protest: An Empirical Test in Two Democratic States." *American Journal of Political Science* 40: 1179–1204.

Gamson, W. 1975. *The Strategy of Social Protest.* Homewood, IL: Dorsey Press.

Gerhards, J., and D. Rucht. 1992. "Mesomobilization: Organizing and Framing in Two Protest Campaigns in West Germany." *American Journal of Sociology* 98: 555–95.

Gillham, P. F., and G. T. Marx. 2000. "Complexity and Irony in Policing and Protesting: The World Trade Organization in Seattle." *Social Justice* 27: 212–36.

Goffman, E. 1974. *Frame Analysis: An Essay on the Organization of Experience.* New York: Harper and Row.

Gupta, D. K., H. Singh, and T. Sprague. 1993. "Government Coercion of Dissidents: Deterrence or Provocation?" *Journal of Conflict Resolution* 37: 301–39.

Katz, E., and P. Lazarsfeld. 1955. *Personal Influence: The Part Played by People in the Flow of Mass Communications*. New York: Free Press.

Klandermans, B., and D. Oegema. 1987. "Potentials, Networks, Motivations and Barriers: Steps toward Participation in Social Movements." *American Sociological Review* 52: 519–31.

Koopmans, R. 1993. "Dynamics of Protest Waves: West Germany, 1965–1989." *American Sociological Review* 58: 637–58.

Kraska, P. B. "Questioning the Militarization of U.S. Police: Critical versus Advocacy Scholarship." *Policing and Society* 9: 141–55.

Kraska, P. B., and V. E. Kappeler. 1997. "Militarizing Mayberry and Beyond: Making Sense of American Paramilitary Policing." *Justice Quarterly* 14: 607–29.

Kraska, P. B., and D. J. Paulsen. 1997. "Grounded Research into U.S. Paramilitary Policing: Forging the Iron Fist inside the Velvet Glove." *Policing and Society* 7: 253–70.

Lichbach, M. I. 1987. "Deterrence or Escalation? The Puzzle of Aggregate Studies of Repression and Dissent." *Journal of Conflict Resolution* 31: 266–97.

Marx, G. 1974. "Thoughts on a Neglected Category of Social Movement Participant: The Agent Provocateur and the Informant." *American Journal of Sociology* 80: 402–42.

McCarthy, J. D., and C. McPhail. 1998. "The Institutionalization of Protest in the United States." In D. Meyer and S. Tarrow, eds., The *Social Movement Society: Contentious Politics for a New Century,* 83–110. Lanham, MD: Rowman and Littlefield.

———. 1999. "Policing Protest: The Evolving Dynamics of Encounters between Collective Actors and Police in the United States." In J. Gerhards and R. Hitzler, eds., *Eigenwilligkeit und Rationalität Sozialer Prozesse,* 336–51. Wiesbaden, Germany: Westdeutscher Verlag.

McCarthy, J. D., C. McPhail, and J. Smith. 1996. "Images of Protest: Dimensions of Selection Bias in Media Coverage of Washington Demonstrations, 1982 and 1991." *American Sociological Review* 61: 478–99.

McClelland, K. 1994. "Perceptual Control and Social Power." *Sociological Perspectives* 37: 461–96.

McPhail, C. 1985. "The Social Organization of Political Demonstrations." Paper presented at the annual meeting of the American Sociological Association, Washington, DC.

———. 1991. *The Myth of the Madding Crowd*. Hawthorne, NY: Aldine De Gruyter.

———. 1994. "The Dark Side of Purpose: Individual and Collective Violence in Riots." *Sociological Quarterly* 35: 1–32.

————. Forthcoming. *Beyond the Madding Crowd: Individual Purpose and Social Organization.* Hawthorne, NY: Aldine De Gruyter.

McPhail, C., and D. L. Miller. 1973. "The Assembling Process: A Theoretical and Empirical Examination." *American Sociological Review* 38: 721–35.

McPhail, C., and D. Schweingruber. 1998. "Unpacking Protest Events." In D. Rucht, R. Koopmans, and F. Neidhardt, eds., *Acts of Dissent: New Developments in the Study of Protest,* 164–98. Boulder, CO: Rowman and Littlefield.

McPhail, C., D. Schweingruber, and A. Ceobanu. 2003. "Variations in Collective Action across Ten Hours among a Half-Million Men: The 1997 Promise Keepers' 'Stand in the Gap' Rally in Washington, D.C." Paper presented at the annual meeting of the Midwest Sociological Society, Chicago.

McPhail, C., D. Schweingruber, A. Ceobanu, and P. A. J. Waddington. 2000. "Analyzing Video Records of Collective Action." Paper presented at the annual meeting of the American Sociological Association, Washington, DC.

McPhail, C., D. Schweingruber, and J. D. McCarthy. 1998. "Policing Protest in the United States: 1960–1995." In D. della Porta and H. Reiter, eds., *Policing Mass Demonstrations in Contemporary Democracies,* 49–69. Minneapolis: University of Minnesota Press.

McPhail, C., and C. W. Tucker. 1990. "Purposive Collective Action." *American Behavioral Scientist* 34: 81–94.

Morris, A. 1993. "The Birmingham Confrontation Reconsidered: An Analysis of the Dynamics and Tactics of Mobilization." *American Sociological Review* 58: 621–36.

Oliver, P. E., and G. Marwell. 1992. "Mobilizing technologies for Collective Action." In A. Morris and C. Mueller, eds., *Frontiers in Social Movement Theory,* 251–72. New Haven: Yale University Press.

O'Malley, T., and D. A. Lund. 1970. "SEADOC: An Overview." *Military Police Journal* (October): 4–10.

Opp, K., and W. Roehl. 1990. "Repression, Micromobilization and Political Protest." *Social Forces* 69: 521–47.

Schweingruber, D. 2000. "Mob Sociology and Escalated Force: Sociology's Contribution to Repressive Police Tactics." *Sociological Quarterly* 41: 371–89.

Schweingruber, D., and C. McPhail. 1999. "A Method for Systematically Observing and Recording Collective Action." *Sociological Methods and Research* 27: 451–98.

Shibutani, T. 1968. "A Cybernetic Theory of Motivation." In Walter Buckley, ed., *Modern Systems Research for the Behavioral Scientist,* 330–36. Chicago: Aldine.

Smith, J. 2000. "Globalizing Resistance: The Battle of Seattle and the Future of Social Movements." *Mobilization* 6: 1–20.

Snow, D., and R. Benford. 1988. "Ideology, Frame Resonance, and Participant Mobilization." *International Social Movement Research* 1: 197–217.

Thompson, J. 1995. *The Media and Modernity.* Cambridge, UK: Polity Press.

Tilly, C. 1979. "Repertoires of Contention in America and Britain, 1750–1820." In M. Zald and J. McCarthy, eds., *The Dynamics of Social Movements,* 126–55. Cambridge, MA: Winthrop.

———. 1981. "Useless Durkheim." In *As Sociology Meets History,* 95–108. New York: Academic Press.

———. 1995. *Popular Contention in Great Britain, 1758–1834.* Cambridge: Harvard University Press.

———. 1996. "The Invisible Elbow." *Sociological Forum* 11: 589–601.

Tilly, C., L. Tilly, and R. Tilly. 1975. *The Rebellious Century, 1830–1930.* Cambridge: Harvard University Press.

Titarenko, L., J. D. McCarthy, C. McPhail, B. Augustyn, and L. Crishock. 2001. "The Interaction of State Repression, Protest Form and Protest Sponsor Strength during the Transition from Communism in Minsk, Belarus, 1990–1995." *Mobilization* 6: 151–72.

Titarenko, L., C. McPhail, and J. D. McCarthy 1999. "Assessing the Impact of Concrete Political Opportunities on Protest during a Transition from Communism: Minsk, Belarus, 1990–1995." Paper presented at the biannual meeting of the International Sociological Association, Toronto.

Waddington, P. A. J. 1993. "Dying in a Ditch: The Use of Police Powers in Public Order." *International Journal of the Sociology of Law* 21: 335–53.

———. 1994. *Liberty and Order: Public Order Policing in a Capitol City.* London: University College of London Press.

———. 1999. "Swatting Police Paramilitarism: A Comment on Kraska and Paulsen." *Policing and Society* 9: 125–40.

Walgrave, S., and J. Manssens. 2000. "The Making of 'The White March': The Mass Media as a Mobilizing Alternative to Movement Organizations." *Mobilization* 5: 217–39.

# 2

# Precarious Regimes and Matchup Problems in the Explanation of Repressive Policy

*Vince Boudreau*

In some circumstances, it may be relatively easy to figure out why state actors resort to repression against social challenges. Where authorities confront a powerful insurgent army that can credibly oppose fundamental state interests, they will respond as they would against external threats—by mobilizing the force necessary to defeat the challenge. Where well-established states face less powerful challenges, state violence emerges more as police or military brutality: between 1968 and 1971, for example, Los Angeles police officers periodically attacked Chicano demonstrators, as other U.S. security forces were attacking African-American, Native American, and Puerto Rican groups elsewhere (Escobar 1993). This violence was increasingly at odds with Washington's formal policies, and at key moments, national forces moved against local authorities to prevent these attacks. Hence, most explanations for this violence, at least from the Johnson administration forward, focus on the orientations, excesses, or pathologies of discrete and usually local government agencies. Although violence differs across the two kinds of cases, in both a kind of intuitive fit exists between the degree of violence, its relationship to central state objectives, and the size of the social challenge. Strong challenges call forth violence from authorities moving to ensure their survival and health. Limited or isolated challenges against secure officials may still trigger brutality—but this violence stands apart from central state objectives. The massive violence of the besieged state may be loathsome, but it is explicable in political terms; the brutality of renegade cops is a problem of police technique and perhaps broader social norms, rather than of state objectives.

Consider, however, different sorts of cases. At times, states have devoted themselves to the brutal suppression, defeat, or elimination of dissent or difference that falls far short of anything like a robust revolutionary challenge. One thinks in contemporary times of the Chinese state's pursuit of Falun Gong, state-backed genocide in Rwanda, or ethnic cleansing in the former Yugoslavia (Calhoun 1993). Similar campaigns occurred in the not too distant past: the Indonesian state murdered nearly one million members of a Communist Party that *had virtually no insurgent capacity*, and had restricted itself to almost purely parliamentary modes of activity. The Burmese military in 1962 detonated a bomb that killed a small and politically isolated group of students supporting the Communist Party. In many places—Manila in 1972, Argentina in the late 1970s (Anderson 1993), and El Salvador in the 1980s (Stanley 1996)—emerging or existing authoritarian states exaggerated or fabricated threats to legitimize repression. In each of these cases, centrally directed state violence attacked relatively weak challengers. How can we explain such attacks?

Now, another set of puzzles: armed insurgency would seem always to pose fundamental threats to state leaders, but sometimes (despite durable insurgent organizations), authorities have adopted markedly *understated* approached to these armies. The same Burmese state that slaughtered protesting students in Rangoon, for instance, at times almost ignored, and even licensed, insurgent organizations on its frontiers (Tucker 2001, 72–74). At various times since the early 1970s, Philippine authorities made few concerted efforts decisively to defeat Muslim or Cordillera-based separatist movements, and concentrated more on containment strategies and regional autonomy negotiations. But authorities that ignore some threats may pursue others with vigor, and this suggests that more than mere incapacity lies behind these acts of apparent tolerance. Indonesia's New Order regime tirelessly chased down regional insurgencies but often ignored urban student challenges (against which the Burmese state invariably leveled violent sanctions).

Both excessive state violence against relatively weak social challenges and surprising state tolerance toward apparently formidable challenges are explicable, I believe, in similar terms. In each example, state violence directed against specific social challengers is embedded in larger programs designed to establish or extend state power. Sometimes, the target is a principal obstacle to extending state power; in most cases, often misleadingly, officials seeking to legitimize coercion present their targets as fundamental challenges to public order or political stability. But these claims, obviously enough, are often invalid, and the attacks a ruse to convince or coerce other social forces to back the state (see Bonner 1987; Stanley 1996). In other situations, the challenging social force does not itself represent a powerful threat, but operates in ways that demonstrate political modes subversive to the established order. In all cases, however, relationships between the extent and nature of state power, on the one hand, and the extent and nature of a social challenge, on the other hand, help us to understand these state attacks and interpret their implications for subsequent politics.

In this essay, I examine state violence against society, with a particular focus on surprising and excessive violence that officials within weak or poorly consolidated states sometimes directed at social challenges. Weak or uncertain state actors (i.e., *not* secure authorities in liberal political settings) often react to social challenges from a position of fundamental insecurity. Authorities may not have the resources to exercise power simultaneously across territory *(broadly)* or over many aspects of social life *(deeply)*. Contentious challenges may undercut modes of state power, or legitimize or inspire other challenges to which authorities cannot respond. Social challenges—protest, insurgency, and separatism—hence pose threats in themselves (i.e., in what they may demand or take away from authorities) and in how the fact of their challenge may disrupt the authorities' efforts to consolidate power and build hegemony. State violence against challengers in these cases, I argue, becomes more explicable if we situate it within balances between states and social forces striving to overcome one another. The goal of my analysis is to provide a generalizable framework for thinking about relationships between weak, poorly consolidated state authorities and social challenges. I hope in particular to illustrate one way of thinking about the context of confrontation between the two groups that explains why apparently innocuous movements often receive brutal treatment and ostensibly formidable groups are often let off the hook.

## Political Order in Contested States

Where political power is highly contested, authorities seeking to thwart social challenges face two separate, but closely related, puzzles. First, over the short term, they must respond to threats against their power, identifying the most formidable, deciding how best to quash them, and (of equal importance) identifying challenges that can be regarded as innocuous (for ignoring some dissent provides a welcome respite to authorities with strained resources). Second, over the long term, authorities set out to build existing power into a more stable hegemony—deepening state influence when it has been superficial to establish more extensive social control, expanding the state's reach where it has been overly short. Accordingly, authorities with deep but centrally isolated power might try building it out toward territorial boundaries, whereas those that exercise weak social control over a broad geographic expanse will try to deepen that power within that territory.

The key to understanding repressive policies lies in the intimate relationship between these two puzzles (i.e., the short- and long-term defense of state power). The designation of any given social challenge as threatening or harmless may depend in the first instance on the power resources that claim makers gather to advance their cause, but it also reflects the challenge's relationship to state actors' program of domination. In most of what follows, I attempt to lay out what I consider the main contours of this interrelationship—illustrating the primarily deductive argument with examples drawn from several countries, including Indonesia, Burma, and the Philippines. Before that, however, let us consider some alternative formulations.

One way of thinking about state reactions to social challenges is to argue that different kinds of regimes have different repressive potentials, or that different kinds of social challenge provoke different levels of repression (Tilly 1978; Marks 1989). Yet authorities within individual states often also apply violence selectively, and this important nuance cannot be measured by a regime's general repressive proclivities (della Porta and Reiter 1998). As the Indonesian military was slaughtering members of East Timorese and Acehnese resistance movements in the 1980s, student protesters—and even rioters—often had very little to fear from authorities. The Chinese state famously repressed national democracy protests in 1989 and the Falun Gong movement after 1998, but has been more circumspect about local and economic-based resistance to, for example, tax policies (Perry 2001, 167). Nor, of course, can we assume that authorities operating in different national areas will be equally repressive. Chanddra and Kammen (1999) argue that Indonesian officers working in territorial commands often pursued conciliatory relationships with local societies that they hoped to join (postretirement). While Burmese soldiers were killing thousands in Rangoon during 1988, large Mandalay protests occurred without similar bloodshed, at least partly because battle-hardened troops were imported to deal with Rangoon's unrest, while local officers handled things in Mandalay (Callahan 2001).

Other work reasons from the character of the social challenge itself. Some assume merely that the frequency of political contention will influence modes of state response—the more frequently unrest occurs, the more decisive, and violent, the state response (Poe and Tate 1994). Yet authorities often develop an ability to contain unrest that can make once-threatening actions almost routine, and protesters may survive repression by playing up connections between their demands and political and social routines. Some human rights demonstrations in Argentina, for example, survived repression by imitating social routines (Arditti 1999). In the year following the People Power transition from Philippine dictator Ferdinand Marcos to Corazon Aquino, protest occurred almost daily, but authorities (and demonstrators) developed such set conventions for dealing with one another that things seldom grew violent or even threatening (Boudreau 1996). Some theories, concentrating on the variety of collective forms, argue that the most disruptive forms of political activity trigger the most powerful state responses (Taylor and Jodice 1983, 77; Churchill and Vander Wall 1990); cross-nationally however, different authorities may view given forms of resistance as more or less subversive, and this undercuts any effort to develop a single scale calibrating modes of struggle.

Christian Davenport's conception of multidimensional threat perception provides important correctives to this work. As with earlier research, Davenport (1995, 686) reasons from the character of a social challenge to that of state repression, but conceives of states' threat perception as based on a variety of dimensions (i.e., the presence of violence, dissident strategies, and deviations from accepted cultural norms). His main point is that authorities pay attention to a variety of factors, rather than the mere intensity (or frequency) of contentious events. Not the least of the work's contributions lies in its efforts, through concepts such as "culturally accepted levels of dissent," to provide some sense of political and social context for contentious interactions between states and societies. Still, Davenport's large-N approach, though helpful in establishing that states perceive threat along several dimensions, of necessity says less about the precise contours of any specific context. He deals with the strategic dimension, for instance, by arguing that as movements deploy a wider variety of strategies, they appear more threatening to states. This is a nice way to establish this principle, but it develops a rather general sense of threat: a social force that is persistent, unwieldy, violent, or inimical to established norms is threatening. But to what or whom are such threats posed? Perhaps to public order or property, to standards of decent or appropriate behavior, or to the institutions of rule and those who occupy them.

The argument does not require that we specify how the threat *threatens,* and this gives the work fairly broad applicability; where state power is particularly contested, however, we need a more specific calculus of threat. Consider, for instance, the different impact of ethnic conflict across different settings. Although anti-Chinese violence occurs in most Southeast Asian countries, in most settings it acts almost as a safety valve, to the point that some political leaders have sometimes encouraged it to deflect attention from other problems. In India, political elites often stir up ethnic conflict to build political power (Brass 1997). In Malaysia, however, efforts to balance ethnic communities lie at the center of the ruling coalition's power, and so protest that mobilizes ethnic constituencies against one another can be fundamentally destabilizing (Roff 1967). Indonesian authorities have been largely unaffected by violence against Chinese, but utterly shaken by the prospects of separatism diminishing the republic's physical realm. The mapping of Thailand, and the growing power of the mapped realm's geo-body, raised unruly frontier politics (in the mind of Bangkok officials) from insignificance to great national concern (Thongchai 1994). Modes of contention acquire status as more or less powerful, and threatening or subversive in relation to particular arrangements of state power and to specific programs to extend that power.

For weak authorities within poorly consolidated states, social challengers require more crucial, more particular, and more specific responses. Such authorities may not be able to dominate or diffuse every challenge, and must decide who really needs fighting, who can be conciliated, and who ignored. Because of this heightened dilemma of security and power, authorities within weakly consolidated states must seek strategies that established authorities elsewhere would not consider. Some may be willing to expand the power of potentially unreliable nonstate powers, or to weaken ostensible state agents. Joel Migdal (1988) demonstrates how Egyptian President Nasser, fearing a too-powerful Arab Socialist Union, undercut the party and reinforced the powers of local leaders. In 1965–66, as Indonesian generals worked to exterminate Communist Party members (and so eradicate the party), they provided unprecedented material and organizational support to student movements and Islamic associations—but withdrew that support when international aid strengthened the regime (Anderson 1983, 489). The Aquino regime in the Philippines eventually retracted its opposition to anticommunist vigilantes from 1987 to 1988, when it became clear that the armed forces were unable to contain communist insurgents, and unwilling *unconditionally* to back the president (Bello 1987). Authorities that have tolerated unpredictable and often armed social forces periodically repress unarmed protest, parliaments, or other less overtly subversive collective forms. Surely, this repression partly demonstrates the comparative ease with which authorities can move against unarmed demonstrators, relative to warlords or armed militia. But officials working to consolidate precarious holds on power evaluate threats strategically, responding to those that appear most formidable, subversive, or immediate. Such designations emerge in the flow of politics. Where power is hotly contested, that flow depends primarily on the balance of forces surrounding the hegemonic project. But asserting that these logics are particular does not require that we give up efforts to discuss them as tractable phenomena.

## Strategies of Repression: Two Heuristic Questions

Two questions help us discern rules governing these state responses to protest and resistance. The first asks about the sorts of social challenges that strike state actors as formidable. Authorities in any state, but particularly one weakened or beleaguered, will not likely respond to *all* social challenges. What influences the kinds of social challenge that call forth pointed state response? I suggest that the answer is not merely a function of a challenger's quantum of power, but rather of that power's structure and operation, in relation to the structure and operation of state domination. Two elements of challenger power, its breadth and depth, help us think about the contest between movements and state authorities: (1) How broadly diffused are forces across time and space? (2) How extensively, or deeply, does the force control society? We can ask these two questions about both states and social challengers. First, authorities and movements may draw their main support from several central points, or may build a geographically broader power base. We can ask of states whether they control mere enclaves of society, or have penetrated rural areas and established their authority. We can ask of movements whether they constitute merely local networks, or whether claim makers link together over substantial territory: are we dealing with a factory-level labor organization, or a national movement, an isolated land occupation, or a national peasant uprising? Second, authorities and movement leaders may extend deep or shallow control over people's lives. Government officials may be barely able to collect taxes, or may even regulate intimate family relationships. Activist solidarity may only encompass shared resentment of increased highway tolls, or may regulate moral and social conduct, and even inspire members to suicide attacks. States and social movements can *each* be broad or narrow, shallow or deep, and confrontations between them can run the gamut from the innocuous (where, for instance, narrow and shallow social movements confront broad and deeply rooted state authorities) to the fundamentally destabilizing (where, for instance, a deeply established social movement challenges authorities with shallow social influence). Modes of challenge can be more or less formidable to different state arrangements. A regional rebellion may threaten a broadly elaborated state more than one with an insular apparatus. An urban protest movement may more deeply undermine an insular state than one with more geographic reach.

The second question investigates the character of the state response. To understand which authorities adopt what responses, and toward whom, we need to determine the political relationship between movement capacities, state capacities, and the political order that officials pursue. Repression unfolds from within larger patterns of politics and conflict. State responses to social challenges can best be understood in terms of their underlying logic. I divide these responses into efforts to eliminate or diffuse specific social challenges, and efforts to revise rules of engagement and eliminate modes of contestation that especially threaten authorities. Whether authorities will tend more toward one or the other of these meta-logics depends on the architecture of state power, and trade-offs between defeating proximate social challenges and shoring up the regime more generally. I will put off specifying these precise relationships for the moment; for now, I wish to stress the separation between the matter of whether the authorities will respond to a social challenge and how they will do so. I discuss the two questions in turn, first considering factors that render specific modes of dissent more or less formidable to authorities, and then the factors that seem most likely to shape state responses to social movements.

## Social Challenges and Threat Thresholds: The First Question

Determining what challenges will provoke a pointed state response involves two separate, but interrelated, matters: first, what capacities social forces control—which I will consider an objective assessment; and second, how *formidable* the social force is—which I will define as *relative* to state power. Social challenges are not more or less formidable merely in their quantum of power, but rather in the degree to which their power resources undermine state actors and institutions. Some kinds of challenge will particularly threaten some kinds of states, and one needs to assess both their quality and the quantity to gauge their *formidability*. To judge a social challenge's proximity to a state official's threat threshold, we consider the currency in which the challenge is coined, and the value of that currency in the regime's economy of power. Let me clarify what I mean by an economy of power before attempting to integrate this understanding into a concept of threat threshold.

First, the elements of power that we identified earlier—breadth and depth—are strongly influenced by levels of organizational and political support. Political organization vastly influences the breadth of social and political power. An individual or group may act without strong organizational resources, but their influence is likely to encounter temporal, geographic, or programmatic limits unless it is organized, institutionalized, and reproduced. The concept of state building to regularize and expand the political apparatus captures what I have in mind here (Tilly 1990), and social movements can also encompass a variety of spatial or temporal ranges, across one neighborhood or several provinces, during several days or over a period of years. Analysts have developed concepts of diffusion (Tarrow 1995, 48–61) and institutionalization to capture these two extensions. Diffusion depends both on levels of ambient connection in a society and on more specific ties within the movement. Some have looked at movement organization as enhancing challenger power (Hobsbawm 1959), as ending movement radicalism (Piven and Cloward 1979), or as a more contingent element of movement politics (Tarrow 1995). Whatever the costs, institutionalization of some kind helps collective action overcome geographic or temporal limitations. States with weak organizational machineries need to compensate for that weakness by alliance with regional power brokers, by undertaking more indirect modes of rule, by concentrating forces in particular regions, or by building differential support among citizens. Movements with weak organizations may rely more on passionate and spontaneous mass activism—after which most probably demobilize. In either case, however, political actors are shoring up a weak flank.

Second, political power can in part be measured in the degree to which the force (state or social) controls social relations (Wolf 1999). Obviously, different capacities allow different modes of control. Military might can underwrite a more coercive social ordering; financial power can provide incentives and inducements. Some capacities rest on political, national, or charismatic appeals to populations that require—and would presumably be constrained by—social support. Although modalities of power may set the table for different kinds of conflict (what happens, for instance, when the politically and economically powerful lock horns?), I will treat different power resources as entirely fungible and discuss a social force in terms of its variable *depth of social control*.

To reiterate: I regard the two most important dimensions of state or social power as describing how broadly and how deeply a force exerts influence. These musings on power may evoke work in other fields of political science: realists among international relations scholars have long depended on power as an independent variable, and more than a few try (more precisely than I intend) to set qualitative and quantitative criteria for determining how much power a state possesses (see, for example, Baldwin 1979; Bueno de Mesquita 1981). These assessments are central to security studies premised on contentious and strategic interactions as a bedrock of world politics. This literature, however, offers only imperfect tools for the task at hand, because of the particular nature of sovereignty in the international system. Sovereign states interact with one another from territorial home bases, and project power to influence others with similar points of geographic reference. A small or weakly organized state will project less power than larger or better organized counterparts—but in their home territories, both are thought to enjoy sovereign control. Hence, the dominant international relations issue is how resources and organization *project* greater or lesser power into the international system. In domestic political contention, however, sovereignty itself is frequently at issue, and various social forces, including state organizations, contest hegemony *within a single realm and over a single population.* The question in such cases is not how much, or how far, one can project power, but rather how degrees of power projected from specific operational bases threaten the hegemonic project or ambitions of others. The structure of one's power, rather than its mere magnitude, is therefore essential to our understanding of the competition.

Let us, for the moment, leave aside the question of social challengers and concentrate on questions of state power. In general, authorities within state organizations will aspire to a degree of power that allows substantial control over society within the entire territorial realm, aspirations that require both organizational reach and capacities within that reach (Migdal 1994, 9–10). In an abstract and heuristic sense, we can represent interactions between these two sorts of power endowments with Figure 2.1, where state building strives toward the upper-right-hand corner from the lower left. Obviously, however, all states (or states in formation) do not begin in the position represented by the diagram's lower-left-hand corner— with weak capacities and inchoate organization—or along the ascending line that I have labeled A. For many, some crisis—a recent transition from colonial rule, economic underdevelopment, famine, revolution, military coups, ethnic conflict—undermines the state-building program and renders their positions precarious. These initially weakened positions, like hegemony itself, can be conceived along dimensions of breadth and depth: weak states can dominate relatively limited territories, can build an apparatus that spans vast territory but exercises little control within that realm, or settle into some pattern of rule that falls within these poles.

In Figure 2.1, the series of concentric arcs (inscribed around a point in the upper-right-hand corner where states exercise strong geographic and social control) represent different levels of state power. Each arc contains an infinite number of points, representing infinite combinations of breadth and depth, each existing an equal distance from the imaginary point of

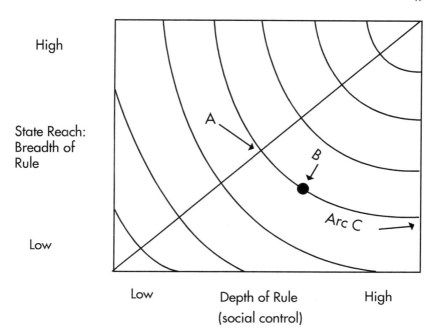

*Figure 2.1. Breadth and depth of state capacity*

complete hegemony. Point B exists along Arc C, along with an infinite number of other points, all representing different hypothetical states (or, indeed, social forces) with equal quanta (but different compositions) of power. In a general sense, of course, actors in any state, no matter where it falls on the diagram, should eventually strive toward conditions indicated in the diagram's upper-right-hand corner—for a combination, that is, of broad and deep social control. However, the immediate tasks required to fulfill this general ambition vary from state to state, depending on their starting points. Some may need to deepen control over resistant and independent society. Others need to bring autonomous and self-governing territories under more central control. What authorities require will initially depend on what they have already mastered, and states with similar levels of power (existing, that is, along a single arc) may nevertheless require different kinds of state building to move toward hegemony. In the absence of significant social challenge, states should take the shortest route between where they are and where they want to be: direct lines, that is, between any point and the diagram's upper-right-hand corner.

Where states and social forces contend with one another for hegemony, however, such a direct route is often not possible, for the state's progress toward hegemony is undercut by its need also to fend off social challenges. Where state forces and capacities are concentrated in the urban capital, officials may not be able to reach into the countryside and exercise influence if they also face powerful urban adversaries. Authorities may not wisely neglect urban challengers to pursue longer-term hegemony if those challengers pose sufficiently grave threats. If the urban challenge is weak enough, however, or is coined in a currency that does not threaten state power in the capital, it may be possible for authorities to meet it with token repression or none at all. Moreover, even a powerful challenge emanating from the countryside may be ignored by such authorities, at least until state power has reached further into rural areas. Hence a discussion that begins with the problem of building state power (where the existing state is precarious) turns the original question of political contention and state repression on its head: rather than asking how authorities respond to protest, we essentially ask what social challenges distract authorities from state-building programs. In this reading, social challenges will be perceived as threats depending on the magnitude and the nature of their power, as its relationship to the magnitude and nature of state power.

Under what conditions will a movement catch a state's attention and pose a threat? In answering, what role must we assign to the relationship between the hegemonic project and the compositions of state and social power? Two sets of assumptions regarding this question seem reasonable. The first deal with the comparative composition of state and social power, and the second with their respective magnitudes. Assume, first, that authorities will be fairly well positioned to defeat adversaries that have constructed their power in terms similar to that of the state. In such cases, challenges must be comparatively powerful to pose substantial threats. Conversely, challenges that mobilize political power in terms sharply different from those controlled by the state can often pose what I will call matchup problems, in which relatively weak challenges pose comparatively strong threats. Second, assume that the weaker states face more desperate trade-offs between fending off challenges and building hegemony than stronger states—and this influences both the location of the threat threshold and its curve. Let us deal with these two sets of assumptions in turn.

Most states, and surely those that are unconsolidated and hard-pressed, have some interest in ignoring episodes of dissent and unrest that they safely can. The question is, according to what principle will it undertake the distinguishing calculations? We began, as does much of the literature, with a consideration of the mere frequency or intensity of the conflict, and then introduced complicating caveats about how relative degrees of state power influence the authorities' ability or need to take account of social challenges. We can imagine these considerations in terms of *threat thresholds,* distinguishing social challenges that are formidable from those that are innocuous, and depicted in Figures 2.2 and 2.3 as lines drawn to the left of states. The way one draws the line representing the threat threshold has important implications for the model, and I will discuss the general principles before explicitly explaining the two figures. Were we to draw threat thresholds on parallel with the arcs indicating state power, they would suggest that amounts of power alone determine the degree to which social challenges threaten states, and movements that mobilize the greatest power will always pose the strongest threats to state officials. The examples cited at the start of this essay, however, pose puzzles precisely because they describe cases when social challenges, by any apparent measure, did not rival state power—and often did not even meet clear standards for criminal behavior or disorderliness. All represent situations in which (either) weak challenges called forth dramatic state repression, or apparently strong challenges were ignored by state authorities. In light of such anomalies, I argue that strategic interactions among forces, rather than the mere calculation of raw power, more thoroughly explain state responses to social pressure.

Specifically, authorities who have based their domination on one or another mode of power—on broadly or deeply elaborated resources, for instance—will be most able to withstand threats posed in those same terms. Authorities that have worked to penetrate frontiers are likely to be well positioned to outflank even relatively strong national movements, or at least to avoid being overwhelmed by the mere fact of their national scope. Where authorities have particularly deep ties with society, they will have the resources to maintain those ties, even when rivals emerge to try to undo them. This is not to say that state actors are invulnerable to challenges that assemble power in ways that resemble the state's, but rather that such challenges, in order to threaten, must be relatively powerful. The converse, however, is also true: challenges that have power attributes that sharply differ from those of the state can be threatening without being as powerful—and so, in relationship to such challenges, the threat threshold drops considerably. A basketball analogy might illustrate what I have in mind.

Sportswriters would have little trouble interpreting a basketball game in which the underdog defeats a team favored by a relatively slim margin. The outcome might be somewhat surprising, but if one or another shooter hits a hot streak, if the rival team goes cold, if several rebounds bounce in the right directions—if luck or fatigue or motivation tend in one direction more than in the other—an upset victory is explicable within the normal range of the teams' capacities. When a league's last-place team pulls off such an upset, however, and particularly when a generally weak team consistently poses problems for a far stronger opponent, commentators often begin to talk about "matchup" problems. In the early 1990s, for example, the New York Knicks were a generally strong team, particularly in their large and aggressive "front line" the center and two forwards). One of the team's hidden weaknesses, however, lay in its guard play. Although generally competent (though never stellar), Knicks guards were no taller than six feet three inches—with some still shorter. At that time, however, a new kind of guard was entering the league in increasing numbers, possessed of the shooting and ball-handling skills the position traditionally required, but also far taller—ranging up to six feet eight inches tall. Several teams, some of them very weak, had such guards—and more often than not, it seemed, even weaker teams with such guards simply torched the Knicks.

In relationships between states and societies, similar "matchup problems" also exist. Let us initially make a simplifying assumption about these matchups: that social threats with power bases that are (across the universe of cases) increasingly different from the state's need less and less net power to cross the threat threshold (as, in the basketball analogy, very weak teams with very tall guards strongly challenged my beloved Knicks). Hence, for instance, a national but weak administrative apparatus may be utterly unequipped to deal with localized insurgency, or even an isolated but strong urban movement. The obverse, of course, is also true: the closer the social challenge comes to approximating the proportions of breadth and depth in the elaboration of power, the closer that challenge must also approach levels of state power to constitute a threat. To capture these considerations, we sketch the threat threshold in Figure 2.2 as an arc curving away from the main power zone lines, requiring the highest levels of power where its combination of resources most resembles the state's. Social challenges that fall to the right of these arcs will attract attention from their associated states. We designate such challenges as threatening because they have attained a significant degree of power, in terms of resources capable of raising government concerns.

The matchup analogy also illustrates another principle. States, and ball teams, that have relatively even mixes of capacities will be least vulnerable to destabilizing challenges from weaker social forces. A team that builds around a single star playing a single position may sacrifice other strengths and become vulnerable to a wider range of matchup problems than a more balanced team without any such star. If a professional team uses its payroll to contract the services of an outstanding center, and fills in the rest of the team with less skilled, bargain-basement players, it could lose to teams that run the floor skillfully and get many points on the fly (for centers typically do not chase down fast breaks), or teams with skilled jump shooters (for centers play defense near the basket), or teams that emphasize precise passing; the concentration of power resources in a single position creates a variety of matchup problems. We can graphically illustrate this same principle in Figure 2.2, in which two states located along the same arc produce individuated threat thresholds. State 1 rests in the center of the diagram, with a relatively proportional mix of deep and broad power. State 2, within that same power zone, has very deep, but geographically isolated, power resources—a strong insular state, for instance, that has not penetrated into the countryside. Drawing arcs related to each point (arcs 1 and 2, respectively) inscribed using similar curves underscores state 2's comparative vulnerability—for more space is opened up to the right of its associated threat threshold. It is such states, moreover, that will be most prone to apparently anomalous incidents of repression—using strong force against relatively weak rivals.

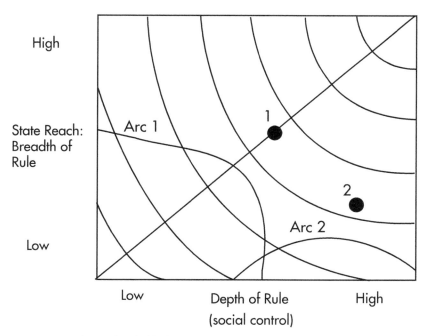

*Figure 2.2. Threat thresholds for two states in same power zone*

The magnitude of state power provides the other important context for contention and repression: social challenges are strong or weak, formidable or negligible, in relation to the power that the authorities themselves control. Weak authorities (i.e., those that can be represented in Figure 2.3's lower-left-hand corner, represented as state 2) would most desperately wish to repress dissent. At the same time, such authorities urgently need to undertake state building. Given the relative weakness of state organizations in this situation, of course, many cannot ignore challenges, and, where they must devote resources to repression, do so. At the same time, where authorities in weak states can ignore some social challenges, conserving resources to undertake the broader state-building program, they will embrace the opportunity. In such cases, the threat threshold will be marked by a sharper curve (arc 2) that drops off more suddenly as it acquires distance from the state position. At the same time, the threshold quite closely approaches the state at the curve's apex, indicating that, when possible, the authorities will ignore or downplay challenges that do not utterly demand a response.

States with stronger power resources (i.e. those that we can locate in the upper-right-hand corner of Figure 2.3, represented here as state 1) are only

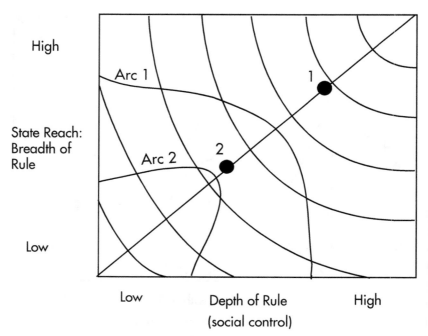

*Figure 2.3. Thresholds for strong and weak states*

truly threatened by movements with vast, state-like capacities, and in many places such challenges are relatively hard to imagine. As suggested earlier, such states may have long since ceased evaluating unrest and dissent in terms of their genuinely destabilizing capacity, and focus more on its criminal or disruptive content. Threats to public order, however, need not be so formidable as those to state power, and so the distance between the threat threshold (arc 1) and the state power position lengthens, even as authorities respond to an increasing range of dissident activity. But accumulating state power also relieves authorities of the need to weigh the resources necessary to address dissent from those necessary to build state power. Indeed, virtually any disruptive protest may call forth attention from authorities—and, in recognition of this, arc 1 flattens considerably compared to arc 2.

There are, then, roughly two ways in which social challenges approach what I have called threat thresholds. The first, and most straightforward, is that they amass sufficient power. Past a certain point, it hardly matters how they mobilize or deploy this power—if challengers are strong enough, state officials will respond. Particularly in immediate postcolonial periods, where the new society is often chaotic, mobilized, and armed, any number of social forces can represent substantial threats to emerging state arrangements—and even after one or another group has clearly come to occupy state offices, challengers may be quite formidable. Second, social challenges that pull together sources of power significantly different from the state's own resource bases also draw state attention—often out of all proportion to the magnitude of the challenge itself. Such dissident forces can develop exceptionally subversive modes of politics without necessarily acquiring great power. Both interpretations of formidability draw on a strategic and contingent reading of the elements of state and social power, and the contests between them.

## Official Responses to Social Challenge: The Second Question

Understanding the conditions under which one or another social challenge draws state attention only gets us partway to learning how authorities will respond. State responses, especially from authorities operating within poorly consolidated states, depend both on the nature of the challenge and on their larger concerns to extend and solidify their control over society. The main questions that analysts ask about negative state sanctions seek to explain state violence. The literature on policing protest investigates the causes and consequences of different police tactics. One strand of that literature emphasizes technology change; another concentrates on police techniques. An interesting and more recent branch of this work attempts to situate techniques of police control in larger relationships between states and society. Della Porta, Fillieule, and Reiter (1998) describe how the idea of the "King's police" gives way to more socially constrained models of community policing. They argue that originally isolated security forces, oriented toward protecting the state, grow more embedded in, and sympathetic to, society and its demands and concerns. Few, however, ask strategically instrumental questions about state repression: what, short of keeping the peace, do negative sanctions attempt to accomplish? In the main, police confronting protest pursue a general maintenance of order, and smaller objectives (in the service of that general goal) elaborated at street level. What of more pressing state-power objectives?

For officials operating within precarious states, negative sanctions support more contested and fundamental interests, such as authorities' survival and institutional reproduction. Figure 2.3 suggests that once authority becomes less vulnerable to social challenge, dissent can be evaluated and engaged as criminal activity or extra-institutional participation: authorities may arrest (or dislike) some demonstrators, compromise with others, but seldom wonder which ones threaten state power (della Porta and Reiter 1998, 24–26). Higher authorities in these same situations respond to contention as they might to elections or public opinion polls: as an indication of popular sentiment about policy. But where strategic calculations of political and material survival lurk behind state repression, and authorities need to allocate scarce resources among tasks that include both repression and state building, the key question is not what drives states to violence, but what is repression designed to accomplish? What does one do on the short end of a matchup problem?

The answer, of course, depends on the matchup, and on the game. To start, we make a distinction between two repressive logics. First, authorities may seek primarily to eliminate or incapacitate particular social threats—and all states that face formidable social threats, *whatever else they do,* must stave off these threats. In its purest form, such attacks concentrate on dissident orientations and identities, and may outlaw or attack groups or individuals based on what activists are, believe, or want, rather than on what they have actually done. The Philippine resistance against Marcos included movements designated (ambiguously, but unfailingly, by both authorities and activists) as "semilegal." The appellation indicated that formally, these groups pursued legal activity, but individuals within them (probably) supported the illegal Communist Party. With some regularity, activists were murdered or arrested, but their groups remained (Weekley 1996; Franco 2000). A second repressive mode manipulates arenas of struggle and styles of social power to privilege state actors and undercut challengers. In this variant, a challenge's political or ideological orientation is irrelevant to the proscription: rather, authorities ban some modes of activity as inherently destabilizing or subversive. Corporatist regulations illustrate a common such proscription. State-corporatist policies de-license modes of association outside of state auspices, and need not specify that communist labor unions, socialist farmers' cooperatives, or radical student organizations are *particularly* banned. By controlling arenas of power, state officials will control associational life, and so diffuse both existing and potential social challenges.

What influences whether authorities adopt one or another of these policies? Several hypotheses seem logical, based on the foregoing considerations. First, states with the most lopsided mix of capacities will tend to impose sanctions that repress *modes of activity* rather than *specific activist projects*. Lopsided power resources give authorities domination in specific areas, and open up potential vulnerabilities in others. Some state authorities may possess either strong but geographically limited resources or national but weak institutions. Officials in such states will seek to drive opponents toward areas in which authorities enjoy a comparative advantage. In some cases, authorities move against these modes of struggle, or activist arenas, in essentially regulatory ways, with laws or rules restricting political rights and freedoms. In other cases, sanctions may be violent—as when security forces murder an activist engaged in proscribed political form. As such murders eliminate particular threats, they also serve notice to others who might have contemplated similar acts of resistance and may eventually close off entire arenas of struggle (Heryanto 1999). Burma's 1962 state murders of student activists did not strike down particularly powerful collectives, but collectives that embraced the particularly subversive form (in Burma, at that time) of the public demonstration. This kind of repression helps authorities resolve dilemmas between short- and long-term state objectives, and so helps build state power: by restricting political modes in which rivals enjoy capacities, state officials clear the field of competitors and open the possibility of extending state power in new directions. The Indonesian military grabbed power in 1965 with a strong organization but weak social connections; following corporatist restrictions that eliminated rivals, the New Order could more leisurely deepen its rule (King 1982).

Conversely, states with more balanced capacities are less inclined to limit one or another dissident mode. For one thing, officials in more balanced states may not have such sharp ideas about what activity will undercut their power—and allowing a variety of dissident activity may introduce (from the regime's perspective) helpful divisions among challengers. Moreover, enjoying deep and broad power in equal (if limited) measure, officials in such states may have no interest in imposing blanket sanctions that could apply to any challenger. It may be more important to cultivate the idea of broad rights and freedoms, and then distinguish specific social forces that the state can depict as having separated themselves from the larger society. All journalists might protest blanket restrictions of press freedom, yet hold their peace when a communist newspaper is singled out for closure. Authorities operating in balanced states may not seek to build a monopoly in one or another mode of power, but instead keep society divided among itself, with repression helping to exacerbate some of these divisions. In such cases, individual activists or activist collectives will be denigrated in a particular fashion—as traitors, criminals, communists, or something else. Some may be arbitrarily (i.e., without clear charge) detained, tortured, or murdered—with such actions never justified in terms of activist activity, but only in terms of activist identity. Marcos's attacks on semilegal activists rooted subversives out of organizations engaged in public activity (strikes and demonstrations) that the regime was reluctant to sanction. Although Marcos-era antisubversion laws prohibited a wide range of political acts, those restricting demonstrations or strikes tended to be temporary; those outlawing communism remained on the books into succeeding, democratic regimes (Franco 2000).

Distinctions between these two objectives are, predictably, not as clearly drawn as I have described. For one thing, efforts to eliminate a mode of activity necessarily also strike at activists engaged in that activity, and subsequently, those who adopt proscribed political forms may set themselves individually apart as subversives. Conversely, repression that clears away a specific activist force will give subsequent activists pause before they pursue similar activity, and in this sense may also inhibit political modes as well as specific social forces. Yet the overlap is neither total nor purely conceptual, and it is in understanding its empirical dimension that we begin to grasp how violence operates. In the respective political ascent of Ne Win and Suharto, for instance, Burmese and Indonesian security forces both used violence against communists. After attacking student demonstrators, however, the Burmese government let survivors slip away—evidence, I think, that authorities were more interested in proscribing the collective form than in eliminating the Communist Party (Boudreau 2001). In Indonesia, soldiers and their supporters hunted down Communist Party members who had long since ceased pursuing any activity, and carried out their murders with an almost mechanical efficiency. Both regimes cut away at specific rival groups, and proscribed modes of political act. Indonesian authorities, however, were more committed to eliminating the Communist Party of Indonesia (PKI) as they regulated dissent, for the PKI possessed political capacities that more evenly balanced those of rising Indonesian authorities. In contrast, while the Burmese state was ill-prepared to respond to urban protest, it was not, in 1962, particularly threatened by urban communists. The Indonesian case, in fact, is particularly interesting because, as conditions evolved, authorities changed from a strategy designed to eliminate a specific rival to one designed to restrict modes of political expression. In 1965, in the closer competition between the military and the rival PKI, efforts to eliminate the communists were paramount. Once the field had been cleared, and the military-led New Order consolidated its monopoly on political organization, its repression concentrated on efforts to restrict political organization, but with respect, at least, to noncommunist Indonesian activists, state violence diminished considerably. The case illustrates the importance of thinking through the logic of threat and rivalry—using the argument outlined in the figures to guide this thinking.

These considerations help us more properly evaluate the frequently invoked concept of intensity, and its relationship to violence. Whether or not the state faces strong and dangerous challengers *does* matter, but it matters in ways we qualify in two respects. First, intensity is relative to threat thresholds discussed earlier—challenges are not intense objectively, but in their relationship to capacities possessed by states. Where matchup problems are most acute, a relatively weak challenge will still be intense. Returning to Figure 2.2, which depicts threat thresholds for 2 states (1 and 2): states toward the center of the arc, which we indicated as more likely to pursue activist specific responses to challenges (state 1), will likely respond to moderate threats (i.e., those that just barely cross the threat threshold) by jailing, harassing, or denouncing activists. States toward the edge of the arc, which we indicated as more likely to proscribe specific modes of politics (state 2), may concentrate on drafting and enforcing new rules regulating political expression and mobilization—and then depend on established and legal procedures to enforce those sanctions; that is, for repression both against activist forces and against political arenas, we can contemplate moderate and violent ranges of activity.

The most profound violence against dissent will most likely occur in precisely the kinds of cases illustrated by the PKI massacre in Indonesia, where authorities sought simultaneously to eliminate a powerful rival and regulate an entire mode of political activity. In such cases, the proximate challenge mandates violence, but that violence must also wipe away entire ways of expressing dissent, and so requires a scope that will resonate across time and territory. Violence in the Philippines under Marcos was erratic but measured, because the state itself stood atop a broader range of power modalities, including murder, patronage, propaganda, and elections, and faced activists mobilizing a broad range of resources as well. Ne Win's postcoup regime used repression to end the possibility of open demonstrations and dissent—using a symbolically shocking act of violence against a politically isolated adversary. But Indonesian generals acted both to eliminate the communists and to prevent future organization.

## Conclusions

These considerations are perhaps more useful, at this stage, as a way of thinking about repression than as a guide to prediction. Underpinning the specific arguments, however, are several points I would like to emphasize. First, in situations where authorities have not established domination, they will need to make trade-offs between efforts to build their power and efforts to defeat rivals. These efforts lead directly to the strategic mode of interpreting social challenges in light of state capacities—and so the weaker a state may be, the more stringent the strategic calculus will become. Second, although many observers assume that the stronger the social challenge, the more likely the state's recourse to violence, I hope to have convinced readers to regard violence, and repression more generally, as one potential answer to a larger question: what strategies might the state adopt to defeat adversaries and extend hegemony? In this light, the relationship between the intensity of a challenge and the violence of state response will depend on deeper readings of the threats posed by particularly structured social challenges to particularly structured state institutions. Some very weak social challenges may nevertheless pose significant threats to some states. Finally, I urge that we attempt to understand negative state sanctions not in the quanta of violence that they level against challengers, but rather in the logic of what they set out to accomplish. Some sanctions eliminate or diffuse particular social forces, but leave the field of play untouched—and typically operate either by justifying sanctions in terms of target identities or by obscuring state culpability in the attack. Other sanctions target not explicitly forces, but rather modes of operation, and may give rise to a legalistic or technocratic definition of proscribed activity.

The most urgent questions at present involve designing a research strategy to test and refine the propositions suggested in this work, to begin measuring the breadth and depth of state rule, or to plot the exact curve of a threat threshold. Simplifying assumptions used in this work, such as the fungibility of power resources, may profitably be relaxed later, to develop more specific relational propositions. Until then, this work will remain an elaborate (if, I think, necessary) injunction that we think strategically both about the interrelationship between state and dissident capacities and about the operations and intentions of negative state sanctions. As it stands, of course, this is no small injunction. But further research might usefully strive to make the conceptual distinctions I have outlined in precise and specifiable fashion. A second, necessary, pending task would be to try to situate individual social forces on a broader field of play. I have developed this argument as if states and challengers squared off in a game of one on one (to revive the basketball metaphor), but of course that's not the case. Each exists within a field of supporting and contending movements, counter-movements, state and social institutions. No account of the strategic calculus undertaken by either party in a contentious exchange would suffice without some thought to the actions and influences of secondary players. Indeed, in some settings, state violence cannot be understood unless we also consider the actions of social elites, whose interests are often defended by the authorities. Still, where state interests are most challenged, state actors make strategic decisions, at least initially, by and on behalf of themselves.

## Works Cited

Anderson, Benedict. 1983. "Old States, New Socieities: Indonesia's New Order in Comparative Historical Perspective. *Journal of Asian Studies* 42: 477–96.

Anderson, Martin Edwin. 1993. *Dossier Secreto: Argentina's Desaparecidos and the Myth of the "Dirty War."* Boulder, CO: Westview Press.

Arditti, Rita. 1999. *Searching for Life: The Grandmothers of the Plaza de Mayo and the Search for the Disappeared Children of Argentina*. Berkeley and Los Angeles: University of California Press.

Baldwin, David, A. 1979. "Power Analysis and World Politics: New Trends versus Old Tendencies." *World Politics* 31: 161–93.

Bello, Walden. 1987. *US-Sponsored Low-Intensity Conflict in the Philippines*. San Francisco: Institute for Food and Development Policy.

Bonner, Raymond. 1987. *Waltzing with a Dictator: The Marcoses and the Making of US Foreign Policy*. New York. Times Books.

Boudreau, Vincent. 1996. "Of Motorcades and Masses: Protest and Innovation in Philippine Protest." In P. N. Abinales ed., *The Revolution Falters: The Left in Philippine Politics after 1986,* 61–82. Ithaca, NY: Cornell University Southeast Asia Press.

———. 2001. "State Building and Repression in Authoritarian Onset." *Southeast Asian Studies* 39, no. 4: 537–57.

Brass, Paul R. 1997. *Theft of an Idol: Text and Context in the Representation of Collective Violence.* Princeton, NJ: Princeton University Press.

Bueno de Mesquita, Bruce. 1981. *The War Trap.* New Haven: Yale University Press.

Calhoun, Craig. 1993. "Nationalism and Ethnicity." *Annual Review of Sociology* 19: 211–39.

Callahan, Mary. 2001. "Civil-Military Relations in Burma: Soldiers as State-Builders in the Postcolonial Era." In Muthiah Alagappa, ed., *Coercion and Governance: The Declining Role of the Military in Asia,* 412–29. Stanford, CA: Stanford University Press.

Chanddra, Siddarth, and Douglas Kammen. 1999. *A Tour of Duty: Changing Patterns of Military Politics in Indonesia in the 1990's.* Ithaca, NY. Cornell Modern Indonesia Project, Number 75. Southeast Asia Program, Cornell University.

Churchill, Ward, and Jim Vander Wall. 1990. *Agents of Repression: The FBI's Secret War against the Black Panther Party and the American Indian Movement.* Boston: South End Press.

Davenport, Christian. 1995. "Multi-Dimensional Threat Perception and State Repression: An Inquiry into Why States Apply Negative Sanctions." *American Journal of Political Science* 39, no. 3: 638–713.

della Porta, Donatella, Oliver Fillieule, and Herbert Reiter. 1998. "Policing Protest in France and Italy: From Intimidation to Cooperation?" In David S. Meyer and Sidney Tarrow, eds., *The Social Movement Society: Contentious Politics for a New Century,* 111–30. Landham, MD: Rowman and Littlefield.

della Porta, Donatella, and Herbert Reiter. 1998. "The Policing of Protest in Western Democracies." In Donnatella della Porta and Herbert Reiter, eds., *Policing Protest: The Control of Mass Demonstrations in Western Democracies,* 1–35. Minneapolis: University of Minnesota Press.

Escobar, Edward J. 1993. "The Dialectics of Repression: The Los Angeles Police Department and the Chicano Movement, 1968–1971." *Journal of American History* 79, no. 4: 1483–1514.

Franco, Jennifer Conroy. 2000. *Campaigning for Democracy: Grassroots Citizenship Movements, Less-Than Democratic Elections and Regime Transition in the Philippines.* Quezon City. Institute for Popular Democracy.

Heryanto, Ariel. 1999. "Where Communism Never Dies: Violence, Trauma and Narration in the Last Cold War, Capitalist Authoritarian State." *International Journal of Cultural Studies* 2, no. 2: 147–77.

Hosbawm, Eric J. 1959. *Primitive Rebels: Studies in Archaic Forms of Social Movements in the 19th and 20th Centuries.* Manchester, England. Manchester University Press.

King, Dwight. 1982. "Indonesia's New Order as a Bureaucratic Polity, a Neo-

patrimonial Regime or a Bureaucratic-Authoritarian Regime: What Difference Does It Make?" In Benedict Anderson and Audrey Kahin, eds., *Interpreting Indonesian Politics: 13 Contributions to the Debate*, 104–16. Ithaca,
NY: Modern Indonesia Project, Southeast Asia Press.

Marks, Gary. 1989. *Unions in Politics: Britain, Germany and the United States in
the Nineteenth and Early Twentieth Centuries*. Princeton, NJ: Princeton University Press.

Migdal, Joel. 1988. *Strong Societies and Weak States: State–Society Relations and
State Capabilites in the Third World*. Princeton, NJ: Princeton University
Press.

———. 1994. "The State in Society: An Approach to Struggle for Domination."
In Joel S. Migdal, Atul Kholi, and Vivienne Shue, eds., *State Power and So-
cial Forces: Domination and Transformation in the Third World*, 7–36. New
York. Cambridge University Press.

Perry, Elizabeth. 2001. "Challenging the Mandate of Heaven: Popular Protest in
Modern China." *Critical Asian Studies* 33(2): 163–80.

Piven, Frances F., and Richard Cloward. 1979. *Poor People's Movements: Why They
Succeed, How They Fail*. New York: Vintage Press.

Poe, Steven, and C. Neal Tate. 1994. "Repression and Personal Integrity in the
1980s: A Global Analysis." *American Political Science Review* 88: 853–72.

Roff, W. R. 1967. *The Origins of Malay Nationalism*. New Haven and London.
Yale University Press.

Stanley, William. 1996. *The Protection Racket State: Elite Politics, Military Extortion and Civil War in El Salvador*. Philadelphia: Temple University Press.

Tarrow, Sidney. 1995. *Power in Movement: Social Movements, Collective Action and
Politics*. New York: Cambridge University Press.

Taylor, C. L., and D. A. Jodice. 1983. *World Handbook of Political and Social Indicators*. 3d Edition, vol. 2. New Haven. Yale University Press.

Thongchai, Winishakul. 1994. *Siam Mapped: A History of the Geo-Body of a
Nation*. Honolulu. University of Hawaii Press.

Tilly, Charles. 1978. *From Mobilization to Revolution*. Reading, MA: Addison-
Wesley.

———. 1990. *Coercion, Capital and European States, A.D. 990–1992*. Oxford:
Blackwell.

Tucker, Shelby. 2001. *Burma: The Curse of Independence*. London. Pluto Press.

Weekley, Kathleen. 1996. "From Vanguard to Rearguard: The Theoretical Roots
of the Crisis of the Communist Party of the Philippines." In P. N. Abinales,
ed., *The Revolution Falters: The Left in Philippine Politics after 1986*, 28–59.
Ithaca, NY: Cornell University Southeast Asia Press.

Wolf, Eric. 1999. *Envisioning Power: Ideologies of Dominance and Crisis*. Berkeley:
University of California Press.

# 3

# The Dictator's Dilemma

## Ronald A. Francisco

"History has already made its judgment. We were simply forced to act. We didn't want to. . . . In ten or twenty years you will come to realize that these measures were necessary for the stability of China and for world peace." Speaking in Austria in 1994, China's prime minister Li Peng defended the 1989 massacre in Tiananmen Square (Reuters, July 1, 1994). Will an evaluation in 2004 show this self-serving statement to be correct? Does a massacre enhance stability and the endurance of dictatorship? How do dissidents and their leaders view these repression events? Do they in fact retreat in model obedience to the state? Or do they lash out at the state and its violence? These questions ground this paper.

It was once accepted that dictatorship was stable and enduring. Recent regime collapses have altered this perception, but dictatorships aplenty still remain—many for decades. Long-lasting autocracies have little or nothing to do with citizen support of the dictator. Instead, long-lived dictatorships imply that the dictator is kept in power by a repressive and monitoring force that has not repressed sufficiently for dissidents to backlash and mobilize (Wintrobe 1998). Dictators do not require "legitimacy" or popular support, much as they might desire it. Control is the vital ingredient here. Yet most dictators are surprised at their lack of control over dissident acts. Unexpected events, harsh repression, and natural disasters can weaken state control over citizens' actions. This study concentrates on harsh repression and consequent citizen backlash. From the dictator's perspective, it investigates the backlash threshold. How much repression is sufficient to deter protest without causing backlash and high-level mobilization? This, essentially, is the dictator's dilemma.

## Definitions and Cases

What is a *dictator*? Thomas Jefferson's definition serves well even in the twenty-first century: "a dictator [is] invested with every power: legislative, executive, and judiciary, civil and military, of life and death over persons and property" (Malone 1948, 360). Given Jefferson's definition, foreign military occupiers of a country are also dictators (e.g., the British in India, Portugal in Guinea-Bissau, or Israel in the West Bank and Gaza Strip). While an eighteenth-century definition works for current dictatorships, dictators' methods of repression changed in the twentieth century. As Hannah Arendt (1973, 6) notes: "A fundamental difference between modern dictatorships and all other tyrannies of the past is that terror is no longer used as a means to exterminate and frighten opponents, but as an instrument to rule masses of people who are perfectly obedient." Mussolini's fascist doctrine is perhaps the clearest definition of dictatorship: "Everything with the State, nothing outside the State, nothing against the State" (Johnson 1988, 25).

What is *repression*? Wintrobe (1998, 34) defines repression as "restrictions on the rights of citizens to criticize the government, restrictions on the freedom of the press, restrictions on the rights of opposition parties to campaign against the government, or, as is common in totalitarian dictatorship, the outright prohibition of groups, associations, or political parties opposed to the government." We are concerned with harsh repression, including massacres, Bloody Sunday (or any other "bloody" day), all involving the one-sided and overwhelming use of state force. Massacres in real civil wars generally lie outside our purview (e.g., the massacres in the English civil war [Coster 1999]).

What is *backlash*? The goal of this essay is to study and analyze at least some instances when the entire population is not perfectly obedient. In particular, it attempts to account for the causes of backlash, that is, massive, rapid, and accelerating mobilization in the wake of harsh repression. Backlash generally forms a point of inflection—that is, the concavity of the mobilization level shifts from down to up (Francisco 1996).

What is a *security police*? All dictators depend on forces of political police, secret police, riot police, prison guards, cadres of military officers, and all judges in courts. As Wintrobe (1998) notes, the security force is often of dubious loyalty and constitutes the main threat to the dictator. The ways a dictator rewards and controls the state security force is a principal determinant of the probability of backlash.

Backlash in democratic countries is easy to understand, but why does it happen in dictatorships? Particularly vexing is the fact that backlash does not *always* occur; that is, in some instances harsh coercion dampens public protest, but in others it accelerates mobilization (Lichbach 1987). This forms the principal puzzle that has been partially solved, but does the solution relate to the problem of mobilization after a massacre?

This essay focuses on a narrow, but heretofore unanalyzed, piece of the repression/backlash puzzle. Although Lichbach (1987) solved the general problem of the relationship of protest and repression, we still find niches or contexts that are not fully explored empirically. Lichbach (1987, 1995) proved that rational dissidents shift tactics based on the level and consistency of state repression. The cases considered in this essay are all single-day harsh repressions perpetrated either by dictators or by foreign military occupiers who play the role of dictator. For every case, the repression is consistent and harsh both before and after the massacre. Under these objective circumstances we would expect to find a strong deterrent to public protest. Indeed, at a high and broad level, this seems to be the case. Yet sometimes dissidents seem spontaneously to act collectively; often this directly follows a massacre or repression of outrageous proportion. Why does this happen? How do dissidents know that others will act as well? Why do risk-averse dissidents come out on the street *after* harsh repression, but generally not *before* it occurs? Above all, why do they seem to act only on the basis of the public good itself, not on the basis of selective benefits (Karklins and Peterson 1993)?

An analysis of these questions includes a set of ten twentieth-century harsh coercions selected for repression events claiming many dissident deaths and injuries, but few regime casualties. Table 3.1 reports the basic information on these well-known middle-level massacres.

The events in Table 3.1 are selected to provide diversity across space and time. They occur in a wide variety of cultural and geographic contexts at widely varying times, although most are urban events.[1] The cases exclude several other twentieth-century massacres, for example, the 1981 massacre at El Mozote in El Salvador (Danner 1993). The El Salvadoran army elite battalion killed everyone in the village except one hidden woman and one fleeing child. There was no one left to lash back. Similarly, few escaped the Japanese army massacre in Nanjing, China, in December 1937 (Honda 1999). The essay also ignores systematic, long-term state genocide such as the Holocaust and ethnically based slaughters, for example, Rwanda in 1994 (Gourevitch

**Table 3.1. Short and long-term results of harsh repressions**

| Event | Date | Killed | Injured | Short-term result | Long-term outcome | Endurance of dictator |
|---|---|---|---|---|---|---|
| Amritsar massacre, India | 4/13/1919 | 530 | 3001 | backlash | Gandhi's campaign | 29 years |
| Bloody Sunday, Derry, Ulster | 1/30/1972 | 13 | 14 | backlash | Provisional IRA terror | 26 years |
| Bachelor's Walk massacre, Dublin | 7/26/1914 | 4 | 29 | backlash | Easter Rising, 1916, and IRA campaign | 7 years |
| Pidjiguiti massacre, Guinea-Bissau | 8/3/1959 | 50 | 101 | retreat | guerrilla war | 14 years |
| Prague repression | 11/17/1989 | 0 | 44 | backlash | resignation | 20 days |
| Sharpeville massacre, South Africa | 3/21/1960 | 67 | 186 | backlash | terror and imprisonment of leaders | 30 years |
| Soweto massacre, South Africa | 6/15/1976 | 1,000 | 3,000 | backlash | continued struggle against apartheid | 14 years |
| Bloody Sunday, St. Petersburg, Russia | 1/9/1905[a] | 175 | 625 | backlash | accession and 1917 revolution | 12 years |
| Tiananmen Square massacre, Beijing, PRC | 6/4/1989 | 2,600 | 3,000 | backlash | little protest; Communist Party still rules PRC | 12+ years |
| Wujek mine massacre, Poland | 12/16/1981 | 16 | 39 | backlash | tactical shift to clandestine protest | 8 years |

*Sources:* Bell 1993; Fein 1977; Forrest 1992; Furneax 1963; Goldstone 1998; Honda 1999; Jackson 1999; Lopes 1987; Mandela 1994; Meredith 1998; Mullan 1997; Nan 1992; Sablinsky 1976; and Suhr 1989.

[a] January 9 is the date on the old calendar. It is equivalent to January 22 on the Gregorian calendar.

1998). Instead, massacre figures shown in Table 3.1 represent populations in which the majority of citizens survived the event and were able to initiate public responses.

## The Dictator's Illusions

Dictators and their agents regularly make assumptions or simply take actions to preserve the stability of their country. Serious and effective repression, they believe, will deter public protest. Additionally, they assume that known dissident leaders foment most protest. Therefore, arrest all the dissident leaders and no protest emerges. The following discussion investigates these policies along with several dictatorships or countries under foreign military occupation.

## Does Harsh Repression Deter Protest?

Does consistently severe repression actually preclude public protest? Consider two examples of short-term deterrence and immediate backlash. On August 3, 1959, Portuguese police confronted a dockworker strike in Pidjiguiti (presently in Guinea-Bissau). Police opened fire, killing fifty workers and wounding more than a hundred. This massacre caused dissidents to retreat but then to reemerge in a guerrilla war against the Portuguese colonial army. There was no immediate public backlash (Forrest 1992; Lopes 1987). Contrast this with the Czechoslovak experience. On November 17, 1989, a rumor circulated that Czechoslovak police had killed one student and wounded dozens in a banned Prague demonstration. In each of the succeeding three days, mobilization accelerated in one order of magnitude per day (see Table 3.2). Within twenty days, protesters overwhelmed the state's repression force and caused the regime to collapse.[2]

The question then becomes what limits the must the dictator recognize. When and how can the dictator repress harshly and dampen repression without backlash? Consider the following illustration of the assumption that harsh repression stills dissent. On April 13, 1919, British general Reginald Dyer ordered the massacre at Amritsar in India in which 530 died and thousands were injured. The general later said: "It was a horrible duty I had to perform. I think it was the merciful thing. I thought I should shoot well and shoot strong, so that I or anybody else should not have to shoot again" (Payne 1969, 340). In the long term, and even often in the short term, it is my conjecture that massacres and other acts of harsh repression are rarely efficacious for dictators. The obverse, of course, is that harsh repression, in the long run, helps dissidents to eliminate dictatorship. If that is the case, the dictator's dilemma is better termed the dictator's illusion. Even if immediate

**Table 3.2. Backlash estimations**

| Event | Mobilization at event | Post-day 1 | Post-day 2 | Post-day 3 | Deaths | Injuries | Sources |
|---|---|---|---|---|---|---|---|
| Amritsar massacre, India | 15,000 | 30,000 | 30,000 | 60,000 | 0 | 0 | Fein 1977; *Times* (London) 4/14–4/30/1919; *Irish Times* 4/14–4/21/1919 |
| Bloody Sunday, Derry | 3,000 | 15,000 | 18,000 | 20,000 | 0 | 0 | *Irish Times* 1/31–2/2/1972 |
| Bachelor's Walk massacre, Dublin | 1,000 | 3,000 | 6,000 | 9,000 | 0 | 0 | De Rosa 1990; *Times* (London) 7/28–7/30/1914 |
| Pidjiguiti massacre, Guinea-Bissau | 1,000 | 0 | 0 | 0 | 0 | 0 | Forrest 1992; Lopes 1987 |
| Prague repression | 50,100 | 2,500 | 20,000 | 528,700 | 0 | 0 | http://lark.cc.ukans.edu/~ronfran/data/index.html |
| Sharpeville massacre, South Africa | 6,000 | 15,000 | 30,000 | 30,300 | 0 | 0 | Pogrund 1991 |
| Soweto massacre, South Africa | 10,000 | 50,000 | 70,000 | 30,000 | 109 | 1,100 | *New York Times* 6/18–6/20/1976 |
| Bloody Sunday, St. Petersburg, Russia | 16,000 | 30,000 | 300,000 | 300,000 | 0 | 0 | Sablinsky 1976; Suhr 1989 |
| Tiananmen Square massacre, Beijing | 6,000 | 30,000 | 30,000 | 500,100 | 30 | 301 | *Ming Pao News* 1989; Salisbury 1989 |
| Wujek mine massacre, Poland | 3,001 | 28,993 | 315,855 | 353,127 | 13 | 1,039 | http://lark.cc.ukans.edu/~ronfran/data/index.html |

backlash does not occur, often clandestine and guerrilla conflict arises. A dictator who faces a daily guerrilla war is not a happy dictator.

## Arrest All the Dissident Leaders

Arresting all the usual suspects, or certainly all the dissident entrepreneurs, is a common dictatorial policy. It is analogous to the United States policy of sentencing criminals and drug dealers to long prison terms. The idea in both cases is that within the controlled environment of prison, inmates can initiate neither public protest events nor communicate with other dissidents easily. Success of the U.S. criminal policy is still undetermined, but incarcerating protest leaders has failed many times.

The idea of forced imprisonment assumes that the current dissident entrepreneurs are the last of their lot. When South Africa sent Nelson Mandela and Walter Sisulu of the African National Congress (ANC) and Robert Sobukwe of Pan-Africanist Congress (PAC) as well as many other leaders to Robben Island, the government assumed victory for apartheid (Mandela 1994; Meredith 1998). This was an illusion of the first order. Conditions that bred Mandela, Sisulu, and Sobukwe had, if anything, increased. Illegal strikes, the Soweto rising, Steve Biko, and other increasingly violent challenges revealed dissident entrepreneurs who were even more virulently antiapartheid than those languishing on Robben Island.

The Shah of Iran likewise thought he had solved his dissident problems. By 1976 the shah's SAVAK security force had either incarcerated or killed 90 percent of the members of the Mojahendin-e Khalq and Fedaii organizations (Colburn 1994). Furthermore, Ayatollah Khomeni was safely exiled in Iraq. But three years later the shah fled Iran, driven out by a coalition of Shia Islamists and middle-class citizens.

There are two concomitant disadvantages of putting dissident entrepreneurs in prison. The first is that a prison sentence confers on the inmate a badge of honor. One reason that Nelson Mandela was feted after his release from Robben Island was the many decades he spent there as a martyr. Vaclav Havel's moral authority was enhanced considerably by his long prison sentence, which lasted from January 1989 until the Czechoslovak revolution began on November 15. In India in the early 1930s, Mahatma Gandhi's Yeravda jail cell became the prime dissident publication source, with Gandhi's writings receiving rapid publication and distribution (Payne 1969). The fact that the writings emanated from prison enhanced their effectiveness as mobilization devices.

A second and related problem of imprisoning dissident leaders is the probability that dissident movements will shift their tactics to increase their productivity (Lichbach 1995). For example, when Charles Stewart Parnell, head of the Irish National Land League in 1881, was imprisoned by the British for treason, he said that "Captain Moonlight" would take his place (Jackson 1999). Captain Moonlight referred to agrarian terror—and it did certainly take place. Under cover of night, aristocrats and British officers were killed in rural areas in Ireland. In South Africa, after Mandela and his colleagues were jailed on Robben Island, black South Africans collectively withheld their labor and organized unions, despite their being forbidden by the state, and forced concessions regarding working conditions and rules.

## The Paradox of Democratic Countries' Repression in Colonies

No one should be surprised that Portuguese police under orders from dictator Salazar shot and killed striking dockworkers in colonial West Africa. Nonetheless, three of our cases are in the colonies of the United Kingdom. Although no such massacres occurred within the United Kingdom, India, Ireland, and Northern Ireland suffered consistent harsh repression during the first three-quarters of the century. Foreign military occupation by democratic countries does not necessarily imply democratic governance in colonies. The tenacity of foreign military occupation is also remarkable. The Portuguese fought a debilitating guerrilla war against insurgents in Guinea-Bissau, steadily losing land over a period of nine years. By 1969, Portugal controlled only one-quarter of the country, but it stayed for five more years. British occupation of India and Ireland was finally ended by dissent, but only after long periods of struggle. Given the findings in this essay, as long as the casualty rate stays at a ratio of approximately ten to one—that is, ten of native dissidents, one of the foreign occupation state—then colonial leaders have no incentive to grant independence to native citizens. Once the ratio moves to a lower level, costs become a significant issue at home.

## The Analytic Problem of Backlash against Consistent Repression

Consistently harsh repression is never optimal for a dictator in the long run—and frequently not in the short run. This view conforms to the theorems Lichbach (1984) proved on optimality policies of a regime. Lichbach's theorems demonstrate that consistent repression necessarily increases the amount of revolutionary zeal in a country. From Lichbach's work, one would expect a consistently repressive dictator to be an embattled dictator. Certainly the notion of a battle-weary dictator relates to the United Kingdom's experience with Ireland and India, to Guinea-Bissau's guerrilla war against the Portuguese army, to the East European dictators in 1989, as well as to the South African dictators' experience. The price of consistent repression is revolutionary action. The price of extremely harsh repression, however, is sometimes even higher. In order to analyze the cases, we must consider the relationship between the dictator and his (there has never been a female dictator) security force.

## Rewarding and Punishing the Security Force

The dictator's relationship to the security force is similar to Calvert's (1987) leadership dilemma that was analyzed with game theory. Calvert attempts to discover how a political leader most effectively sanctions followers' uncooperative behavior. Directly concerned about legislative leaders, Calvert even denies that his paper has any relevance to a national leader. Nonetheless, the problem is analogous to those faced by dictators. A leader must have cooperative behavior of his minions. If a follower rebels, the dictator faces a choice. To deter future defection, punishment is in order. Yet punishment might jeopardize the dictator's unassailable leadership position. Calvert shows that only the leader can know the initial cost of a follower's punishment. Consequently, dictators will punish when the cost is minimal. Disgruntled followers learn ever more about costs over time, but a resolute dictator can establish a reputation that deters rebellion.

Considering Calvert's outcome, we can assume that dictators both readily reward and punish their security forces in order to develop a consistent reputation. Joseph Stalin solved the dictator's problem with the security force by subdividing his security and military ministries into several separate divisions. Stalin punished severely any section that he thought disobeyed him, thereby establishing a reputation of ruthlessness that in turn kept other sections in line (Hingley 1974; McNeal 1988). South African dictators attempted to protect themselves from the majority population by recruiting black police to control black African villages and townships. The disadvantage of this approach, of course, was the relative ease of persuading black police to defect during instances of conflict in black villages or townships. Defection of the police or militia was a major factor in the Russian Revolution of 1917, the Iranian revolution of 1979, the Philippine revolution of 1986, and almost all of the East European revolutions in 1989 (see, for example, Süß 1999). In all of these circumstances, dictatorial regimes fell because the security force could not or would not repress dissident citizens.

The obvious solution to these problems is to reward a security force well for obedience (i.e., consistent repression), while at the same time maintaining a reputation of toughness and ruthlessness (Wintrobe 1998). Even under these circumstances, however, loyal security personnel can go too far by repressing dissidents so harshly that backlash against the state occurs. Backlash is a perilous event for a dictator. By definition it involves large and accelerating mobilization. Any mobilization approaching 4 percent of a population, or even of the urban population, is usually sufficient to overwhelm security forces. As Lichbach (1995) notes, no more than 5 percent of any population is ever mobilized, so 3 or 4 percent of a local population is a formidable challenge to any government. Dictators know all of this, of course, but they cannot always elude backlash.

## Why Do Rational Dissidents Backlash after Harsh Repression?

The real puzzle resides with the dissidents. Why do they emerge after harsh coercion—in these cases, massacres—by a consistently repressive state? Backlash seems to contradict what we know about mobilization. First, usually no dissident entrepreneur appears to be present during backlash. Dissidents emerge on their own—seemingly spontaneously. Second, no visible selective incentive is apparent in backlash mobilization. The public good itself stands as the solitary putative cause of action. Third, there is neither regime accommodation nor inconsistent regime action. The regime policy in all of our cases is consistent harsh repression against dissent. Finally, the risk of action is large. If the regime has just committed a massacre, why would it not commit another? In the absence of accommodation from the regime, why would dissent action accelerate?

Answering these questions necessitates a close examination of the ten cases in this study and of previous literature findings. We have four puzzles from the dissident perspective: no mobilizing leader, no selective incentive, consistent regime policy of repression, and great danger of injury or death. Let us take these four puzzles in turn and attempt to understand the mechanism of backlash in a dictatorship.

### No Mobilizing Leader

Except perhaps for the Bachelor's Walk massacre, dissident leaders organized all ten of our basic repression events. Punjab Sikh leaders amassed fifteen thousand citizens to stand quietly holding hands in an Amritsar park before General Dyer ordered them shot. The Northern Ireland Civil Rights Association organized the Bloody Sunday demonstration, after leaders had secured assurance from the Irish Republican Army (IRA) that it would stay away from the demonstration in order to remove all possible provocation (Mullan 1997). The Bachelor's Walk incident was inspired by the Irish Volunteers' success in importing illegal firearms. A great crowd assembled when, at 6:30 p.m., troops misunderstood a command and fired into the crowd. Many fell or were injured in the ensuing chaos. The African Party for the Independence of Guinea and Cape Verde organized the dock strike that triggered the Portuguese army action in 1959. In Prague, forces in Charter 77 and incipient dissident organizations formed the November 17, 1989, demonstration that led to harsh repression. The Sharpeville massacre was one tragic result of a nationwide mobilization by the Pan-Africanist Congress against a new policy in South Africa requiring women to have passes. Student leaders organized the Soweto rising of students against the hated Afrikaans language requirement. Father Gapon, an idealistic cleric, led the 1905 Bloody Sunday demonstration in St. Petersburg in order to secure more food and better living conditions for his flock. The Federation of Beijing Autonomous Unions set up almost all of the protests that culminated in the Tiananmen Square massacre. Finally, the Wujek mine workers protesting against martial law in 1981 were all members of Solidarity.

There was no absence of leadership, then, at the outset of these events. What happens *after* the massacre? Does leadership vanish? Surprisingly, it seems to continue in almost all of these cases. Subsequent to the Amritsar massacre, Punjab union organizations led strikes and sabotage. Religious leaders urged all citizens in Punjab to perform *hartals*, a religious ritual of fasting and desisting from daily business that became an Indian version of a general strike against the British (Fein 1977). And, of course, Mahatma Gandhi used the massacre to build momentum for his own nonviolent, *hartal*-based campaign.

Backlash in Derry after Bloody Sunday took the form of a general strike, terror in Belfast, and then a vigil and funeral procession in Derry. The general strike was apparently universal among Catholics, to the point that grocery stores and banks opened for only a few specified hours, and then immediately closed. Clearly, there was extreme coordination power within the Catholic region. Planning began two hours after the massacre. A crowd gathered in a vacant shop. An official IRA member moved for a general strike; the motion was seconded by a provisional IRA member. The motion passed unanimously. It was then transmitted to journalists, who broadcast the call over Northern Ireland and Ireland itself (McCann 1992).

In the 1914 Bachelor's Walk incident in Dublin, a similar pattern emerged. First, it was a continuous backlash. Young men milled around British soldiers' barracks all night after the massacre. Second, in a union meeting, rank-and-file police refused to disarm Irish Volunteers, even as two thousand armed Volunteers appeared on the street in protest of the massacre. Dublin police met again on the third day to demand reinstatement of police who were fired for refusing to disarm Volunteers. Finally, a massive funeral procession moved slowly through Dublin on the third day.

The situation in Guinea-Bissau is the stark exception in the ten cases. The independent leadership that organized the strike learned from it. The African Party for the Independence of Guinea and Cape Verde ordered a retreat and reorganized the movement as a guerrilla war against the Portuguese (Forrest 1992; Lopes 1987). Leadership was constant throughout the massacre—and that is the reason no backlash occurred. The dissidents' leaders realized that urban protest would never be successful against Portuguese colonial police.

The accelerating demonstrations in Prague in November 1989 had organized leadership that was abetted by knowledge of what was happening in East Germany, Hungary, Poland, and other collapsing Communist countries in East Central Europe. The demonstrations were accompanied by a massive and almost complete student strike—including not only university students, but high school students as well. This was a tremendously effective adaptation tactic. How could the police reach every apartment to force students into school? The combination of demonstrations and student strikes brought the regime to its knees.

Pan-African Congress (PAC) leadership remained intact during and after the Sharpeville massacre. In fact, the PAC was the principal mobilizing force in the backlash demonstrations. The African National Congress also grew more active in the wake of the massacre, even though its leadership was under constant pressure from the apartheid state. Students initially controlled the Soweto rising with backlash, mainly strikes, occurring throughout the country. Riots continued for more than two days and were met with brutal repression, resulting in more than a hundred dead and eleven hundred injured. Fighting finally ebbed on the third day, mainly owing to the repression, but also because of extremely cold weather and a severe shortage of food.

In St. Petersburg in 1905, Father Gapon suddenly and mysteriously disappeared after shooting began. In his wake, students and militant workers mobilized the building of barricades. Thereafter, Menshevik revolutionary leaders directed the backlash—Bloody Sunday had transformed a welfare-based religious movement into a revolutionary force dedicated to reducing and even removing the tsar's power (Sablinsky 1976). They succeeded through general strikes to force the tsar to create a Duma (an elected legislature).

The Tiananmen Square massacre failed to destroy totally the student movement. Two days after the event, an estimated half-million dissidents blocked a critical bridge, even as the army roamed throughout Beijing firing indiscriminately at any challengers. Eventually, the obstruction dissolved and the state arrested or deported most of the student leadership.

Finally, the Wujek mine massacre emerged from a protest against the imposition of martial law. Coal miners had refused to leave the mine, refused to acknowledge martial law, and refused to recognize the banning of Solidarity. Workers continued to resist when security forces marched in to clear the mines; in response, police opened fire and sixteen men lay dead. Other mines and factories held out for as much as two more weeks. By then, Solidarity had adapted to the repression by changing its structure and tactics. Thus was Underground Solidarity born; it came to dominate all planning and implementing of dissent within Poland for the next four years.

It is apparent that leadership after a massacre either remains intact or new leaders emerge almost immediately. Typically, the new dissident entrepreneurs are more radical than those they supplant. In none of the cases studied was backlash mobilization bereft of leadership and direction.

### Mobilization without Selective Incentives

Muller and Opp (1986) argued that the public good itself is the most important incentive to perform rebellious action. Karklins and Peterson (1993) also note the absence of selective incentives in the Eastern Europe revolutions. But although selective incentives are a major factor in Olson's (1965) collective action theory, Lichbach (1995) demonstrates that these incentives are merely one of scores of approaches to the solution of collective action. One relevant example of Lichbach's (1995, 141–55) alternative mobilization approaches is a preexisting organization within the contract solutions. In most of the cases studied here, labor, civil rights, or other dissident organizations were present before the massacre, even if many were clandestine organizations. Lichbach (1995) also demonstrated that community solutions often substitute for pecuniary or selective incentives. After a massacre, many citizens have a personal incentive to signal the regime that it should not shoot people in cold blood.

Moreover, Karklins and Peterson (1993) underscore the special nature of severe repression. They call it a "focal event," an event that marks a critical tipping point in a society. Lohmann (1994) goes even farther. She notes that extreme public repression of dissident citizens sets in motion an informational cascade that reveals to an ever-widening public increasing evidence of the hidden malign nature of the regime.

A massacre or Bloody Sunday is likely to provide that moral tipping point. Kuran (1995) argues that most citizens in a dictatorial regime rationally falsify their public preferences. These preferences remain false as long as the regime shows no vulnerability. When the regime commits a serious error, such as a public massacre, Kuran (1995, 248) contends that many citizens break through a revolutionary threshold to mobilize dissidents quickly and to accelerate their own participation. Should they be able to sustain their activity, they can quickly imperil the dictatorial regime. If immediate large-scale organization is impossible, the specter of a massacre still matters—dissident leaders mobilize more easily on anniversaries of massacres. The act of harsh repression focuses a spotlight on the regime and makes mobilization less problematic than if coercion had not occurred.

### Mobilization under a Consistent Repression Policy

Lichbach (1984, 1987) demonstrates that a consistent repressive policy reduces violent dissent. The cases in our sample had (or have in the case of the People's Republic of China [PRC]) a consistent repressive policy. Even the United Kingdom was consistent. After a massacre, the first step was to rationalize the troops' actions and defend the state. The second step established an inquiry committee, which inevitably exonerated the forces that killed the dissidents. Even General Dyer was found innocent of killing 530 unarmed Sikh Indians in 1919.

Governability models show that consistent repression reduces violence but augments revolutionary activity (Lichbach 1984). Karklins (1987) examined the dissent/coercion nexus in the USSR and discovered that the Soviet Union allowed some dissent, as long as it did not exceed prescribed limits. In almost all, if not all, of the cases in this essay, authorities perceived dissidents as having exceeded the country's low limit of protest. Yet, in every case, the dissidents were unarmed and nonviolent. Thus, when state-sponsored shooting began, a focal event emerged. After a massacre, any tacit bargain with the state is null and void. Such a signal event changes the threshold level of action. As Geifman (1993) notes, Russians were ebullient after the Bloody Sunday massacre. A Russian source explained, "Surprisingly, no one among the Russians was depressed. . . . On the contrary, [they] were in a lively, uplifted mood. It was clear that 9 January would be the signal for a victorious struggle" (Geifman 1993, 263). Massacres appear to generate a life beyond simple consistent repression. The real question remaining, then, is the level of risk that backlash dissidents accepted by acting.

### The Repression Risk of Backlash Action

Do backlash dissidents know the probability of repression when they decide to act in response to particularly harsh repression? They have good reason to

be wary. After all, our cases document massacres. If we assume that protesters are risk-averse but are nonetheless incensed, what options do they have
for venting their anger? Tables 3.2 and 3.3 show backlash mobilization levels, casualties, and the dissidents' clear shift of tactics. The numbers in Table
3.2 are basic estimations of mobilization and casualties from the sources indicated. At minimum, they represent a probable proper order of magnitude.

The principal tale of Tables 3.2 and 3.3 is that after a massacre dissidents adapt their tactics to elude repression while they continue to protest.
This adaptation generally is effective. Tables 3.4 and 3.5 show paired two-
sample t-tests between the percentages of death and injuries in the original
event and backlash protest. In each table are the original ten-case t-test
as well as resampling with the bootstrap with one thousand repetitions.
Differences of injuries and deaths are not statistically significant with only
ten cases, but each difference is significant with the resampling. Zero is not
in any of the bootstrap confidence intervals of Tables 3.4 and 3.5. Backlash
adaptation does appear to help to elude repression. The deaths during backlash are easily explained. The only known deaths after the Tiananmen Square
massacre occurred in Shanghai when thirty dissidents lay down on the rails
challenging a stationary train. State agents ordered the engineer to drive
forward and all thirty protesters were killed. In Soweto, it was rioters who
died after the first day of protest—any person who confronted the police
and the army was likely to be shot. Most backlash, however, took the form
of strikes. Protesters adapted after the Wujek mine massacre. But because
the state previously had imposed martial law, mobile riot police (ZOMOS)
and the army rooted miners out of mines and workers out of factories and
eventually arrested the dissidents.

Despite all the problems in backlash mobilization, this investigation shows that dissidents, at least in these ten cases, solve the difficulties
naturally. Leadership either continues after massacres or is replaced by still
more zealous leaders. The massacre itself becomes a focal event, rendering
the public good against the state more salient than ever. Perhaps the most
remarkable finding is the general acceleration of mobilization over the three
days after the massacre. Tables 3.6 through 3.8 show paired two-sample
t-tests and resampling t-tests of mobilization between the massacre day
and all three post-days. The day following the massacre exhibits tentative
mobilization—so tentative that not even the bootstrap t-tests are statistically significant. Nonetheless, subsequent numbers of dissidents are significant
and generally demonstrate acceleration. The difference between massacre
mobilization and the third day after the massacre is statistically significant
even with only ten cases (Table 3.8).

## Table 3.3. Event and backlash tactics

| Event | Event tactics | Post-event tactics |
|---|---|---|
| Amritsar massacre, India | rally | *hartals* (general strike) and railroad strike |
| Bloody Sunday, Derry, Ulster | demonstration | general strike; funeral procession |
| Bachelor's Walk massacre, Dublin | march | rallies and funeral processions, accompanied by Irish Volunteers |
| Pidjiguiti massacre, Guinea-Bissau | strike | none; reorganized for guerrilla war |
| Prague repression | demonstration | strikes and demonstrations |
| Sharpeville massacre, South Africa | demonstration | rallies and strikes |
| Soweto massacre, South Africa | stone throwing and demonstrations | rioting and strikes |
| Bloody Sunday, St. Petersburg, Russia | demonstration | general strike |
| Tiananmen Square massacre, Beijing, PRC | occupation | civil disobedience |
| Wujek mine massacre, Poland | occupation | occupation |

## Table 3.4. Paired two-sample t-test: event deaths and postevent deaths; raw data and bootstrapping tests

| t-statistic | N/ repetitions | Mean | Standard error | 95% confidence interval | |
|---|---|---|---|---|---|
| 1.686 | 10 | 430.4 | 255.2787 | -147.0805 | 1007.88 |
| 1.686001 | 1,000 | 430.4 | 0.4971479 | 1.076285 | 2.393544 (bias corrected) |

## Table 3.5. Paired two-sample t-test: event injuries and postevent injuries; raw data and bootstrapping tests

| t-statistic | N/ repetitions | Mean | Standard error | 95% confidence interval | |
|---|---|---|---|---|---|
| 1.8273 | 10 | 759.9 | 415.8594 | -180.8394 | 1700.639 |
| 1.8273 | 1,000 | 759.9 | 0.8817809 | 0.1009356 | 3.582225 (bias corrected) |

The apparent absence of selective incentives is less important than in conventional mobilization. There is an elevated chance of making a difference by acting, and the public good can be enhanced to include the defeat of the state (as in Czechoslovakia in 1989 or St. Petersburg in 1905). Finally, the risk of repression after a massacre is real, but it is mitigated effectively by adaptive tactics and refusal to cooperate with the repressing state.

## Modeling Revolutionary Backlash

One of the cases in our sample led to almost immediate dissolution of the Czechoslovak Communist state because of enormous backlash mobilization. The same pattern occurred throughout East Central Europe in 1989 and early 1990: after a particularly egregious repression event, the dictator

**Table 3.6. Paired two-sample t-test: event mobilization and post-day 1 mobilization; raw data and bootstrapping tests**

| t-statistic | N/ repetitions | Mean | Standard error | 95% confidence interval | |
|---|---|---|---|---|---|
| 1.2662 | 10 | 9339.2 | 7375.739 | -26024.28 | 7345.881 |
| 1.266205 | 1000 | 7375.739 | 1.97753 | -5.89242 | 0.6912 (bias corrected) |

**Table 3.7. Paired two-sample t-test: event mobilization and post-day 2 mobilization; raw data and bootstrapping tests**

| t-statistic | N/ repetitions | Mean | Standard error | 95% confidence interval | |
|---|---|---|---|---|---|
| 1.8338 | 10 | 70875.4 | 38648.62 | -158304.6 | 16553.85 |
| 1.83384 | 1000 | 70875.4 | 0.654137 | -3.135592 | -0.54739 (bias corrected) |

**Table 3.8. Paired two-sample t-test: event mobilization and post-day 3 mobilization; raw data and bootstrapping tests**

| t-statistic | N/ repetitions | Mean | Standard error | 95% confidence interval | |
|---|---|---|---|---|---|
| 2.6337 | 10 | 172012.6 | 65313.19 | -319761.3 | -24263.9 |
| 2.633658 | 1000 | 172012.6 | 0.7692145 | -4.4669 | -1.449867 (bias corrected) |

loses control of state security forces, dissident leaders mobilize easily in a repression-free environment, and the state collapses under the overwhelming protest. The level of revolutionary mobilization in Czechoslovakia expanded exponentially from late November through the regime transition on December 10, 1989 (see http://lark.cc.ku.edu/~ronfran/data/index.html). A total of 8,767,913 Czechoslovak citizens protested between November 17 and December 10.

As we have seen, these exponential bursts in mobilization are not uncommon after especially harsh repression events. How can we understand the mechanism of these often startling events? Conventional action–reaction or predator–prey models are inappropriate for the sudden emergence of huge mobilization levels. Instead, a more appropriate model is one that explicitly incorporates exponential growth from a small initial base. One such mathematical formalism is the insect outbreak model (Murray 1993). This is a relatively simple logistic single-equation model that can be estimated from the data available on Czechoslovakia:[3]

$$\frac{dN}{dt} = aN\left(1 - \frac{N}{K}\right) - bR$$

where N = mobilization levels,
a = the logistic rate of mobilization in the absence of repression
K = the carrying capacity of the environment
b = the declining rate of mobilization due to repression

This is a biological model, of course, so we must modify it for our purposes. First, we cannot assume continuity. Dissidents do not remain constantly on the street. Therefore, we transform the model from a differential to a difference equation (Elaydi 1996). Second, the notion of a carrying capacity is irrelevant for our purposes—the street can contain sufficient numbers of dissidents given the 5 percent rule (Lichbach 1995). We eliminate the carrying capacity, leaving us with the following difference equation:

$$\Delta N = aN(1-N) - bR$$

where N = mobilization levels,
a = mobilization in the absence of repression,
b = the rate of decline of mobilization due to repression,
and R = repression (arrests, injuries, and deaths)

This model was estimated with Czechoslovak daily-aggregated data from January 1, 1980, to regime transition on December 10, 1989. The results of this test are shown in Table 3.9.

## Table 3.9. Results of the model estimation

| Parameter | Parameter estimate | Standard error | t-value | p(t) |
|---|---|---|---|---|
| a | 0.00000017 | 0.000000004515 | 36.88 | <0.0001 |
| b | 20.342 | 78.7954 | 0.26 | 0.7963 |

*Note:* Durbin-Watson = 1.9999

In this estimation, repression does not appear to matter, but of course it was a single repression event that triggered the enormous backlash mobilization, with virtually no repression thereafter. The logistic parameter *a* is nonetheless highly statistically significant, indicating that the model mechanism of exponential growth fits well to this sort of backlash sample. Repression did not "remove" many dissidents after the burst in mobilization and that accounts for its nonsignificance in the estimation procedure. This model might be useful in more general terms of protest and repression. It assumes that once dissent reaches a threshold level, repression intervenes. If mobilization is able to continue through the repression, as in Czechoslovakia, then we have the kind of results noted in Table 3.9. If, however, repression contains the dissent, then mobilization either reaches a plateau or approaches it asymptotically.

## The Efficacy of Harsh Repression and Backlash Mobilization

This essay investigates ten instances of massacres by a state and argues that such egregious repression is never really efficacious for a dictator. The arguments, at least in the cases investigated here, are compelling. Let us start with the logical outcomes of massacres. What are the possibilities after particularly harsh repression? First, nothing—the repression was effective. Second, backlash—the repression mobilizes dissidents. Third, a delayed reaction with a tactical shift—the repression moves dissidents to do two things: change tactics in order to elude future coercion and mobilize more dissidents (Lichbach 1987). Two of these three possibilities are bad for the dictator. Moreover, even deterrence may be temporary at best. Durable dictators must then have an uncanny sense of how to use and limit repression for deterrence alone. But this seems unlikely. Consider the triggers of backlash in Table 3.1. In Prague, it was a rumor of one student shot and killed. In Amritsar, in contrast, it was 530 shot dead and thousands wounded. Context matters, as does the number of citizens killed and injured. Pragmatically speaking, it is very difficult for a dictator to judge accurately his country's tolerance level of repression.

Protest, random in nature, is usually triggered by an event. Repression is committed by a security force that cannot always be controlled. A dictator can require training, but instructors cannot anticipate well which kind of event might occur. Natural disasters can upset equilibrium, as can other sorts of events: Hungary's decision to open its border in 1989 knocked the foundation out from under the German Democratic Republic (GDR). Once the GDR lost control of emigration, it lost its basis as a government. Almost anything can trigger an event that later might be depicted as a massacre or bloody day. Once such an event occurs, life changes for a dictatorship. No longer can a dictator ignore the loyalty issues his security force presents. An embattled dictator faces episodic challenges of the sort that occurred in South Africa, India, Ireland, and the guerrilla war in Guinea-Bissau. A regime may have fighter jets, armored personnel carriers, and helicopter gunships, but it still must fight hard to hold the ground it claims.

Table 3.1 lists the post-massacre tenure of the dictators in the ten cases under study. For the most part, their years in power are impressive. Bueno de Mesquita and Siverson (1995) investigated the office tenure of political leaders who engage their nations in war. Their data suggests that dictators are far more robust than democratic leaders—they enjoy lengthier leadership and they defray many of the costs associated with war that often topple democratic governments. Losing a war, however, especially one with high costs, is an equal hazard for political leaders of all stripes.

International war exposes dictators to widespread attention, to the consequences of losing, and to heavy costs in general. In contrast, harsh domestic repression, finely tuned to context, apparently carries small risks to tenure. Because the focus is domestic, outside attention is limited and publicity inside the country is under state control. Dictators can limit their risks in these ways, but after a massacre, they have a high probability of embattlement. In our single ongoing regime case, the PRC, the government must continue to negotiate with an international community resistant to harsh repression and with ongoing challenges from internal groups such Falun Gong. One easy way to reduce the risk of overthrow is to avoid using harsh repression.

What is the efficacy of backlash protest from the dissidents' perspective? In the case of Czechoslovakia, it was quick overthrow of the dictatorship (twenty days). For most other cases, though, backlash mobilization was either a first or a continuing effort against the regime. Against a resolute dictator dissidents can hope at best for a state of continued embattlement. The key for dissidents is to minimize losses as they attempt to maximize the productivity of adaptation tactics. Dissidents stay away from work and schools, they engage in work slowdowns, and in other ways signal noncooperation with the state. To the extent that a large number of community members participate, they can inflict significant damage to the dictator's prestige, reputation, and economic collateral. Dissidents achieved this minimum goal in all ten cases.

Massacres appear to strengthen dissident leadership and mobilization. Organizing a dissident movement is much easier after a massacre. Pre-existing associations tend to become at once stronger and more radical, and resources tend to increase as well. A close examination of historical sources and contemporary newspapers reporting on the ten events studied here leads to a rich catalog of solutions to the rebel's dilemma (Lichbach 1995).

Extreme levels of repression help dissidents to remove the mask of benevolence from a dictatorial regime. Sablinsky (1976) notes that Russians no longer regarded the tsar as their natural leader after January 9, 1905. Gandhi's campaign against the British used the Amritsar massacre and its whitewash as an important mobilization device (Payne 1969). Derry's Bloody Sunday accelerated the IRA terror campaign that led to prison hunger strikes and the deaths of British soldiers in the Netherlands, Germany, and elsewhere in Europe during the 1980s. In South Africa, the 1976 Soweto rising signaled apartheid's eventual demise. The students' cause was clearly just and the repression meted out was sufficiently harsh as to lead to widespread international criticism and withdrawal of investment from the South African economy. Similarly, St. Petersburg's Bloody Sunday initiated the tsar of Russia's downward spiral. From the disastrous Japanese-Russian war through World War I, the tsar lacked the broad base of support from his subjects that would have conferred legitimacy to his reign.

Even when the regime faced few repercussions from backlash (e.g., Poland, Tiananmen, and Guinea-Bissau), the initial repression caused great difficulties for the regime in the long term. In Poland it was the Underground Solidarity movement that daunted and humiliated Jaruzelski's martial-law regime. China saw huge international and domestic political costs arising from the massacre in 1989. "Tiananmen Square" echoes repeatedly whenever China seeks better accommodation in international organizations. For the Portuguese, more than a decade of guerrilla war and significant losses in Guinea-Bissau threatened Salazar's dictatorship at home.

The point of this essay is that large-scale public massacres hurt dictatorships in the long run. The long run is sometimes very long, but not as long as in the case of a strong dictator such as Stalin. Stalin killed huge numbers of people, but not in massacres. He starved them, executed them after secret trials, sent them to Siberia, and worked and tortured them to death, but did not shoot large numbers of citizens dead in a public square.

Even the Bachelor's Walk massacre, "unintended" as it was, resulted from the British military occupation of Ireland, something most Irish agreed was a dictatorship.

The beginning of this paper quoted PRC leader Li Peng's assertion that history would verify China's response during the Tiananmen Square demonstrations. Recently released transcripts document the Chinese Communist Party debate about controlling protest in Tiananmen Square (*New York Times,* January 6, 2001). The transcripts reveal two factions, one recommending slight accommodation, the other demanding harsh repression. The latter group prevailed, but history refuses to vindicate the PRC. In fact, all over the world Chinese dissidents continue to mark June 4 as a signal mobilization date.

## Notes

I am grateful to the National Science Foundation (NSF) (award SBR-9631229) and the Kansas General Research Fund for partial support of the data in this essay. I also thank Joshua B. Forrest for his assistance on the Guinea-Bissau case.

1. These cases represent most of the best-known massacres in the twentieth century. In a later study, eighteen additional cases did not alter the findings in this essay, lending probability that these ten cases are representative of all harsh repressions.

2. When examples from 1980 through 1995 in Europe occur with no citation, then the data comes from NSF coding; see http://lark.cc.ukans.edu/~ronfran/data/index.html.

3. The data stems from my coding project funded by the National Science Foundation. The URL for all of the data in the project is http://lark.cc.ku.edu/~ronfran/data/index.html. Sixteen years of twenty-eight countries are coded by five hundred sources in Reuters.textline with interval data and event descriptions.

## Works Cited

Arendt, Hannah. 1973. *The Origins of Totalitarianism.* New York: Harcourt Brace & Co.

Bell, J. Bowyer. 1993. *The Irish Troubles: A Generation of Violence, 1967–1992.* New York: St. Martin's Press.

Bueno de Mesquita, Bruce, and Randolph M. Siverson. 1995. "War and the Survival of Political Leaders: A Comparative Study of Regime Types and Political Accountability." *American Political Science Review* 89, no. 4: 841–55.

Calvert, Randall L. 1987. "Reputation and Legislative Leadership." *Public Choice* 55: 81–119.

Colburn, Forrest. 1994. *The Vogue of Revolution in Poor Countries.* Princeton, NJ: Princeton University Press.

Coster, Will. 1999. "Massacre and Codes of Conflict in the English Civil War." In Mark Levine and Penny Roberts, eds., *The Massacre in History,* 89–105. New York: Berghahn Books.

Danner, Mark. 1993. *The Massacre at El Mozote.* New York: Vintage Books.

De Rosa, Peter. 1990. *Rebels: The Irish Rising of 1916.* New York: Doubleday.

Elaydi, Saber N. 1996. *An Introduction to Difference Equations.* New York: Springer-Verlag.

Fein, Helen. 1977. *Imperial Crime and Punishment: The Massacre at Jallianwala bagh and British Judgment, 1919–1920.* Honolulu: University Press of Hawaii.

Forrest, Joshua B. 1992. *Guinea-Bissau: Power, Conflict, and Renewal in a West African Nation.* Boulder, CO: Westview Press.

Francisco, Ronald A. 1996. "Coercion and Protest: An Empirical Test in Two Democratic Societies." *American Journal of Political Science* 40, no. 4: 1179–1204.

Furneaux, Rupert. 1963. *Massacre at Amritsar.* London: George Allen & Unwin.

Geifman, Anna. 1993. *Thou Shalt Kill: Revolutionary Terrorism in Russia, 1894–1917.* Princeton, NJ: Princeton University Press.

Goldstone, Jack A. 1998. *The Encyclopedia of Political Revolutions.* Washington, DC: Congressional Quarterly.

Gourevitch, Philip. 1998. *We Wish to Inform You That Tomorrow We Will Be Killed with Our Families: Stories from Rwanda.* New York: Farrar, Straus & Giroux.

Hingley, Ronald. 1974. *Joseph Stalin: Man and Legend.* New York: Konecky and Konecky.

Honda, Katsuichi. 1999. *The Nanjing Massacre.* Armonk, NY: M. E. Sharpe.

Jackson, Alvin. 1999. *Ireland 1798–1998: Politics and War.* Malden, MA: Blackwell Publishers.

Johnson, Paul. 1988. *Intellectuals.* New York: Harper and Row.

Karklins, Rasma. 1987. "The Dissent/Coercion Nexus in the USSR." *Studies in Comparative Communism* 20, no. 3/4: 321–41.

Karklins, Rasma, and Roger Peterson. 1993. "Decision Calculus of Protesters and Regimes: Eastern Europe 1989." *Journal of Politics* 55, no. 3: 588–614.

Kuran, Timur. 1995. *Private Truths, Public Lies: The Social Consequences of Preference Falsification.* Cambridge: Harvard University Press.

Lichbach, Mark I. 1984. "An Economic Theory of the Governability: Choosing Policy and Optimizing Performance." *Public Choice* 44: 307–37.

———. 1987. "Deterrence or Escalation? The Puzzle of Aggregate Studies of Repression and Dissent." *Journal of Conflict Resolution* 31, no. 2: 266–97.

———. 1995. *The Rebel's Dilemma.* Ann Arbor: University of Michigan Press.

Lohmann, Susanne. 1994. "The Dynamics of Informational Cascades: The Monday Demonstrations in Leipzig, East Germany, 1989–1991." *World Politics* 47, no. 1: 42–101.

Lopes, Carlos. 1987. *Guinea-Bissau: From Liberation Struggle to Independent Statehood*. Boulder, CO: Westview Press.

Malone, Dumas. 1948. *Jefferson the Virginian*. Boston: Little, Brown.

Mandela, Nelson. 1994. *Long Walk to Freedom*. Boston: Little, Brown.

McCann, Eamonn. 1992. *Bloody Sunday in Derry: What Really Happened*. Dingle, County Kerry, Ireland: Brandon Book Publishers.

McNeal, Robert H. 1988. *Stalin: Man and Ruler*. New York: New York University Press.

Meredith, Martin. 1998. *Nelson Mandela: A Biography*. New York: St. Martin's Press.

*Ming Pao News* staff. 1989. *June Four: A Chronicle of the Chinese Democratic Uprising*. Fayetteville: University of Arkansas Press.

Mullan, Don. 1997. *Bloody Sunday: Massacre in Northern Ireland*. Niwot, CO: Roberts Rinehart Publishers.

Muller, Edward N., and Karl-Dieter Opp. 1986. "Rational Choice and Rebellious Collective Action." *American Political Science Review* 80, no. 2: 471–87.

Murray, James D. 1993. *Mathematical Biology*. New York: Springer-Verlag.

Nan Lin. 1992. *The Struggle for Tiananmen: Anatomy of the 1989 Mass Movement*. Westport, CT: Praeger.

Olson, Mancur. 1965. *The Logic of Collective Action*. Cambridge: Harvard University Press.

Payne, Robert. 1969. *The Life and Death of Mahatma Gandhi*. New York: Konecky and Konecky.

Pogrund, Benjamin. 1991. *Sobukwe and Apartheid*. New Brunswick, NJ: Rutgers University Press.

Sablinsky, Walter. 1976. *The Road to Bloody Sunday: Father Gapon and the St. Petersburg Massacre of 1905*. Princeton, NJ: Princeton University Press.

Salisbury, Harrison E. 1989. *Tiananmen Diary: Thirteen Days in June*. Boston: Little, Brown.

Suhr, Gerald D. 1989. *1905 in St. Petersburg: Labor, Society and Revolution*. Stanford, CA: Stanford University Press.

Süß, Walter. 1999. *Stattssicherheit am Ende* [State security at the end]. Berlin: Christoph Links Verlag.

Wintrobe, Ronald. 1998. *The Political Economy of Dictatorship*. New York: Cambridge University Press.

**Part II
Moving Beyond, Moving Into:
Developing New Insights**

# 4

# When Activists Ask for Trouble:
# State–Dissident Interactions and the New Left Cycle
# of Resistance in the United States and Japan

*Gilda Zwerman and Patricia Steinhoff*

This study examines the relation between repression and mobilization of resistance from the latter part of the New Left protest cycle in the late 1960s through the 1990s in two countries, Japan and the United States. It focuses on a subset of activists who joined the movement in the later militant phase of the cycle and continued to engage in violent confrontations with the state long after the protest cycle had ended. The study finds that the activists' commitment to violence was sustained by deployment of new strategies and structures that enabled them to absorb high levels of repression. By analyzing the activists' responses to the escalation of state repression in detail, we identify the formation of a new mobilization of resistance in both countries, with its own characteristics and trajectory. The resistance movement is both embedded within and separate from the New Left mass protest cycle.

## Introduction

Documentary studies of both public and covert government efforts to stifle political dissent (Blackstock 1975; Churchhill and Vander Wall 1988; Donner 1980; Goldstein 1978; Marx 1973; O'Reilly 1989; Schultz and Schultz 2001; Skolnick 1969; Wolfe 1974) have expanded the knowledge base about the relationship between state and social movements. No longer do we assume that actions by social-control agents and state officials are irrelevant to the dynamics of protest. In the late 1960s and 1970s, special investigations of policing and intelligence practices in the United States (United States 1968, 1970 [Eisenhower Commission 1968; Church and Pike Senate Judiciary Committees 1975, 1976]) found that during the protests in the sixties, the constitutional rights of activists were routinely violated and in some instances government operations provoked more disorder than they prevented (McPhail, Schweingruber, and McCarthy 1998).

Although there are no comparable independent investigations of state agencies in Japan, the agencies' self-reports concerning the management of protest and security matters contain revealing information about their practices. Research on these practices found strong similarities in methods of social control of social movements used in the United States and Japan during the 1960s through the 1980s (Hōmu Sōgō Kenkyushō 1969, 1970; Hōmushō 1969, 1970, 1971, 1972; Katzenstein 1998; Katzenstein and Tsujinaka 1991; McKeon 2001; Steinhoff 1991b, 1996a, 1999). Research on social movements during the sixties era has relied heavily on expository media accounts of government misconduct, the release of legislative records, and the availability of Freedom of Information files in specifying the costs of repression to the New Left. Studies identify repression as a primary cause for the overall decline of the protest cycle (Freeman 1983; Oberschall 1978). They cite correlations between deployment of aggressive intelligence and police practices and the constriction of opportunities for legitimate protest activity early in the cycle (McAdam 1982); the destruction of specific social movement organizations (Balbus 1973; Gitlin 1980; Marx 1973; Wolfe 1974); the fracturing of social and political solidarity among activists (Gamson 1990); and the diversion of the movement's material resources away from political mobilization to legal defense.

Gurr (1970), Snyder and Tilly (1972), and Tilly (1978) were among the first to identify specific characteristics internal to the social movement environment that serve to modulate the magnitude and intensity of repression. Building on Tilly's interactive model, Loveman's (1998) study of human rights activism in Latin America has shown that the influence of repression on political mobilization varies depending on the relationship between the type of strategies deployed by social-control agents and the density of interpersonal networks that are embedded in the protest movement. Similarly, Davenport's (1995) analysis of government repression and the Black Panther Party specifies the impact of state actions on decision-making processes inside the protest arena and on the physical and emotional health of individual activists.

However, the shift toward an interactive model still privileges only one side of the conflict; that is, power and agency are largely attributed to state actors and governmental structures. It is assumed that the rational social movement actor simply does his or her best to stay out of harm's way: to change course in order to avoid repression, to develop strategies that modulate repression, or to retreat when repression is severe. Although we know much about what the state has done to social movements, we understand little about the ways in which activists provoked, absorbed, and resisted repression and how these proactive processes differ across time, space, and various cohorts of social movement actors.

Studies of high-risk activism in the American New Left protest cycle have complicated this picture of the uses and outcomes of repression on the social movement side of the equation. For instance, McAdam's (1986) study of activists who participated in the 1964 Freedom Summer project shows that those who were willing to bear the consequences of repression (e.g. physical confrontation, jail, and even death) actually contributed to expanding political space within the civil rights movement. Adanack and Lewis (1973), Young (1983), and Gitlin (1987) refer to confrontational events that occurred in the United States at the peak of the 1960s protests in which activists emerged more affirmed in their oppositional identities. In a study of the aftermath of the bombing of the Bank of America in Santa Barbara, California, Flacks and Whalen (1989) suggest that activists who participated in mobilizations during periods when both activism and repression were intense were more, not less, likely to escalate their commitment and were more, not less, likely to remain connected to the movement longer.

Finally, research on clandestine organizations that formed at the peak of the New Left protest cycle (della Porta 1995; Melucci 1988; Steinhoff 1991a, 1992; Zwerman 1994, 1995) found that as state–dissident conflict reached a crescendo in 1969–70, the overall effect on the movement was deleterious, causing most activists to retreat or seek out more tempered avenues of social change. But for a persistent few, draconian responses on the part of the government served as a stimulant. Instead of surrendering, these activists raised the bar on militancy and redoubled their commitment to the movement. While the mass movement receded, they went on the offensive. Beginning in 1967, they embraced revolutionary ideologies that justified violence (Zwerman, Steinhoff, and della Porta 2000) and engaged in armed campaigns against the state that included bombings, ambushing and assassinations of police, and prison breaks. In many cases, protagonists sustained their commitment to armed insurgency for two decades.

For these insurgents, repression represented something other than an obstruction to dissent or a reason to run. Rather, the restrictions on legitimate forms of protest imposed by unjust authorities were seized as an opportunity to intensify the struggle: to test the individual's mettle as a revolutionary, to escalate the militancy, to deepen the level of support among comrades, and to ensure that the revolutionary potential glimpsed at the end of the 1960s would be realized "the next time around."

By tracing the trajectories of those who joined armed underground organizations at the peak of the protest cycle, stayed, and engaged in a "war" with the state within the framework of "mobilization-repression-remobilization," we contend that the turn to violence is not most fruitfully understood as merely an unsettling page in the final, demobilization chapter of the New Left protest cycle. Rather, the capacity of clandestine organizations and their supporters to regenerate and develop strategies that challenge and resist intense state repression over an extended period of time represents a small but distinct new movement: a mobilization of resistance against state repression with its own characteristics and trajectory.

## Methods

This study is the product of many years of field research conducted independently in the United States by Zwerman (1988, 1989, 1992, 1994, 1995) and in Japan by Steinhoff (1976, 1989, 1991a, 1991b, 1992, 1996b, 1999) on insurgents who remained active despite severe repression as the protest cycle of the late 1960s waned. In the late 1990s, we began comparing and pooling our knowledge in order to search for broader patterns that seem consistent despite the differences in national conditions and the variations among the groups (Zwerman, Steinhoff, and della Porta 2000). Our understanding of the insurgents and their interactions with other movement actors and with the state are based on several hundred interviews (some very lengthy and some repeated many times with the same informant), on thousands of pages of accounts and documentary materials produced by the organizations and their members, on field notes from hundreds of hours of trial sessions and support group meetings, and on extensive documentary research into state practices of social control.

As researchers accustomed to interviewing individuals and immersing ourselves in the details of each organization's history, we are most comfortable making our arguments with the fine-grained historical evidence of our individual cases. In the limited confines of this essay, we cannot recount the details of each group's history of resistance. Even counting the number of organizations in our pooled "sample" is difficult, because the groups themselves were in an almost constant state of fission and fusion, and our argument also encompasses the many support groups and defense committees that formed when activists were arrested and put on trial.[1] Instead, we trace the trajectory of the interactive process and identify its key factors, offering as evidence the fact that we found very similar overall patterns in the two societies.

## Outline of the Argument

Our strikingly parallel findings for the United States and Japan contest the master narratives of New Left decline in two ways. First, we find that the standard equation of increased repression producing a decine in mass protest and the splintering of the major protest organizations is missing a critical explanatory factor: the infusion of a new micro-cohort of younger activists at the peak of the protest cycle. These militant activists joined the movement when both violence and repression were escalating and they participated heavily in the emergence of public insurgency organization within the New Left's mass protest organizations.

Second, we find serious oversights in the prevailing view that as repression increased, most public protest participants withdrew entirely, leaving short-lived armed clandestine groups as the last whimper of the postrepression New Left protest cycle. By following what happened to the second micro-cohort, we find continuing resistance not only in the armed underground, but also in the nature of state–dissident interaction in the courts, in the prisons, and in exile. To the relatively small numbers of people directly involved in these activities must be added the legal, public support provided in varying degrees by New Left activists, which helped to sustain their resistance for more than two decades after the decline of the New Left protest cycle.

The character of resistance mobilization is indeed external to the universe of traditional political discourse and the conventions that typically define protest politics; that is, although it emerges from within a popular movement, derives a portion of its constituency from the veterans of mass movement organizations, and adheres to ideological frames that were prevalent at the peak of the protest cycle, the mobilization of resistance becomes partially dislodged from the norms and institutions of civil society. It mobilizes primarily in secret, its targets are primarily symbolic, and its oppositional character is fueled, not by the responses of the mass movement nor the constituencies they claim to represent, but by the responses of state authorities who seek to destroy them—a type of recognition through violation. Yet the separation from civil society is never complete, because the resistance movement also mobilizes a strong conscience constituency that supports resistance in the name of civil liberties and democratic values, in explicit opposition to the escalation of state repression.

In both Japan and the United States, the mobilization of resistance appears as a function of the constriction of political opportunities caused by a sharp escalation of repression, coupled with the entry of a new, second-generation micro-cohort of activists into the protest arena. As the movement turned militant and the government turned against the movement, these young activists filled small insurgency groups that formed as mass organizations dissolved or retreated. Although in the context of the mass protest cycle the insurgency trajectory was short-lived, we contend that it continued to evolve through the broader mobilization of resistance. Key sites of mobilization included (1) the insurgency organizations that formed during the peak of the mass protest cycle; (2) the armed, clandestine organizations formed inside insurgency organizations and the semiclandestine cells of radicalized prisoners and incarcerated militants that formed behind prison walls; and (3) the defense committees or support groups—a loose, almost borderless network of aboveground activists and legal workers who provided ongoing support for defendants, fugitives, prisoners, and other casualties of the war with the state as public insurgency organizations dissolved.

Our thesis rests on strong similarities found in the two national cases and repeated in multiple organizations within each nation. The focus on resistance, instead of victimization, provides a unique opportunity to examine power and agency on the dissident side of the state–dissident conflict nexus. It lends empirical support to those (Denardo 1985; Gupta and Sprague 1993; Lichbach 1987) who have challenged the repression as cost thesis. It advances the development of a dynamic and interactive approach to the study of repression and social movements. It also challenges narratives of New Left and post–New Left terrorism (including some of our own previous analyses) that characterize New Left violence as a short-lived byproduct of the decline phase in the cycle of mass protest.

We contend that, taken together, these phenomena constitute a new resistance movement that emerges out of the New Left protest cycle but develops a strong life of its own. Accordingly, our argument has two parts. We first reconsider the dynamics of repression and its impact on New Left protest. We emphasize the role of the militant micro-cohort of younger activists within New Left organizations in factioning and the emergence of public insurgency groups. We then ask where these activists went as the New Left protest cycle faded away.

Within the escalation of violence and repression in the late 1960s, we find the roots of the mobilization of resistance by focusing on the people who were the most immediate targets of repression. We show how they transferred their resistance into new venues and developed new ways to sustain it, both within the New Left movements and by going beyond them. At the same time, these innovations provided new avenues of resistance for other New Left activists who did not participate personally in violence or illegal activity. They also brought new actors into the resistance movement, further broadening its scope. We conclude with a discussion of the implications of the mobilization of resistance as a consequence of heightened repression in a waning protest cycle.

## The Dynamics of Repression Revisited
### Escalation of State–Dissident Conflict

In both the United States and Japan, the cycle of protests in the 1960s was launched in an environment in which a democratic regime had renewed its commitment to constitutional rights following a period of severe repression of the Communist Party and its "popular front" organizations active during the 1930s through the mid-1940s. One key difference between the two was that repression of the Communist Party continued in the United States through the 1960s, whereas in postwar Japan the Communist Party was legalized (ironically, by the U.S.-led occupation) and became, along with the Socialist Party, a minority voice in parliamentary politics and a strong voice for the protection of the newly established constitutional protections that permitted ideological dissent. Hence, in the United States it was the long legal tradition of civil liberties protections, whereas in Japan it was a strong Old Left defending new and fragile civil liberties, that created the political opportunity for more public dissent at the beginning of the sixties.

However, by midpoint in the decade, several factors converged to bring about an escalation of conflict between the dissidents and the state in both countries. On the dissidents' side, rejection of peaceful protest and passive resistance as a strategy sharply increased the use of violent rhetoric and the threat of confrontation at demonstration sites. Increased exposure to contemporary Third World insurgency frames—the writings of Frantz Fanon, Mao Zedong, and Che Guevara—contributed to a reserve of ideologies and practices with which young militants narrated the turn to proactive forms of violence. The commitment to violence was further reinforced by personal contact between the New Left and Third World revolutionary movements, which occurred at international conferences and through gestures of mutual support.

In both nations, the period between 1967 and 1970 marked a dramatic decline of the government's overall policy of tolerance toward protest (della Porta and Reiter 1998, 4). Both governments deployed measures that involved an unprecedented degree of aggression and intrusion in social movement organizations and a higher level of resource allocation toward policing and intelligence operations, as well as practices that encompassed a broader range of social-control and military agencies. At the legislative and executive level, the governments deployed new laws, innovated in the application of existing laws, and reactivated measures used to repress the left in earlier periods. Although new measures were introduced as an emergency response to a particular crisis of the state, the escalation was deliberate and institutionalized. As control measures became more aggressive, key decisions were made in secret. Even when changes in the rule of law and the democratic game were announced publicly, their implications for reframing protest, strategic decision making, and personal risk calculations could not be fully evaluated by dissidents until the new laws and procedures were implemented in actual security investigations and criminal cases. Then the impact on the movement was sudden and severe.

### The Militant Micro-Cohort

During this period of the late 1960s, the turn to militancy appeared to be a dynamic of the movement as a whole, as if it were the same movement as in 1960, only bigger and more defiant. Less obvious was an emerging ideological divide: between those who forced the turn to militancy and those who warily made the turn and then, within a relatively short span of time, turned around. Indeed, after 1967, many of the activists who had been politicized by the moral imperative of nonviolent direct action in the early sixties began to retreat. They expressed concerns about adventuristic actions that outpaced the consciousness of the masses, about the application of Third World models of revolution to Western democratic states, and about the severe repression that was certain to continue.

Yet the militants persisted, breaking with the ideology of passive resistance (in the United States) and peaceful protest (in Japan), challenging leaders who insisted that mass organizations keep to the discipline of nonviolence, and forming new insurgency-based groups from the small factions that survived the intense internal strife. However, critical to sustaining the militancy over time was the availability of a second generation of activists—those who entered the highly charged protest arena from 1967 on, and for whom confrontation and violence were assumed to be part of the risk calculation of joining the movement. As Whittier (1997) has shown, a cycle of protest produces internal "waves" of activism. With each wave a new micro-cohort enters: they join a "different" movement and bring a distinctive set of sociological characteristics into the protest arena.

For students who joined New Left groups at this time, protests were already configured as confrontations with massive contingents of riot police (and the National Guard in the United States) in which violence erupted quite predictably. Mass demonstrations in both countries between 1967 and 1969 were generally followed by clashes between police preventing access to a symbolic protest site and demonstrators trying to penetrate the barrier. In Japan, riot police armed with full-body aluminum shields and nightsticks, backed by high-powered water cannons or tear gas, fought helmeted student demonstrators who wielded wooden poles, threw stones, and occasionally set police vehicles on fire. In the United States, the picture was the same, except for minor cultural variations in weaponry and protective gear. In some instances, clashes would be followed by yet another burst of street violence as demonstrators left the site and rampaged through public thoroughfares.

Deceleration in the pace of social reform from 1964 on and escalation of the war in Vietnam, coupled with more severe repression in the latter half of the 1960s, produced a deepening level of disaffection. The longer the war went on, the less it looked like an accident, the more like a symptom of a system unalterable through reform. Frustrated activists in both countries came to recognize that issues that seemed separate had a relationship to one another, and found potent explanations in Third World revolutionary rhetoric.

Indeed, those who filled new insurgency organizations were not the same activists who had shaped the movement in the early 1960s. In the United States, this second cohort was markedly more diverse than the first: it included not only white and black activists with backgrounds similar to that of the first generation, but a significant portion of students from poor and working-class and other minority backgrounds, recruited from public and community colleges, antipoverty organizations, and street gangs. In Japan, a movement begun by relatively elite college students now attracted and welcomed young workers, marginalized drifters, and Korean residents born in Japan, who constituted a minority without citizenship rights.

Despite differences in nationality, culture, and the economic and educational background of these second-generation activists, the narratives of those who ultimately joined insurgency organizations reflect a common theme. The more violent second-generation micro-cohort confronted repression very early in their movement careers, and found it more of a piece with their expectations about the high-risk nature of movement participation. These activists emphasize the effect that state repression—experiencing it, witnessing it, and or closely identifying with its victims—had at every point in their political development. Specifically, the repression propelled their initial decision to join the movement, the decision to escalate from reactive to proactive forms of violence, and the decision to stay in the movement while others left. Moreover, because they joined the movement late, when repression was already intense, these decisions were made in rapid succession; that is, the second micro-cohort did not evolve slowly from activism to armed struggle but moved with great speed from peripheral or no engagement in activism to total immersion in revolutionary politics.

### Public Insurgency Organizations

Urged on by the militant second micro-cohort's taste for direct action, splinter groups began to engage in more provocative actions within mass-based public protests. Smaller insurgency organizations emerged as a result of internal conflicts over strategy and tactics in mass-based protest organizations, as violence between protesters and police escalated. Although insurgency organizations represent the first stage of the transition from public protest to armed, clandestine groups, we emphasize here the semi-public nature of the phenomenon and its direct connection to public parent organizations. The features of these insurgency groups and the expectations they placed on individual members were critical to the process of socializing militants for long-term resistance.

Foremost, recruits were encouraged to sever ties from mainstream institutions—to leave school, to avoid careers and conventional jobs, and to diminish contact with their family and with nonpolitical friendship networks. The revolution required nothing less than total commitment to the revolutionary organization. Second, the insurgency group consumed their lives. Entire days were filled with meetings, strategizing sessions, fundamentalist-like indoctrination in political education seminars, and endless rounds of criticism, self-criticism, and debriefing sessions in the aftermath of an action. In this way, individuals had little chance to think independently about what they were doing. They became acclimated to a high level of emotional tension, physical discomfort, fear, and exhaustion. And finally, these young insurgents were encouraged not only to bear the pain of confrontation with the state, but to seek it out. At demonstrations they were expected to initiate clashes with police, to form militant "breakaway" contingents from otherwise peaceful protests, and to meet force with force. They were also expected to develop ways of steeling themselves in the face of return fire—the beatings, arrests, and violent shakedowns that followed confrontations.

Initially, the violence associated with public insurgency–based organizations involved relatively low-grade provocations on the dissidents' side. As insurgency organizations became more disciplined, militants were required to develop physically and militarily. They trained in the martial arts; they sent representatives for one-on-one training in the use of firearms with former members of the armed services or tried to conduct such training exercises themselves; and they pored over recipes for bomb making. Schooling themselves in the arts of subversion, they learned how to forge identification documents, disguise themselves against police surveillance, and procure resources through illegal means. As a result, their actions gradually became more complicated and audacious. Repression intensified in response. Government agents of social control held the entire movement accountable for the violence enacted by the insurgents.

## The Mobilization of Resistance

Against the backdrop of mass legal protests, which continued through the early 1970s, the insurgents focused most of their attention on repression. They developed new forms of resistance that were more difficult for the state to control. Following the more violent second micro-cohort and some of their elders as repression intensified, the path leads to three new arenas of resistance: the courts and prisons; the underground; and exile. In these arenas activists were able to continue their resistance, recruit new participants, and sustain their own activity and identity based on repression, long after the main New Left protest cycle had ended in the early 1970s. We contend that these three new arenas, taken together, define a new mobilization of resistance that developed its own trajectory, independent of the waning of the original protest cycle. The state responded to the mobilization of resistance with new forms of repression, which in turn prompted adaptive forms of resistance.

### From the Streets to the Courts and Prisons

In both the United States and Japan, one immediate and obvious result of the escalating repression of the late 1960s was the creation of a new class of political criminals. They were most often arrested and charged with violations of ordinary criminal laws, so the criminal justice system could adamantly deny that there was anything political about the situation. To the movement, the arrests and prosecutions of activists were unmistakably political. Defense committees and support organizations for political trials were the main vehicles for the protest mobilization. Our findings from the

United States and Japan are strikingly similar overall, although the specific characteristics of the movement from the streets to the courts and prisons also reflects national variations in culture and institutional practices.

Japan's New Left trial support system was organized systematically as a direct response to the escalation of state repression in late 1968, when felony charges began to be applied to demonstrators and concurrently, under a new and unannounced government policy, students were jailed indefinitely after being arrested at street demonstrations. Thousands of student demonstrators were suddenly being held in isolation under severe pressure to confess, apologize, and leave the movement. These conditions forced the New Left to develop a volunteer coordinating organization with a hotline where arrested persons could request legal representation and obtain support during the first critical weeks of interrogation in the police jail. In addition to providing immediate support to help activists resist confession pressures, the volunteers later formed trial support groups to provide personal and paralegal support during the long period of intermittent trial sessions, when defendants were held in isolation cells in unconvicted detention. The coordinating organization supplied lawyers, taught people how to organize trial support groups, and lent them experienced organizers (Steinhoff 1999).

Because of the rapid development of the new support system, the police crackdown on street protest in Japan did not end resistance by taking protesters off the streets and intimidating them into staying home. Rather, it shifted resistance into the criminal justice system. Thousands of arrested students refused to submit docilely by confessing and apologizing as expected; instead, they demanded their full legal right to contest the charges in an open trial, thereby clogging the criminal justice system for several years. Hence the support system was envisioned, and in fact functioned, as a way to facilitate continued resistance to the state. This resistance movement required the defendant to adapt to the isolation of life in unconvicted detention, but at the same time, it engaged large numbers of sympathizers as volunteers providing support from the outside. The system of trial support not only served the prisoners, but became a social movement activity in its own right, sustaining the participation of support group members for many years after the main New Left movement had faded.

In the United States, persons arrested for minor insurgency moved quickly through the criminal justice system, but defense committees were organized to support high-profile defendants facing serious felony charges. The defense committees that formed between 1967 and 1970 were supported by the public aboveground organizations but drew members from a broad assortment of student, antiwar, and minority-based groups. Their activities included fund-raising, securing attorneys, attending trials, writing to and visiting the defendants in jail, and placing support for the defendant or prisoner on the agenda of other organizations. The defense committee structure sustained a network of activists after the dissolution of the public organizations. Later in the 1970s, after the exposure of government abuses of power in repressing movements during the 1960s, a new generation of radical lawyers took the lead in forming "law collectives" and new defense committees to pursue new litigation on behalf of political prisoners who had been the target of these abuses of power.

In both countries, as the overall New Left movement declined in the early 1970s the trial support groups and defense committees remained active, giving voice to the prisoners they supported by facilitating the publication of their writings. On the smallest scale this occurred through the publication of letters from prisoners in support group newsletters. However, many of the prisoners became celebrities, writing books and magazine articles that are read well beyond their own New Left circles. Some had a strong identity as political ideologues before their arrest, and have simply been able to continue writing from prison. Others were quite unknown before they were arrested, but have become famous through their autobiographical prison writings. This personal and public identity based on repression has kept the ideas and emotions of the New Left generation alive long after it ceased to be an active, self-generating political movement in its own right.

The ramifications of the movement of resistance into the courts and prisons are even broader. In both Japan and the United States, the infusion of a generation of largely middle-class political activists into the prison system brought to light a number of issues they and their supporters otherwise might not have noticed. This in turn sparked movements for prison reform in both countries and also helped to turn some nonpolitical prisoners into political activists.

In the United States, the radicalization of prisoners in the late 1960s drew inspiration from a number of sources, including the organization of religious study groups and religious services by Black Muslims in the 1950s and early 1960s; the jail-ins mobilized by the civil rights movement; and, perhaps most essentially, personal contacts between movement militants and nonpolitical prisoners that blossomed into political associations. These relationships developed through mutual efforts to improve conditions inside and through the establishment of radical groups and chapters of movement organizations inside the jails. These activities not only linked nonpolitical prisoners to the movement, they also gave rise to new movement organizations outside that focused on prison reform, civil litigation contesting prison conditions, and high-profile cases of rebellion. The formation of prison-based and prison reform groups both expanded the borders of the movement and extended protest well into the 1970s.

In Japan, as political prisoners met other nonpolitical prisoners on the inside, they began to identify miscarriages of justice involving false confession, which were then taken up by the New Left's support system. Political prisoners formed a prisoners' union that organized both political and nonpolitical prisoners and has carried out a number of resistance activities inside Japanese prisons, using the New Left's outside support system to facilitate communication and to provide lawyers and other services. In addition, groups supporting particular New Left prisoners became involved in spin-off movements for prison reform and amelioration of prison conditions because of the problems their own prisoners faced, including movements to improve medical and psychiatric care for prisoners. When a number of former New Left activists were given death sentences at the end of their long trials in the 1980s, their support groups also linked up with the small anti-death penalty movement.

A further impetus to continued resistance arose with the release of radicalized ex-convicts and hardened militants from 1969 on, supplying a reserve of recruits into the armed underground organizations who were ultimately responsible for generating a second wave of armed clandestine organizations in the mid-1970s. In Japan, this release of radicalized militants from prison came about through international hijackings by "free the guerrilla guerrillas" who took their comrades into overseas exile to engage in further international incidents.

### Armed Clandestine Groups

The clandestine cells that formed at the peak of the New Left protest cycle emerged in both societies within the context of public insurgency organizations, not as a result of the dissolution of those groups. Insurgency organizations served as a recruitment base for the clandestine cell, as a base of public support for the actions carried out by the cell, and as a support network for cell members who were arrested or on the run. Thus, for the individual activist, the transition from participation in an insurgency group to participation in an organization that was entirely underground was not especially dramatic.

The armed, clandestine groups that emerged out of the New Left protest cycle shared a set of ideological and strategic convictions drawn from Third World revolutionary writings, which they applied to contemporary conditions in their own industrialized societies. While others in the New Left used the same rhetoric for armchair political critique or questioned whether it applied in their societies, a subset of activists found in these ideas a compelling basis for action. Hence, although some of the impetus for going underground was reactive, the proactive impulse to live out the guerrilla life was equally powerful. Throughout the 1970s, such clandestine groups carried out hijackings, kidnappings, bank robberies, and bombings with startling frequency. The members of these armed, clandestine groups had to adapt to the new exigencies of life underground, where long periods of boredom, secrecy, and struggling for daily survival were punctuated by occasional moments of high drama (Zwerman, Steinhoff, and della Porta 2000).

Although the existence of the armed clandestine groups is a direct result of the increased repression of the late 1960s mass protest movement, these groups posed new problems for state authorities precisely because they had been pushed underground, where they could not be monitored as easily as the public insurgency groups that preceded them. The result was a greatly increased concentration of state resources on a much more elusive and unpredictable target, which led to further repression and loss of civil liberties for the broader movement and the general public. Similarly, people who had gone underground because of their personal ties to fugitives were soon drawn into illegal activity and became vulnerable to arrest themselves.

The invisibility and elusiveness of the clandestine groups enhanced their aura and led to exaggeration of their numbers and their power. Many armed clandestine groups, particularly those with personal ties to public protest or insurgency organizations, received a fair amount of support from their associates aboveground, which also served as recruiting fields for new members to replace those who had the misfortune to get arrested. As repression increased and their links to aboveground organizations weakened, the clandestine groups drifted into more overtly criminal behavior with increasingly tenuous ideological rationale, which further discredited them in the eyes of the more moderate New Left.

Yet even after many public protest organizations had weakened or dissolved, the armed underground could still count on some support from individuals with whom they had previously participated in movement activity, whether because of shared political commitment, personal friendship, or a sense of guilt and obligation toward those who were still carrying on the battle. Once arrested, whatever the charges, they could also count on a resurgence of support as they moved through the criminal justice system. To a surprising extent, people who completely dissociated themselves from the criminal acts committed by armed clandestine groups stepped forward to become active in the defense committees and support groups that formed as soon as the perpetrators were arrested. Thus, the underground acted as a continuing catalyst for the mobilization of resistance, both for those who went underground and for those who were mobilized to help support them.

### Protected Exile

The defense committees and support groups represented a structure within the social movement environment with a unique capacity to recruit across ideological and organizational lines and to sustain a diverse network over a long period of time. However, the support these groups offered came after the damage was done—after had an indictment had been issued, after a subpoena had been served, or after sentence was pronounced. Also, as conflict between the state and dissidents spiraled and the ranks of the new political criminals swelled, the defense committees' resources were overstretched. An insurgent in trouble could not be certain that a strong support network would in fact be mobilized on his behalf. Thus, some insurgents chose an alternative to resisting in the courts and prisons. They sought asylum from foreign governments that were friendly toward the movement.

By 1967–68, members of the second micro-cohort of insurgents were seeking contact with socialist states and revolutionary movements abroad. On political tours and at movement-to-movement summit conferences, insurgents met with representatives from national liberation movements in North Vietnam, Africa, Algeria, and other parts of the Third World. Initially, the motive for establishing contact was based on the desire to build political solidarity with more advanced revolutionaries and to build an international context for action. As repression intensified, matters of security and resistance took precedence. The nature of exile was somewhat different in the U.S. and Japanese cases, but in both societies it involved new adaptations that mobilized and sustained resistance well beyond the end of the New Left protest cycle.

For the U.S. movement, the Organization of Latin American Solidarity (OLAS) conference in 1967 was pivotal in creating the possibility of asylum for black and Puerto Rican insurgents. In this venue, U.S. counterinsurgency strategies were evaluated and the prospects for guerrilla warfare inside the United States were explored, inspiring some groups to escalate insurgency with the promise of wider support. In the late 1960s, Cuba granted asylum to hijackers. In the decades since, Cuba has continued to provide a reliable base of exile, offering fugitives and prison escapees protection from U.S. government agents seeking their arrest. Members of the Black

Panther Party, Republic of New Afrika, Black Liberation Army, FALN, and Los Macheteros have remained free in Cuba, despite demands by U.S. law enforcement officials for their extradition. During the same period, large numbers of students who were resisting the draft found exile in Canada.

For American activists, exile provided an escape and sometimes an opportunity to rethink strategy before returning to the United States, but it has not generally provided an external base for continued resistance. The opposite has been true for Japan, where exile has been pursued explicitly in order to continue resistance from a protected base where repression was less severe and mobilization could continue. As the exiles have adapted by expanding their insurgent political activity in cooperation with international partners, the Japanese government has adamantly continued to track them all over the world in order to bring them home and prosecute them.

In 1970, nine members of a prominent Japanese insurgency organization, the Red Army Faction, carried out Japan's first domestic airline hijacking to North Korea, where they were allowed to remain and were promptly reeducated. During the 1970s, North Korean agents lured several young Japanese women to North Korea, where they, too, underwent reeducation and were forced to remain and marry the Japanese hijackers. Members of the expanded group subsequently engaged in covert activity in Europe, Japan, and Southeast Asia, including luring several other young Japanese to North Korea and forcing them to stay. Although both the North Korean government and the Red Army group under their protection adamantly denied the kidnappings for many years, in 2002 the North Korean government admitted its role and apologized to the Japanese government. Meanwhile, some of the group's members have been located outside of North Korea and brought to trial in Japan, the women and children are now returning voluntarily with help from their supporters in Japan, and the remaining exiled men have announced that they will soon return to face trial (Steinhoff 2004).

In the early 1970s, other Red Army Faction members began working with a branch of the Palestinian Liberation Organization in Lebanon, combining public support for the Palestinian cause with guerrilla training for a string of young Japanese who joined them. Initially under Palestinian guidance and later acting on their own as the Japanese Red Army, the group became involved in high-profile armed attacks, international hijackings, and hostage-taking incidents, many of which were designed to rescue their own members and other activists from Japanese prisons and offer them exile. With each new incident, the Japanese government placed those directly involved, plus any other Japanese suspected of associating with them, on international wanted lists. Nonetheless, the exiles continued to receive protection in the Middle East because of their service to the Palestinian cause. Like their counterparts in North Korea, the Japanese Red Army members in the Middle East have married and raised children, and have engaged in a variety of covert activities all over the world since they stopped their high-profile attacks in the late 1970s. Since the late 1980s, a steady stream of persons on international wanted lists as Japanese Red Army members have been arrested in various places and put on trial in Japan, where old networks and new recruits have been mobilized to support their continuing resistance in the Japanese criminal justice system.

At this writing, a number of trials of these former exiles are in progress in Japan, and trial support for the defendants is expected to continue for at least a decade. As the second-generation offspring of the exiles have returned to Japan, the New Left support groups for their parents have also embraced and supported them. This generational transfer of support to the children of imprisoned activists has also occurred among support organizations in the United States.

## Conclusions

This analysis suggests that the radicalization of a small minority, which previously has been regarded as simply a minor side effect of the relatively successful application of repression to curtail the New Left protest cycle, has in fact generated a much longer mobilization of resistance whose broader outlines are only now becoming visible. The resistance mobilization is directly connected to the conditions found at the peak of the New Left protest cycle, but has developed its own structures and strategies. The scope of the mobilization of resistance is only visible when its constituent elements, which have heretofore been regarded as small and separate phenomena, are aggregated and related to their origins in the New Left protest cycle. To explicate these connections, we have emphasized a new element for analysis of the New Left protest cycle: the participation of a more militant second-generation micro-cohort of activists who entered the New Left protests at a critical point, responded to repression with greater resilience, and sparked a mobilization of resistance with surprising longevity.

One major implication of this analysis is that repression may have serious long-term costs not just for the activists it represses, but for the state that imposes it—that, indeed, the cost of repression may be borne by the state for decades after its apparent end. Just as the political process approach to social movements (McAdam 1982) suggests that a relatively long historical approach is needed to understand the origins of major social movements that precipitate a protest cycle, we suggest that the costs and ramifications of repression can only be understood by taking an equally long historical approach to the tail of the cycle and what follows from it.

The emergence and development of this mobilization of resistance have been shown to be quite parallel in two cases of New Left protest cycles, in Japan and the United States. Similar patterns may be found in the European countries, such as Germany and Italy, that experienced very similar New Left protest cycles during the same time period. However, the conditions of repression that set this dynamic in motion are limited to relatively democratic societies with an underlying commitment to the rule of law, even though it may be breached in practice. We suspect that these conditions are further limited to industrialized societies, but it is not clear whether similar patterns might emerge in other protest cycles that meet roughly similar basic conditions. In short, we do not know how historically circumscribed these findings may be. Nonetheless, we suggest that disaggregating the participants at the peak of a protest cycle in order to identify new, more militant micro-cohorts, and following these participants past the apparent end of the protest cycle, may lead to new understanding of the dynamics of repression in many protest cycles, and not just the New Left protest cycle of the 1960s.

## Notes

1. For the record, the main organizations studied in the United States are Students for a Democratic Society/Action Faction, Weatherman, Weather Underground, Prairie Fire, May 19th Communist Organization, Black Panther Party, Revolutionary Action Movement/Republic of New Africa, Black Liberation Army, Movement for Independence (Movimiento por Independencia), Armed Liberation Commandos (Comandos Armadas de Liberación), FALN (Fuerzas Armadas de Liberación Nacional), Armed Revolutionary Movement for Independence (Movimiento Independencia Revolucionario Armado), Statewide Correctional Alliance for Reform, United Freedom Front, plus numerous defense committees supporting individual defendants in the U.S. criminal justice system. In Japan, the main organizations studied include Bund (Kyōsanshugisha Dōmei), the Red Army Faction (Sekigunha) and its exiled Yodogo group in North Korea, the United Red Army (Rengō Sekigun), the Japanese Red Army (Nihon Sekigunha), the Japan Communist Party Kanagawa Committee Revolutionary Left Faction (Kakumei Saha), East Asia Anti-Japanese Armed Front (Higashi Asia Han-Nichi Busō Sensen), and the Central Core Faction of the Revolutionary Communist League (Chūkakuha), plus the Relief Contact Center (Kyūen Renraku Sentā), which is the central support agency for individuals arrested for political activities related to the New Left,

and numerous support groups formed under its umbrella to assist with individual cases in the Japanese criminal justice system.

## Works Cited

Adanak, R., and J. Lewis. 1973. "Social Control, Violence and Radicalization: The Kent State Case." *Social Forces* 51: 342–47.

Balbus, I. 1973. *The Dialectics of Legal Repression.* New York: Russell Sage.

Blackstock, N. 1975. *COINTELPRO.* New York: Vintage Books.

Churchhill, Ward, and Jim Vander Wall. 1988. *Agents of Repression: The FBI's Secret War against the Black Panther Party and the American Indian Movement.* Boston: South End Press.

Davenport, C. 1995. "Multi-Dimensional Thread Perception and State Repression." *American Journal of Political Science* 38: 1056–78.

della Porta, D. 1995. *Social Movements, Political Violence, and the State: A Comparative Analysis of Italy and Germany.* New York: Cambridge University Press.

della Porta, D., and H. Reiter. 1998. "The Policing of Protest in Western Democracies." In *Policing Protest: The Control of Mass Demonstrations in Western Democracies,* ed. D. Della Porta and H. Reiter, 1–32. Minneapolis: University of Minnesota Press.

Denardo, J. 1985. *Power in Numbers: The Political Strategy of Protest and Rebellion.* New York: Cambridge University Press.

Donner, F. 1980. *The Age of Surveillance.* New York: Alfred A. Knopf.

Flacks, R., and J. Whalen. 1989. *Beyond the Barricades.* Philadelphia: Temple University Press.

Freeman, J. 1983. *Social Movements of the Sixties and Seventies.* New York: Longman.

Gamson, W. A. 1990. *The Strategy of Social Protest.* Belmont, CA: Wadsworth.

Gitlin, T. 1980. *The Whole World Is Watching: Mass Media in the Making and Unmaking of the New Left.* Berkeley: University of California Press.

———. 1987. *The Sixties.* New York: Bantam.

Goldstein, R. 1978. *Political Repression in Modern America.* Urbana: University of Illinois Press.

Gupta, D., and T. Sprague. 1993. "Government Coercion of Dissidents: Deterrence or Provocation?" *Journal of Conflict Resolution* 37: 301–39.

Gurr, T. 1970. *Why Men Rebel.* Princeton, NJ: Princeton University Press.

Hōmu Sōgō Kenkyūshō. 1969. *Kensatsu Tokubetsu Shiryō.* Vol. 34. Tokyo: Hōmushō.

———. 1970. *Kensatsu Tokubetsu Shiryō.* Vol. 35. Tokyo: Hōmushō.

Hōmushō. 1969. *Hanzai Hakushō.* Tokyo: Hōmushō.

———. 1970. *Hanzai Hakushō.* Tokyo: Hōmushō.

————. 1971. *Hanzai Hakushō*. Tokyo: Hōmushō.

————. 1972. *Hanzai Hakushō*. Tokyo: Hōmushō.

Katzenstein, P. 1998. "Left-Wing Violence and State Response: United States, Germany, Italy and Japan, 1960s–1990s." In *Working Papers of the Institute of European Studies*. Ithaca, NY: Cornell University Press.

Katzenstein, P. J., and Y. Tsujinaka. 1991. *Defending the Japanese State: Structures, Norms, and the Political Responses to Terrorism and Violent Social Protest in the 1970s and 1980s*. Ithaca, NY: East Asia Program, Cornell University.

Lichbach, M. I. 1987. "Deterrence or Escalation? The Puzzle of Aggregate Studies of Repression and Dissent." *Journal of Conflict Resolution* 31: 266–97.

Loveman, M. 1998. "High-Risk Collective Action: Defending Human Rights in Chile, Uruguay, and Argentina." *American Journal of Sociology* 104: 477–525.

Marx, Gary T. 1973. "Thoughts on a Neglected Category of Social Movement Participant: The Agent Provocateur and the Informant." *American Journal of Sociology* 8: 402–42.

McAdam, D. 1982. *Political Process and the Development of Black Insurgency, 1930–1970*. Chicago and London: University of Chicago Press.

————. 1986. "Recruitment to High-Risk Activism: The Case of Freedom Summer." *American Journal of Sociology* 92: 64–90.

McKeon, M. 2001. "Ogino Anna's Gargantuan Play in Tales of Peaches." In *The Father-Daghter Plot: Japanese Literary Women and the Law of the Father,* ed. R. L. Copeland and E. Ramirez-Christensen, 327–68. Honolulu: University of Hawaii Press.

McPhail, Clark, David Schweingruber, and John McCarthy. 1998. "Policing Protest in the United States: 1960–1995." In *Policing Protest: The Control of Mass Demonstrations in Western Democracies,* ed. D. della Porta and H. Reiter, 49–69. Minneapolis: University of Minnesota Press.

Melucci, A. 1988. *Nomads of the Present*. Philadelphia: Temple University Press.

Oberschall, A. 1978. "The Decline of the 1960s Social Movements." *Research in Social Movements, Conflicts and Change* 1: 257–89.

O'Reilly, P. 1989. *Racial Matters: The FBI Secret File on Black America*. New York: Free Press.

Schultz, Bud, and Ruth Schultz. 2001. *The Price of Dissent: Testimonies to Political Repression in America*. Berkeley: University of California Press.

Skolnick, Jerome H. 1969. *The Politics of Protest: Report to the National Commission on the Causes and Prevention of Violence*. New York: Simon and Schuster.

Snyder, D., and C. Tilly. 1972. "Hardship and Collective Violence in France." *American Sociological Review* 42: 105–23.

Steinhoff, P. G. 1976. "Portrait of a Terrorist: An Interview with Kozo Okamoto." *Asian Survey* 16: 830–45.

————. 1989. "Hijackers, Bombers and Bank Robbers: Managerial Style in the Japanese Red Army." *Journal of Asian Studies* 48, no. 4: 724–40.

————. 1991a. *Nihon Sekigunha: Sono Shakaigakuteki Monogatari (Japan Red Army Faction: A Sociological Tale)*. Tokyo: Kawade Shobō Shinsha.

————. 1991b. "Political Offenders in the Japanese Criminal Justice System." Paper presented at American Society of Criminology annual meetings, San Francisco.

————. 1992. "Death by Defeatism and Other Fables: The Social Dynamics of the Rengo Sekigun Purge." In *Japanese Social Organization,* ed. T. S. Lebra, 195–224. Honolulu: University of Hawaii Press.

————. 1996a. "From Dangerous Thought to Dangerous Gas: A Frame Analysis of the Control of Social Movements in Japan." Paper presented at American Sociological Association annual meetings, New York City.

————. 1996b. "Three Women Who Loved the Left: Radical Women Leaders in the Japanese Red Army Movement." In *Re-Imaging Japanese Women,* ed. A. Imamura, 301–23. Berkeley: University of California Press.

————. 1999. "Doing the Defendant's Laundry: Support Groups as Social Movement Organizations in Contemporary Japan." *Japanstudien, Jahrbuch des Deutschen Instituts für Japanstudien* 11: 55–78.

————. 2004. "Kidnapped Japanese in North Korea: The New Left Connection." *Journal of Japanese Studies* 30, no. 1 (winter): 123–42.

Tilly, C. 1978. *From Mobilization to Revolution*. Reading, MA: Addison-Wesley.

U.S., Kerner Commission. 1968. *Report of the National Advisory Commission on Civil Disorders*. New York: Bantam Books.

U.S., President's Commission on Campus Unrest. 1970. *The Report of the President's Commission on Campus Unrest; Including Special Reports: The Killings at Jackson State, the Kent State Tragedy*. New York: Arno Press.

Whittier, N. 1997. "Political Generations, Micro-Cohorts and the Translation of Social Movements." *American Journal of Sociology* 62, no. 5: 760–78.

Wolfe, A. 1974. *The Seamy Side of Democracy*. New York: David McKay.

Young, T. R. 1983. "Underground Structures of the Democratic State." *Mid-American Review of Sociology* 8, no. 2: 67–80.

Zwerman, G. 1988. "Special Incapacitation: The Emergence of a New Correctional Facility for Women Political Prisoners." *Social Justice* 15, no. 1: 31–47.

Zwerman, G. 1989. "Domestic Counterterrorism: U.S. Government Responses to Political Violence on the Left in the Reagan Era." *Social Justice* 15, no. 2: 31–63.

————. 1992. "Conservative and Feminist Images of Women Associated with Armed, Clandestine Organizations in the United States." *International Social Movements Research* 4, *JAI Press*: 133–60.

———. 1994. "Mothering on the Lam: Politics, Gender Conflict and Maternal Thinking in Women Associated with Armed, Clandestine Organizations in the U.S." *Feminist Review* 47: 33–56.

———. 1995. "The Identity-Vulnerable Activist and the Emergence of Post-New Left Armed, Clandestine Organizations in the United States." *Studies of Social Change, The Working Paper Series*: 1–25.

Zwerman, G., P, Steinhoff, and D. della Porta. 2000. "Disappearing Social Movements: Clandestinity in the Cycle of New Left Protest in the United States, Japan, Germany, and Italy." *Mobilization* 5: 85–104.

5

# Talking the Walk:
# Speech Acts and Resistance in Authoritarian Regimes

*Hank Johnston*

Repressive states distort patterns of communication and association that are the basis of mobilization in Western democracies. Models of mobilization based on Western cases take for granted communication among social movement participants, but in authoritarian states free communication and dissemination of political information are not only highly problematic but carry risks such as interrogation, arrest, blacklisting, and imprisonment. Increased risk combines with the constrained patterns of social organization characteristic of authoritarianism, such as the one-party state and its colonization of daily life, to give rise to innovative oppositional adaptations. At the heart of these adaptations is the centrality of talk as political resistance.

Following Scott's analysis (1985, 1990) of how subordinated populations challenge authority and the work of scholars who have elaborated the role of free spaces in social movement development, I argue that *oppositional speech acts* are key elements of nonviolent political contention in authoritarian regimes. In the Communist regimes of Eastern Europe, in the minority national republics of the USSR, in Basque and Catalan regions of Spain during Francoism, in Pinochet's Chile, the opposition talked a lot. Looking at the long span of oppositional development, and especially early on, it was more what was said than was done that defined the opposition. Indeed, when political opportunities are severely constricted, much of the *doing* of contentious politics is *talking* about it.

A speech act is what one does when speaking rather than what one says. Speaking and doing are related, of course, but a speech-act focus looks at what is behaviorally accomplished by uttering words—the pragmatic intent of talk instead of the surface meaning. A speech-act perspective draws on the work of linguistic philosophers John Searle (1969) and John Austin (1962) by stressing that interactional goals guide what gets said, and tacitly understood rules guide how it is said. In the nuanced and between-the-lines speech contexts of authoritarian societies, knowing what is intended is crucial to interpreting what is said. Oppositional speech acts are strategic responses to authoritarian distortions of communication and information flow. Moreover, as state repression begins to relax, speech acts and other coded assertions of opposition serve as the basis for mobilizations that increasingly rely on the contemporary modular repertoire. In this essay, I identify the common forms of oppositional talk, where it tends to occur, and several more public processes that also have coded elements.

My observations are based on studies of oppositional politics in several different authoritarian contexts. They come mostly from my own field research in the Estonian Soviet Socialist Republic and in Francoist Spain, where, over the course of the last decade, 154 activists and dissidents were interviewed about their oppositional activities under authoritarianism (see Johnston 1991; Johnston and Snow 1998; Johnston and Aarelaid-Tart 2000; Johnston and Mueller 2001). I also base my observations on studies of the Polish opposition, and the opposition in several titular republics of the USSR, in Eastern Europe, and Latin America. The goal is to take a step beyond Scott's observations about oppositional speech in peasant societies and apply them to contemporary authoritarian regimes—to do an initial mapping of contentious speech acts, and their clustering, with the goal of situating them within a broader understanding of antiauthoritarian mobilization.

## Oppositional Speech Acts and Free Spaces

Social movement research in Western democracies has recognized the role of less obtrusive contention in movement development but has not accorded it a central theoretical place. In the panorama of the twentieth century's major movements, empirical research about the preparatory labor of premovement groups and activists often is overshadowed by events of greater historical significance. Still, several seminal studies have probed the behind-the-scenes phenomenon of movement seed planting: Morris (1984) has pointed out how *movement halfway houses* helped prime the U.S. civil rights movement; Mueller (1994) has identified the *cultural laboratories* of the women's movement; Hirsch (1990) analyzed the urban community movements' *havens,* and Rupp and Taylor (1987) looked at *abeyance structures* of feminist politics. The more widely used concept in this literature is free spaces, which describes gathering places where intimate association foments collective identity, shared grievances, oppositional frames, and tactical innovation. Polletta (1999, 13) has reviewed the free-spaces literature and noted that emphasis has been on spatial separateness and intimacy of the networks, at the expense of what get said and done in those networks. Interest in free spaces most recently focuses on how the Internet may be used in mobilization. Yang (2002), for example, looks at the virtual free space of the Internet and its role in the Tiananmen Square protest to draw a distinction between physical space and communication networks.

An opposition accomplishes important cultural work in free spaces: reframing what is possible, defining collective identities, articulating grievances, preserving oppositional norms and values, reshaping mobilization structures through network bridging and network extension. Polletta (1999) identifies three patterns or types of free spaces in which these functions are performed. A *transmovement free space* preserves oppositional values during periods of abeyance and often functions as "movement midwives," such as the Fellowship of Reconciliation (Smith 1996) or the Highlander Folk School (Morris 1984). An *indigenous free space* similarly nurtures oppositional values and ideologies, but grows out of the unique configuration of the culture and society in question, such as the African-American churches in the civil rights movement. Finally, *prefigurative free spaces* are intentionally formed groups that provide alternative models for what society could be, such as feminist collectives or anarchist communities. They are cook pots of new collective identities for members, and loci of speech acts that articulate grievances and reframe possibilities. Polletta calls for greater emphasis on the performative roles of free spaces and less on their structural characteristics—a focus on what they do rather than on where they occur. This is an important insight because, as is obvious with oppositional activities via the Internet, culture, structure, and space are three distinct analytic dimensions; and we lose purchase by conflating them. It is also a perspective that helps highlight the differences between free-space forms and functions in liberal democracies and those in authoritarian regimes.

The authoritarian state transforms the relationship between the content, structure, and location of free spaces. In contrast to the West, where legal rights permit many radically contentious groups to exist free of overt repression, in authoritarian regimes it is essential that free spaces be shielded from state scrutiny. In the West, a free space might take the form of a small organization with a charter and tax-exempt status, or of an informal autonomous collective. In authoritarian regimes, the constraints of repression mean that open, free, and structured organization is often impossible. This gives rise to innovative adaptations that tend to cluster according to variable combinations of the space, culture, and structure. For example, Polletta, noting that spatial separation by itself is insufficient to create a free space, observes that no one sees the Boy Scouts as free spaces for social movements (1999, 13). She is right, of course—in the West. But in Communist Poland, Boy Scout groups were indigenous free spaces where oppositional values were passed to new generations (this was also true of Boy Scout groups in British-mandate Palestine and in Francoist Spain). Under the Communists, scouting's lessons about patriotism were coded as Polish nationalism instead of socialist internationalism.

This is an example of a noncontentious organizational structure in a noncontentious space infused with a contentious cultural code that existed alongside scouting's apolitical content. Authoritarian regimes often provide organizational spaces—loopholes of administrative freedom—where contentious words are uttered along with noncontentious ones. As we shall see, it is not uncommon that when an organization's official business is over— a historical society, for example—conversations sometimes can push the limits of acceptable speech. In several Communist states the shell of what had been the established church often provided place and opportunity for indigenous free spaces to take root. It is not an exaggeration to say that, for a time, the Polish church was the most extensive free space in all of Eastern Europe. In this case, an understood cultural code of opposition led to the occasional duplicitous use of space and organization for oppositional activities.

Another innovative response to repression is that spatial dimension is transcended by the creation of temporary free spaces. These are the movable feasts of authoritarian opposition, such as renditions of prohibited songs at concerts, or when a crowd politicizes a soccer match through songs, chants, and intense cheering. These temporary free spaces must be distinguished from spontaneous outbursts of protests that occur in the West. Although there is clearly an element of protest in both, they are much less spontaneous in authoritarian states because these event seizures—as I call them— are often planned and initiated by dissident groups in response to a closed political milieu. What looks like spontaneity, say, at a soccer match, in fact reflects planning and strategic instigation. For the mass of bystanding participants, taking part in these temporary free spaces is a relatively low-cost collective action that breaks patterns of fear and continual self-monitoring common to public life.

A third innovation is when both spatial and organizational dimensions are transcended by the creation of diffuse free spaces via oppositional speech acts. Authoritarian society creates a citizenry that is acutely aware of the split between public and private spheres (Habermas 1984). Social gatherings, neighborhood associations, labor organizations, and so on, bring together a wide variety of people who manage this split in different ways and degrees. The private sphere may break the surface of public discourse and be openly voiced, depending on participants' assessment of the setting's safety and the group's composition. The emergent definition of an interactional setting as safe is basic to the creation of an *oppositional speech situation.* These are a kind of prefigurative free space—to use Polletta's term—in the sense that they augur a future society of free and open communication, but without the structure or fixed location characteristic of those in the West. Moreover, there is an additional authoritarian caveat that spies and agents provocateurs are always possibilities. Much as fog is composed of microparticles of water in the air, oppositional speech situations pervade daily life when the authoritarian state begins to lose legitimacy but maintains social control. They are temporary free spaces in that they are dependent on the moment, defined by the interlocutors, the topic, and the assessment of trust.

In all of the cases on which this report is based, the authoritarian state liberalized prior to democratic transition. During the halting and often recurrent process of internal liberalization, opposition groups develop out of these free-space configurations. When the authoritarian state first eases repression, such as the de-Stalinization campaigns in the USSR or the Polish October of 1956, it is typical that these innovative free spaces condense from the authoritarian fog into the morning dew of proto-oppositional groups and associations. These groupings are composed of people who are willing to assume more risk, and who are more innovative in confronting the state. For example, in the Estonian SSR it was well known that many local history groups had anti-Soviet leanings, or, in Poland, that certain Catholic circles and confraternaties were anticommunist. These compose the tentative structure of an emerging opposition—free spaces in the more typical spatial sense where protest entrepreneurs are schooled to take advantage of the next opening or weakening in the regime. Running parallel with these groups is the intelligentsia, which also benefits from liberalization by gaining new freedoms, better living standards, and more travel opportunities. Some intellectuals become a loyal opposition within the regime, some cultural critics, some dissidents, but they all talk with one another. They seize upon new freedoms and, based on the cases I have observed, never completely relinquish them should the cycle of liberalization contract, as it often does. These circles and associations are islands of oppositional talk, where talk constitutes most of the action that takes place—because open protest still remains severely constrained.

### Oppositional Speech Situations

Away from surveillance by authorities, oppositional speech can occur almost anywhere: the kitchen, the coffee shop, barhopping at night, informal discussions at a book club or a cinema society, and those small circles of friends that linger for hours after the proceedings of more formally structured groups and organizations. Informal politicized talk in kitchens and coffee shops has been frequently commented upon by area scholars but not placed within a broader theory of the authoritarian state (Shlapentkokh 1989; Laba 1991; Taagepera 1993; Ries 1997). For social movement scholars, the tendency is to focus on the volcanic eruptions of protest, rather than the subterranean magna of oppositional speech.

Yet, the widespread nature of oppositional kitchen talk suggests that something important is going on. It would be incorrect to dismiss it as mere grumbling of the kind that is ubiquitous in the West because complaints about authoritarian systems carry consequences. Kitchen talk is a twentieth-century urban manifestation of Scott's "hidden arbors" where peasants and slaves speak freely, knowing that they are outside the scrutiny of the master, the landowner, or the police. Drawing on speech-act theory, these places are marked by shared understandings of the situation—specific rules of speech, that is, what is appropriate to say and how far one can go in criticism, how to say it, and to whom. These are not political discussions of the kind that occur in the liberal democracies because partisan and tactical positions are irrelevant, and actual contention for power is not practicable. Nevertheless, sustained criticism against the regime, the party, and/or society is prohibited by the state, and therefore automatically politicized. In the words of one observer of Russian discourse:

> While talk is a central locus of value production in all societies, in Russia it has long been highly marked; consider, for example, the constant references to the "kitchen" as the most sacred place in Russian/Soviet society. There, over tea or vodka, people could speak their minds, tell their stories, and spill their souls openly. . . . The Soviet state was, of course, a critical agent in the continuous sacralization of private talk, since only in these quiet communicative exchanges did most people feel free to communicate honestly and openly. (Ries 1997, 21)

Nancy Ries has documented the varieties of Russian discourse during the late 1980s (see also Pesmen 1995). She observes that litanies of complaint, suffering, and victimization were common forms of talk in a large repertoire that included husband tales, drinking tales, laments of sacrifice and social breakdown, and sexual jokes. Only a small number, Ries observes, were politicized statements about the system or criticisms of the party or state.

A *speech situation* is a sociolinguistic concept that recognizes that there are understood rules about what gets said, how, and by whom. They are numerous in everyday life, embracing common encounters (such as the polite talk of people waiting in a queue) as well as more specific subcultural encounters (such as an office visit of a student to a professor, or an intellectual chat at the commons with a colleague). For these types of interactions, there are tacitly understood rules that are learned and become part of one's speech repertoire. Similarly, in authoritarian regimes, the rules of oppositional speech situations are learned as part of unofficial, private-sphere socialization. A poignant example comes from an Estonian informant who recounted an incident as a student under the Soviets. A teacher saw a nationalist rhyme written in her workbook ("I am an Estonian, I am proud to be an Estonian, and an Estonian I will ever be") and quietly informed her, "Yes, we all feel this way but we must never say it in public."

Sociolinguistic research informs us that definitions of speech situations frequently change, often in the course of the discussion as new topics are introduced or as new members are added. Also, definitions may change in light of broader political or cultural change. For example, as an authoritarian regime liberalizes, interlocutors recognize that new boundaries for what is said may be possible. Pushing and testing these boundaries is a subtle process linguistically, depending on the composition of the group and perceived levels of tolerance and trustworthiness among the participants. Shifts in speech situations are marked by the introduction of new themes and variations of intonation and prosody (Gumperz 1982), and continual monitoring of these cues is typical. If interlocutors are relatively new and untested, if they voice topics that raise questions about their trustworthiness, others may give cues to indicate their discomfort and caution, or try to change the direction of the conversation. For the most part, participants in oppositional speech situations are known and trusted, but, as regime policies change, during either liberalization or contraction, the rules become more fluid. Respondents have told of cases when a participant openly stated that the discussion should not continue in its present direction because taking part would compromise him.

The concrete topics of oppositional speech situations are potentially innumerable, but certain themes can be identified: criticisms and complaints about the party, leaders, and state; ideological debate about society and the economy; discussion of emigration, of world events, of situations in open societies; ethnic-national issues; the secret police and repression; nonofficial, nonpropagandized information about contemporary society or historical events. A common element is underground humor, which embraces these topics and more, but which also performs key functions in the developing definition of oppositional speech. A scholar of Soviet jokes notes that "jokes were told eagerly in people's homes and kitchens. . . . Political jokes acquired such wide currency, despite the fact that before the collapse of the Soviet Union *anekdoty* were never circulated via official media and were never uttered by comedians [on the stage]" (Krylova 1999, 246).

Psychologists see jokes as escape valves for various kinds of repression and/or anxiety. It is plausible that this in part accounts for why political jokes are widespread in repressive regimes. But a speech-act approach focuses our attention not on the psychology of jokes, but rather on what they accomplish within the context of broader discourse. In oppositional speech situations, jokes can be part of the substance of talk, but not all of their tellings indicate that oppositional speech situations are present. Linguistically, jokes and humor perform two pragmatic functions: They foster solidarity and trust between the interlocutors by pointing to shared frames of interpretation and signaling goodwill. They also are useful conversational devices for saying things indirectly because they are deniable. The teller can always invoke the defense, "I was only joking" (Tannen 1986, 69). This defensive quality means that jokes can be used strategically in conversational settings to gauge the trustworthiness of participants before full-blown oppositional speech begins. If there are doubts, mildly political jokes that test the waters can be diverted, for example, to sexual jokes. It makes sense, therefore, that political jokes represent the first budding of contentious speech, and often mark tentative steps into oppositional speech situations. Because of their deniability, political jokes are less risky than full-blown oppositional speech, and seem to perform prepolitical, secondary, and/or antecedent functions in the development of oppositional speech situations.

### The Network Structure of Oppositional Speech

Interviews in both Soviet Estonia and Francoist Spain point to a network structure of oppositional speech situations that cuts across webs of friendship, neighborhoods, and occupational groups. The concept of preexisting mobilizing networks has been widely applied to authoritarian oppositions (Lipski 1985; Johnston 1991; Laba 1991; Opp and Gern 1993; Mistzal and Jenkins 1995; Flam 1996), but mostly regarding identifiable groups such as dissident circles, samizdat cells, theaters, and church groups. Opp and Gern (1993) cite informal networks as the basis of groups that formed Neues Forum in the German Democratic Republic (GDR). Johnston and Aareleid-Tart (2000) found a reticulated structure of contacts among the Estonian national artistic elite. Although oppositional speech situations do not have formal structure, four characteristics are relevant to developing opposition insofar as they lead to more formally structured collectivities.

First, oppositional speech situations frequently bring together people with diverse occupational and ideological positions vis-à-vis the state and party. On the one hand, this imparts a pluralistic quality to the discussions of ideology and strategy. Debates are sometimes intense, although, practically, the stakes are small; but interlocutors are united by a common understanding of a shared oppositional frame. On the other hand, several respondents reported to me that participants were sometimes linked to the regime and party, and that these party connections were especially important as the opposition developed. These people were internal contacts who had access to resources and permitting procedures that are essential for more organized and public contention.

Second, there is an individual element to oppositional speech in that, within the segment of the disaffected population, some are willing to incur more risk than others. Some are innovative in how they think about opposition, and/or may have a more opportunistic view of the political structure. The diverse and crosscutting structure of oppositional speech networks means that these more contentious souls come into contact with friends and acquaintances who are less outspoken, either because their toleration of risk is lower or their perception of opportunities is narrower. Through these linkages, the more radical members can disseminate their own activist orientation and spur others to action. In particular, their personal influence comes to fruition as state repression eases and some of these more militant members move to what I call hit-and-run protests.

Third, in the long term, oppositional speech situations tend to cluster in certain locales as the authoritarian state liberalizes. The more assertive interlocutors in what had previously been diffuse oppositional speech gravitate and/or create emerging free spaces—well-known coffee shops and bars, or the duplicitous groups and organizations that I discuss later. As these groups form, key activists establish new linkages, often based on more contentious goals, but this does not mean severing old ties. In network terms, these activists become more central in the diffuse oppositional milieu of contentious talk. This is a slow process, but not necessarily an incremental one. The opening of political opportunities in authoritarian states is never unidirectional and linear but represents the complex interrelation of internal regime factors such as elite conflict, resources, and policy issues in the economic and strategic realm. It makes sense that the clustering of speech situations in specific locales and the emergence of movement entrepreneurs follows the fits and starts of state policy and can be linked with specific kinds of changes in the regime (a fruitful line of inquiry for the future, but not the focus of this essay).

Fourth, in the absence of open media, these network-central activists serve as transmitters of information linking disaffected and alienated citizens at different levels of militancy. Networks of oppositional speech situations provide communicative channels whereby information not available in the official media is disseminated. As testified to by the widespread occurrence of samizdat publications in Eastern Europe and the titular republics of the USSR, this information function is critical in the development of an opposition movement against authoritarianism. These networks represent verbal samizdat channels prior to when samizdat publications are distributed, and which continue to function in tandem with them afterwards.

In sum, Soviet and East European scholars in the early 1980s interpreted the growth of dissident activities among intellectuals and the new middle classes as representing widespread dissatisfaction with the Communist system: the tip of the iceberg (Korbonski 1983; Kusin 1983; Sharlet 1983; Zaslavsky 1979). In the repressive context, oppositional speech acts are a less demanding and less risky form of collective action, standing for a part of the iceberg below the waterline but linked to those above it by networks of oppositional speech. In the West, conscience constituencies and potential social movement participants can sign petitions, donate money, attend meetings, stuff envelopes, carpool, and take part in numerous forms of less risky collective action that are essential to public performances such as marches, strikes, and sit-ins (Oliver and Marwell 1993). In authoritarian regimes, these activities are not available, and oppositional talk in these quasi-public situations functions as a low-risk proxy.

### Duplicitous Organizations

In Eastern Europe, in the titular republics of the Soviet Union, and in the Basque and Catalan regions of Francoist Spain, some groups and organizations assumed a duplicitous character by using their official status as an excuse to gather, talk, and sometimes take part in activities that pushed the limits of what the regime defined as acceptable. These groups were not social movement organizations. They filed official budgets and political reports, and met in public buildings. Often they clustered around certain activities that stressed national identity or had roots in earlier periods of in- dependence or democracy, which imparted oppositional symbolism to their activities. Many who were quiet opponents of the regime flocked to these activities, compounding their oppositional quality and making them places where oppositional speech situations frequently and densely clustered. It is significant that Estonian and Spanish respondents had no trouble identify- ing groups and organizations known for their mildly oppositional milieus.

Three categories of duplicitous groups can be identified that are gener- alizable across authoritarian regimes (see Johnston and Mueller 2001 for a fuller discussion).

## Social and Recreational Groups

Officially sanctioned groups that focused on the national histories and traditions often carried an a vague oppositional meaning for participants: folk-dancing groups, ethnographic study groups, folk-music groups, local historical societies, drama clubs, and so on. Choral societies in Estonia, which had its "Singing Revolution" in 1991, played a major role because there was a repertoire of prohibited songs associated with the independent republic (1918–40). The same was true in Catalonia, where a repertoire of national songs (in the Catalan language) from periods of autonomy drew participants. In Estonia, beekeeping societies and horticultural groups were traditional peasant activities that asserted independence from the kolkhoz system, and therefore were widely recognized as having a vague independence from the Communist state. In Euzkadi and Catalonia, ex- cursion groups, outing groups, and geography associations that explored the national countryside had mild oppositional milieus. Activities walked a tightrope of toleration and repression. When activities crossed the line of acceptance or when regime policies tightened, these groups were some- times closed down, and the leading members fined, but rarely were they imprisoned or deported.

## Churches and Religious Groups

Authoritarian regimes are commonly confronted with a contradictory situation regarding religious practice. In some cases, the regime draws le- gitimacy from its association with the church, as was the case in Francoist Spain, Pinochet's Chile, and Brazil under military rule (Johnston 1989). This presents opportunities for lower levels of the ecclesial hierarchy or parts of the church organization far from the capital to act independently and contentiously. In Eastern Europe, the free spaces for churches were much more constrained, although this varied among countries. In general, the Communist states exercised close administrative control over officially recognized churches and were intolerant of grassroots religious practice. Repression of believers, co-optation of church hierarchy, and covert actions by secret police were common. Nevertheless, the organized church played key oppositional roles in the GDR (Rein 1990), and, to a lesser extent, in Czechoslovakia and Hungary. The Catholic church in Poland occupied a position that was unique in all Eastern bloc countries. In the early stages of Solidarity, churches were used as meeting places (Szajokowski 1983; Borowski 1986). Several chapters of Rural Solidarity grew out of the militant sectors of the Catholic Oases movement (Mucha and Zaba 1992). Solidarity itself drew upon religious imagery and, in its early stages, church resources. In the USSR, the Catholic church was an important free space in the Lithuanian SSR, which published the *Chronicle of the Catholic Church in Lithuania* between 1972 and 1982, the most important samizdat publication for the dissident community. In other titular republics, national churches played oppositional roles, as in the western Ukraine (Hvat 1984, 280–89), and in Georgia and Armenia to a lesser extent.

It is important to recognize that religious practice and opposition to the state overlap only partially and for periods when political opportunities are relatively closed. Because churches are the only social institutions outside of party and state control, they can function as free spaces where resources such as meeting places, copy machines, and communication networks are furtively made available. Nevertheless, the main focus of church organization is religious faith, which can become politicized when the state denies freedom of practice. Most people opted for less risky strategies. Several Estonian respondents mentioned that religious faith was maintained in family practice and celebrations rather than public worship, and it makes sense that this was true in other national republics. One measure of this might be that a high proportion of underground political jokes from the Soviet Union and Eastern Europe have religious themes.

## Intellectual and Cultural Groups.

Because the repressive state stifles the exchange of ideas and creative freedoms on which art and literature thrive, it is common that some literary and fine art intelligentsia networks are loci of contentious talk. In Estonia, a reticulated structure of contact was discernible among artists in the capital of Tallinn and the university city of Tartu. For example, artists whose abstract impressionism challenged socialist realism gathered at each other's homes, or took summer vacations together in the country. Within official groups too, such as the creative unions of writers, artists, and musicians, there were cliques of members whose work was more avant-garde and innovative. Union officials had to balance support for these members with the demands of watchdog party officials in the culture ministries.

The groups and circles are numerous. I found that many were informal, such as jazz circles, literary salons, book clubs, and language study groups, especially in non-Communist authoritarian states, where there was more free space for civil society (such as small classes in Catalan and Euzkerra during Francoism, or theater clubs in Santiago de Chile under Pinochet). But informality has liabilities in terms of resources, and some cultural and intellectual associations assumed formal organization to take advantage of state and party resources. Theater groups and cinema societies were common free spaces in the titular republics of the USSR. In Estonia, the English Language Circle and the Book Lovers Club provided opportunities to gather in a mildly oppositional milieu. One member of an English Language Circle recounted how the group enjoyed summer retreats at resorts, paid for by the state. She told how they dutifully filed their reports and practiced English, but when they gathered, there was a freedom of discussion where, "under the surface was the truth."

Like social and recreational groups, members had to be careful about what they said because their words might carry to untested ears. Penalties were not severe for crossing the line: groups could lose their charter, have budget cuts, lose vacation or outing privileges, or have spies placed among them to rein in their activities. Artists might not have their work displayed, or, under extreme circumstances, could be expelled from the union, which meant that they had to earn a living doing other things. In Estonia, artists sometimes ended up as boiler tenders or farmworkers if they pushed too far.

### Dissidence

Dissidence as a form of contention arises when individuals, many of whom come from intellectual and scientific communities, reframe what is possible for their oppositional talk to achieve. Contentious speech is the lifeblood of dissident activities, as men and women gather in private homes to ideologize and strategize ways to challenge regime policies (Flam 1996, 1998). Indeed, a great proportion of antiauthoritarian dissidence is dissident talk—to be differentiated from the talk of artists or folklorists who actively monitor and limit their public performances. Dissidents, in contrast, "openly proclaim dissent and demonstrate it in one way or another to compatriots and the state" (Medvedev 1980). There seem to be two key reasons for this shift: first, dissident talk breaks the surface of public life when authoritarian regimes take small steps toward liberalization; second, dissident figures draw upon their own elite, sometimes international, status as intellectuals and/or scientists to insulate themselves from severe retribution. Dissident activities were especially characteristic of the 1970s and 1980s in the Soviet bloc, when cracks in the repressive system allowed these men and women to gain a notoriety (Joppke 1995); but dissident circles can be identified in Latin American authoritarianism, and were present in Catalonia and Euzkadi under Francoism, suggesting that dissidence is a common genre of antiauthoritarian opposition.

The varieties East European and Soviet dissidence can be traced to the Sinyavsky–Daniel show trial in the Soviet Union in 1965 in which two authors were tried for publishing works abroad that "maligned and slandered" the Soviet system. Intellectuals, artists, and scientists who under Khrushchev had enjoyed relative freedom, saw these charges as heralding a return to Stalinism and rallied to support them. Many of those who spoke out were members of the Communist Party. Their challenges were wholly reform-oriented and within the Communist worldview. They encountered an especially heavy wave of repression between 1966 and 1972, reflecting the hard-line, inflexible response to the 1968 Prague Spring.

In the East bloc, dissidence sometimes developed out of frustrated reform initiatives within the Communist Party, and sometimes out of claims of continuity with pre-Leninist society—especially in Eastern Europe and the Soviet Baltics. Flam's study of Polish dissidents (1996) points to a hierarchy of status in dissident circles. High-visibility elites faced great risks, but their fame often mitigated punishment. In many cases, they had come to terms already with loss of jobs, expulsion from the party, and denial of any privileges for themselves and their families. Fear permeated the lower levels of the hierarchy, whose participants often did the legwork, such as passing papers, making contacts, and gathering information. These activities could lead to prison, or, for young men, immediate drafting into the military. Passing information to the Western media could mean exile or psychiatric punishment.

Typical dissident activities were the drafting of open letters and petitions, defending activists' actions, disseminating information about arrests and illegal police activities, proposing new laws and democratic reforms, challenging official history and economic theory, passing information to foreign media, or giving interviews. Samizdat publication was critical because dissident activity could only assume political importance insofar as it was disseminated to the larger public. In general, the trajectory of dissidence is partly determined by the party's tactic of trying to manage internal dissent, and partly by the inherent contradictions of state administration of intellectual and creative production. Periods of liberalization raise expectations and spur creativity and debate. When party apparatchiks judge that innovation has gone too far, new freedoms are tenaciously held on to and can spur tactical innovation by dissident circles. Severe repression, such as exile and prison for dissidents, may quell the public arena but drives dissent temporarily into less public oppositional forms, such as oppositional speech in duplicitous organization. When political contexts opened under Mikhail Gorbachev's programs of glasnost and perestroika, dissidence as a repertoire became increasingly outdated, although dissidents themselves did not. Indeed, public awareness of their risk-taking behaviors and quixotic campaigns at times when penalties for such behaviors were still severe frequently imparted a notoriety that advantaged them when the opposition moved into more open forms of contention along the lines of the Western repertoire, and later when political competition broke out in full. The list of countries is long—Estonia, Lithuania, Chile, Ukraine, Latvia, Georgia, Catalonia—in which prominent dissidents occupied positions of political leadership after the democratic transition.

### Hit-and-Run Protests

Hit-and-run protests are often the first buds of public contention. They are intended to catch the eye of casual observers and passersby before the police dismantle, eradicate, or obscure the traces of the action, which is typically very soon. They are less based on speech acts than the previous examples, but preserve continuity with the coded talk of clandestine gatherings in two ways. First, the public manifestations of opposition are often not direct but symbolic, that is, meaningful to those who can draw upon an unstated interpretative frame to grasp the full meaning of oppositional content. In this sense, they are an elaboration of the between-the-lines readings characteristic of some oppositional speech acts. Second, hit-and-run actions are done by small circles of young men and women who have "talked their way to action." My fieldwork in Spain and Estonia provides evidence that the duplicitous groups mentioned earlier are hatcheries of these small, clandestine actions. In several cases, protest entrepreneurs were schooled and nurtured in these groups. One legacy of long-lived repressive states, especially the Communist regimes of Eastern Europe, is the absence of experienced compatriots. In this vacuum, duplicitous groups are incubators of innovation. They are places where friendships and solidarity mitigate the risks of going public. Although many hit-and-run actions superficially appear to be spontaneous one-person events, my interviews suggest that most are planned and executed by a small circles of activists who discuss logistics, material requirements, timing, and division of labor in oppositional speech situations. Moreover, as part of their education, these activists seek information about protest actions from outside sources (such as during international youth conferences in the USSR). These experiences frequently position these activists to become actors in the emerging social movement organizations when the opposition takes off. Based on my fieldwork and on secondary sources, several patterns of hit-and-run protests can be identified.

## Graffiti

Probably more than the other hit-and-run tactics, graffiti appear to be the work of a single person, but it is my contention that this is usually not the case. In Francoist Spain, *pintadas* or painting sprees were commonly organized by youthful activists. I was told that select members of a Catholic youth group frequently organized to paint anti-Francoist slogans in Barcelona. As Francoism eased in the late 1960s, political graffiti was a common sight in Barcelona, Bilbao, Madrid, and other cites. At the minimum, short graffiti containing one or two words, such "Free Pujol" (supporting a jailed Catalan activist) or "Charter 77," requires a lookout. For more elaborate graffiti, such as the painting of a prohibited Basque or Estonian flag, more lookouts are needed. The more elaborate the graffiti, the more time is of the essence, and the more likely several artists participate based on prior planning.

John Bushnell (1990) studied Moscow graffiti during the late Soviet period, most of which was youthful fan graffiti for sports teams and rock groups, and not coded oppositional acts. One specific genre, however, had political connotations, namely, the graffiti of entry 6, No. 10 Bolshaia Sadoviaia Street. This entryway led to apartment 50, where the writer Mikhail Bulgakov lived in the early 1920s and which he incorporated into in his novel *The Master and Margarita*. Written in the 1930s but not published until 1965–66, the book is a complex commentary about Stalinist society. Bulgakov uses a group of supernatural characters, led by Woland (Satan) and Behemoth (usually appearing as a giant cat), who expose the corruption of Moscow through magic pranks. Bulgakov also incorporates religious themes in sections about a conversation between Jesus and Pilate. Much of the graffiti carried an obvious political message (Bushnell 1990, 184). References to the novel were common: "Woland, come back, too much crap has piled up." Many graffiti were intricate paintings of the novel's characters, most commonly the giant cat, Behemoth, and Woland. Many statements were long quotes. Although Bushnell does not have information about who the writers were, except in the few cases when they were signed, or how the graffiti were done, it is plausible that much of it was done in small groups composed of the graffiti artists, text writers, lookouts, lantern holders, and others along for the excitement.

## Clandestine Placements

A common hit-and-run tactic, again usually symbolic, was nighttime placement of flowers, flags, crosses, and candles. This happened in Poland with placement of flowers to commemorate the workers killed at the Gdańsk shipyard strike. Flowers appeared overnight at the gates of the shipyard and at the square where the workers were killed on the anniversary of their deaths. Similarly, in Catalonia, at the site of the statue of Rafael Casanovas, a hero in Catalonia's struggle for autonomy, flowers appeared regularly on the national day, September 11. The location was in the center of a traffic circle, and another hit-and-run tactic was to circle the site several times that day, honking auto horns and yelling "Visca Catalunya!" In Tallinn, Estonia, at the site of a statue of a national hero demolished by the Soviets in 1940, flowers sometimes appeared on the anniversary of the republic, February 24. The statue stood across from the Reaalgümnaasium School. Rumor was that the flowers were placed by groups of youth at the school. Also in Tallinn, students placed candles on Christmas Eve at the grave of Julius Kuperianova, a hero of Estonia's war of independence against the Russians (1918–20). In downtown Kanaus, Lithuania, students regularly placed excrement in the outstretched hand of a Lenin statue. A loaf of bread was placed in the hand he held behind his back.

In both the Basque region and Catalonia, the placement of the respective national flags was a political statement against the centralizing authoritarian Francoist state. In the course of fieldwork, I interviewed older militants who nostalgically recalled youthful escapades with their friends, climbing to rooftops in order to raise the Catalan national flag. Usually they were torn down by 10:00 a.m. the next day, but for people on their way to work these flag placements were symbols of the opposition and reminders that there was an active resistance. It is a suggestive proposition that these symbolic actions had their greatest effect as markers for the larger population of cracks in the regime's legitimacy. In Lithuania, there was a continual battle between the secret police and dedicated Catholic groups who placed crosses at the mountain of Sinuali—the police regularly tore them down did not hinder their replacement at all.

Like graffiti, some of these placements were surely done by isolated individuals, but my interviews suggest that the majority were carried out clandestinely by small circles of activists. Also, it was common that activists encouraged others to participate, by reproducing and distributing clandestinely reproduced notices. In Barcelona a campaign like this was organized to protest the Francoist newspaper *La Vanguardia*. One respondent told of carbon-copied (this was 1954) ribbons of paper lying on the ground appealing to people to rip up their copies of *La Vanguardia* the next day in protest against the Francoist chief editor. For a week, strips of the destroyed paper blew around the city. Eventually, a boycott campaign was organized, again using similar notices, and which eventually ended in the dismissal of the editor.

## Event Seizures

An event seizure is protest action that relies on the risk taking of a few militants and the spontaneous participation of bystanders who are not initiated into the action but whose support is assumed. Militants risk personal safety by precipitating the action, and hope that others will see that risks are low (there is safety in numbers), join in, and transform the occasion into a significant protest event. Event seizures are important in the developing anti-authoritarian opposition because they give a taste of protest participation to a previously quiescent mobilization potential. A second effect is that these events often serve as markers for reframing oppositional possibilities for the wider population because they involve a relatively large number of people. Superficially, event seizures seem to be spontaneous outbursts of opposition, and although sometimes this may be the case, most are planned by small groups of activists. Scattering small notices or leaflets is often important to prime the potential supporters for action. However, many event seizures require secrecy up until the last moment, which makes prior notice impossible. Although tactics may vary, five types of event seizures are common across authoritarian regimes.

*1. Symbolic songs and anthems.* In 1964, the audience at the Barcelona Music Palace sang a prohibited Catalan anthem at a concert attended by Generalissimo Francisco Franco. The action was planned by several anti-Francoist militants, all members of duplicitous groups associated with the Catholic Catalan opposition. Several militants had placed themselves throughout the audience and at a prearranged point began to sing the song. Several others, for whom the action had been passed by word of mouth, then joined in. The result was that most of the audience understood the significance of what was happening and also began to sing, so many that the police were able to do nothing. The generalissimo walked out, scandalized; and news of the action rapidly spread. It led to the arrest of one of the leaders, Jordi Pujol (later president of the Catalan autonomous government), and the printer of a satirical flyer protesting Franco's visit to Barcelona, written by Pujol but which did not mention the action, for obvious reasons. These events at the concert and Pujol's arrest precipitated a graffiti campaign to free Pujol that lasted several months, and signaled a more militant collective action frame for the opposition.

Planning to sing prohibited songs at public events is a common event seizure. It happened throughout the Baltic republics of the USSR during the late 1980s, where choruses are a strong cultural tradition. In 1987, at the Baltic Nights festival in Tallinn, militants began to sing the prohibited anthem of the independent republic. In Poland, the prohibited anthem "Pose cos Polska" (God, who saves Poland) was often heard during the millennium celebrations in 1966 (Kubik 1994, 128).

*2. Concerts.* Related to the hit-and-run intonation of prohibited anthems are oppositional performances by well-known singer-composers. As censorship eases, it is common that a handful of performers acquire oppositional stature by virtue of veiled regime criticism in their songs. Lluis Llach and Raimón in Catalonia, Kwold Biermann in the GDR, and Boris Grebenshchikov in Moscow come to mind. Each country in the Eastern bloc had a collection of daring singers, composers, and performance groups. Among respondents in Francoist Spain and Estonia, the lore about how performers circumvented and tricked censors was frequently recounted. I was told of concerts in Barcelona in which toned-down repertoires were submitted to censors with the intention of adding more contentious songs on stage. Another variation was that performers played only the music of their prohibited songs, but the audience sang the words, which had been committed to memory because of their daring. Under these circumstances, there is little that the police can do except sanction the performers, which only increases their popularity. The folklore of the opposition had stories of red-faced police frustratedly waving hands and screaming at thousands in the audience to stop.

*3. Parodies of official events.* Activists may take advantage of official gatherings, such as state parades and commemorations, to stage counter-demonstrations. Because these are public, they are risky; but they use irony and parody to lessen the risk. Repression is more difficult because the manifest actions mirror the official ones, and because there is often a sense of goodwill. The Orange Alternative (Alternatywa Pomaranczowa) in Poland was a clandestine group that was especially adept at using irony.[1] On the forty-fourth anniversary of the Civic Militia in 1988, demonstrators took to the streets with signs proclaiming "Long Live the Military," "Democracy is Anarchy" and "The Youth is with the Party" (Uncensored Poland News

Bulletin 1988b, 3). Similarly, on the eve of the October Revolution anniversary the group marched in the streets shouting, "Lenin is with us" and "We love the police." Notice of these actions was passed by leaflets or by word of mouth. The text of a flyer for this action gives a sense of the irony:

> Comrades, dress up in your best, in red. Put on red shoes, red hat, red scarf. . . . We Reds (red faces, red hair, pants, and lips) will stand fast at 4 pm under the clock.
> Comrades, let us meet at the rally to honor the Revolution!!! The ideas and practice of Leninism and Trotskyism live on!!! (Uncensored Poland News Bulletin 1988a, 17)

*4. Sporting events.* Sporting events are sometimes seized and given symbolic political connotations. This most commonly happens with soccer matches, in which uncommonly intense crowd enthusiasm, chants, and songs (including prohibited ones) impart a clear sense to authorities that something beyond fan support of their team is occurring. A match between the USSR and Czechoslovakia, held in Tallinn after the 1968 Soviet invasion to quash the Prague Spring, invoked especially strong support for the Czechs. Similarly, matches between Russian teams and other national teams in the Eastern bloc sometimes were seized this way. The matches between Real Madrid and Barcelona were often politicized. These matches also became part of the oppositional folklore, invoked in the course of interviews as measures of anti-Soviet, anti-Russian, or anti-Castilian sentiments in the population. I have not interviewed respondents who confirm that they instigated chants or songs at soccer matches, but I believe that these occurrences are common enough that at least some are provoked by activists to make political points.

*5. Diversion of funerals.* This hit-and-run genre typically redirects the funeral of a well-known dissident from its manifest intent, burial and mourning, to overt political symbolism. Contemporary images show this frequently in the politicization of funerals in Gaza and West Bank, but the deaths of (sometimes martyred) dissidents were occasions for politicized funerals in Poland, the GDR, and South Africa. Similarly, in Francoist Barcelona, the casket of a well-known opponent to the regime, Don Aurelio María Escarré, was seized by mourners and diverted from the funeral route to the main streets of Barcelona.

Hit-and-run actions represent a middle stage in the progression from oppositional speech to mass protest. They have fewer participants than duplicitous organizations, but are more audacious, and, because they are public, bring a wider audience into (perhaps their first) oppositional actions.

They presage future mobilizations through reframing what is possible for a wider audience and by schooling cadres of oppositional activists in tactics and organization.

## Symbolic Mobilization

To be precise about terms, I take true symbolic protests to be events that are manifestly about one set of claims but that also serve as proxies for a direct political contention against the regime. In other words, the coded and indirect elements characteristic of oppositional speech acts are reflected in the content of protest events before direct antistate political contention occurs. Symbolic protest takes place when the authoritarian state has eased repression enough that openings are presented for collective action on certain issues. These mobilizations are about peace, ecology, or women's issues that the party and state chose not to repress for ideological reasons or for reasons of international politics. Organizers go through official channels, apply for and receive permits to use parks and squares, and reserve the right-of-way for marches: there are strong similarities to the contemporary Western repertoire. However, paralleling the activities of duplicitous organizations, these protests focus on one theme, but simultaneously are given a more general oppositional meaning by many participants—not all, but many. Like songs and poetry that must be read between the lines, the antiregime subtext is coded, invoked by widely recognized symbols, and interpreted by applying the tacitly understood rules of the antiregime code.

True symbolic protest is a common form of opposition in the later stages of the authoritarian state: campaigns for language rights (in Catalonia, Euzkadi, titular republics of USSR); ecology protests (the Basque campaign against the nuclear power plant in Lemoiz, Guipúzcoa; the Estonian antimining campaign); memorial campaigns (remembrance of Stalin's victims in titular USSR republics, campaign for a memorial to slain workers in Gdańsk; campaigns to make public the Molotov–Ribbentropf pact in the Baltic republics of the USSR). Finally, Polish Solidarity began as a working-class movement but, of course, became much more. Nevertheless, its early essence as a labor movement symbolically challenged the party's leading role, and many workers knew it. So did a great many Poles as the union branched into spheres of society far from the shipyard and industrial shop floor.

Symbolic protests, like hit-and-run actions, are the schools for protest experience as the opposition shifts from talk to action. A representative example is the Estonian antimining movement that began in the late 1980s. Large-scale mining of phosphorites had seriously harmed the ecology of northeastern Estonia. In 1987, a new mine was planned my Moscow to exploit recently discovered deposits. The mine was located on the watershed and threatened to contaminate water supplies for a large portion of eastern and central Estonia. A group of Estonian scientists issued a protest in March 1986, and later that year the Estonian Writers Union publicly spoke against the project. The importance of these groups is that many members were embedded in networks connected with duplicitous organizations and some dissident circles. In my research, the same names came up again and again, suggesting a link between earlier organizations that were loci of oppositional speech and the antimining movement. There was a unspoken subtext in the ecological theme, namely, that this was a plan hatched in Moscow, and that it meant the importation of ten thousand non-Estonian workers to eastern Estonia, further Russifying the region linguistically and culturally and diluting the native Estonian population. Ecological issues were intertwined with cultural and national ones, and opposition to the mining operations was also symbolic of a broader challenge to Soviet dominance for many participants.

The symbolic quality of the campaign was also crucial for the developing opposition because it enabled numerous official groups to support it. Less duplicitous and more tentative organizations could participate, such as the Estonian Naturalist Society, and Komsomol at Tartu University. Articles in state-supported magazines appeared, and even debates occurred on state TV, suggesting support by editors and media managers. There were event seizures at the May Day demonstrations. Street protest increased during the spring and summer. By October, the Estonian CP withdrew its support for the mining project. According to one observer, many Estonians

> learned how to test the unknown gray zone between the allowed and the forbidden in a way that allowed for tactical retreat but also unexpected advances. They practiced focusing on one specific issue at a time. They discovered that many others shared their secret yearnings, while outwardly all of them had gone through the same proregime motions. Above all, the mood of "It cannot be done" changed into "We'll do it anyway." All this new experience could be applied to other issues besides ecology. (Taagepera 1993, 124)

Discussions of symbolic protest usually stop at descriptions of innovative practices, and do not attempt to situate them in the broader sweep of antiauthoritarian mobilization. On the surface, these protests seem to be only secondarily related to the white-hot mobilization periods prior to the fall of the regime. But their widespread occurrence suggests that these protests are a key link in the progression from talk to action. In some cases, there is a straight-line progression of activists as they move from being participants in event seizures and painting sprees to activists in language campaigns or ecology protests. In other cases, the mechanism of contention works via the creation of an oppositional milieu through talk, which emboldens others to action, again depending on the claim. Paralleling how oppositional speech acts created networks that frequently congealed in the form of duplicitous groups, it is often through symbolic protests that mildly oppositional groups shed their duplicitous character, and that contentious groups and organizations become interlinked through activist members.

Finally, the coded and symbolic character of these mobilizations is also suggested by the almost unanimous membership of their constituent social movement organizations (SMOs) in the broad umbrella movements that bridge the transition for antiauthoritarian opposition to pluralistic politics. These broad oppositional fronts, such as the Estonian Popular Front, Sajudis in Lithuania, Assembly of Catalonia, or Ruhk in Ukraine, carve the emerging topography of partisan competition in the final months of the authoritarian state. A significant proportion of their membership is made up of women's groups, peace organizations, ecology SMOs, and antinuclear activists.

## Conclusions

Based on a wide range of cases, I have described several patterns of unobtrusive and coded oppositional action against authoritarian states. Speech acts occurring in the hidden arbors of authoritarianism—kitchens, coffee shops, card games—are the basic templates for this kind of opposition: namely, collective acts that are private, coded, indirect, rule-governed, and continuously monitored for surveillance. These kinds of actions are the most common in authoritarian states, but probably do not represent the entire spectrum of resistance. The ones I have identified are widespread, but usually neglected in contemporary social movement research.

This essay began with speech acts as the first tentative constructions of a collective opposition. At a later point, we encountered the clustering of interlocutors in duplicitous groups. Dissident circles also appear. KOR (Committee for Workers Defense) and ROPCiO (Movement for Defense of Human Rights and the Fatherland, or Ruch Obrony Praw Czlowieka i Ojczyzny) in Poland, the Heritage Society in Estonia, Ethnographic Circles in Latvia and Lithuania, and Centre de Recerc i Investigació in Barcelona are just a few examples of these kinds of groups. This sequence suggests a pattern of increasingly public and contentious actions, a pattern that is not unidirectional or without setbacks, but that, from a long-term perspective, is suggested by all of the cases. Alhough the processes of regime liberalization and its causes have not been the focus of this essay, they are fundamental to understanding the development of antiauthoritarian oppositions: KOR in Poland was formed in 1976, not 1956; prohibited Estonian songs were rarely sung in 1955, but often in 1985; respondents did not speak of between-the-lines meaning of poetry under Stalin, but they did under Khrushchev; Basque Itaskolas (clandestine language schools) formed in the early 1960s, not the early 1940s, right after the Spanish civil war. Certainly, high levels of repression constrain oppositional speech and increase the risks that some groups must face, just as they do in protest actions.

I close this discussion by tentatively proposing a general map of the topics discussed—a schema to guide future elaboration of antiauthoritarian resistance. A fuller treatment must include the relation of these topics to regime dynamics, such as elite divisions and alliances, policies of civic responsiveness and regime access, policies of intellectual and cultural production, international contact and exchange. Extraneous factors such as international pressures, and cross-national diffusion of strategies and repertoires, will also prove to be determinants of how the prepolitical opposition is configured. For present purposes, the shape of this opposition can be correlated to general characterizations of regime repressiveness and political opportunities. The greater the political space for the developing opposition, the less the opposition focuses solely on speech and its free spaces, and the more it focuses on collective action—less talk and more walk. This is summarized in Figure 5.1.

The constraints of graphically summarizing the process may mislead readers to think that liberalization in authoritarian regimes is an incremental process. It is not, as I have indicated. To reiterate, opening political opportunities occur in fits and starts according to internal competition in the party and state, economic factors, and international pressures. Moreover, authoritarian states and their agencies of repression are not unitary actors (White and White 1995). The relation between the opposition and the state is a dark dance—each tactically responding to the other according to past experience, current perceptions, incomplete information, and the idiosyncrasies of what agency confronts what dissident circle (see Kurzman 1996; Rasler 1996). For some agents of repression, it is a job, not a calling, that creates openings that depart from policy. For the opposition, it is a calling; and they seize advantages and hold them tenaciously. A useful metaphor is that liberalization proceeds by two steps forward, one step back. Activists creatively force and seize upon new liberties and do not relinquish easily. As one anti-Francoist militant told me, their strategy was "palos a las ruedas,"

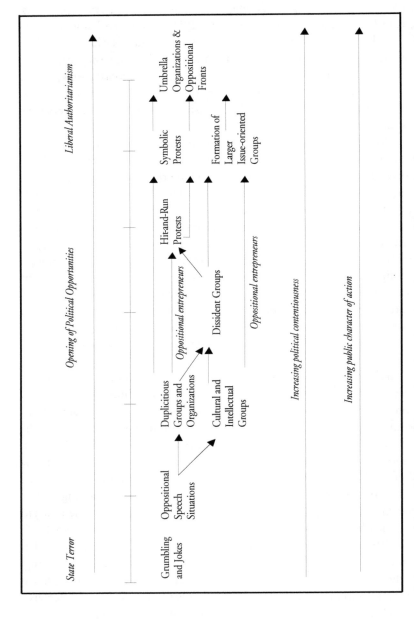

*Figure 5.1. Relationships among forms of unobtrusive contention*

meaning putting wooden planks behind the wheels of a wagon so that it does not roll back.

As Figure 5.1 depicts, oppositional speech acts tend to predominate when repression is strong. They continue to exist in more open regimes, but here there are opportunities for other, more public forms, such as duplicitous groups and hit-and-run protests. The arrows suggest network linkages that are possible paths of influence among different forms, but not full determinants by any means. Policy change and political opportunities do not occur in vacuums, and it is important to recognize that diffusion and strategic borrowing occur across authoritarian regimes, as happened among Eastern European states. Strategic innovation in one country or region can diffuse to others where the political context may be more repressive. The mechanisms, timing, and empirical generalizability of these processes await further research.

The socialization and emergence of protest innovators occurs as political opportunities open. This is represented by the two arrows labeled *Oppositional entrepreneurs,* located at the center of the figure. As changes in regime policy occur, some members of duplicitous organizations take greater risks and acquire notoriety for their opposition. Interviews in Spain and Estonia point to networks of protest innovators who first came to know one another through a variety of links in duplicitous oppositional groupings. Some move on to circles that stage hit-and-run actions, which function as schools for protest innovation. Their hit-and-run actions are typically the initial notice to the broader population that a de facto opposition exists where, de jure, it is illegal. Taken together, these unobtrusive forms of collective action help define anew what is possible in challenging the state and party—a master oppositional frame adapted to the constraints of authoritarianism.

Dissidence is a phenomenon that requires a minimal opening of free space in the public sphere. It is located at the center of Figure 5.1, paralleling the appearance of more openly oppositional duplicitous groups, and performs functions similar to hit-and-run protests, namely, contributing to the master collective action frame. But dissidents are known for their concrete ideological and tactical work (see Oliver and Johnston 2000 for a discussion of frames versus ideology). They disseminate their ideas in samizdat publications and signed letters. Selected interviews (with the foot soldiers, not the dissident stars) indicate that membership in dissident groups overlapped with duplicitous groups. Respondents spoke of how they managed what they said because their participation in dissident activism might compromise the duplicitous groups. Also, those groups were less trustworthy—

speaking of dissident activities incurred risks. Looking forward, it was not unusual that key dissidents participated in the broad oppositional fronts that later develop and became leaders of political parties.

Growing mass protests build upon the hit-and-run repertoires and increasingly seize official and unofficial opportunities to gather. It is common that mass protests at this point pose indirect challenges to the state, such as the antinuclear protests in the Basque region, antishale-mining and environmental protests in Estonia, the peace movement in the GDR, protests for economic devolution in the Soviet Baltic republics. Many hit-and-run protest innovators typically are visible, which gives them broader notoriety and situates them for leadership in the broad oppositional fronts that eventually form. Risk-taking party members begin to relinquish their cards, some in recognition that change from within the party is impossible, others for more Machiavellian reasons.

These broad oppositional fronts represent the beginning of the end of the authoritarian state, with their organizational base, coalitions, conflicts, and proto-party structure composing the next chapter in oppositional development against authoritarianism. They fall between unobtrusive contention, which I have analyzed here, and the white-hot mobilization that is closer to the Western repertoire. These processes too need systemization, for they fall just prior to the broad literature in democratic transition.

## Notes

1. Colin Barker kindly provided information about the activities of the Orange Alternative.

## Works Cited

Austin, John. L. 1962. *How to Do Things with Words.* London: Oxford University Press.

Borowski, Karol H. 1986. "Religion and Politics in Post-World War II Poland." In *Prophetic Religions and Politics,* ed. Jeffrey K. Hadden and Anson Shupe, 228–44. New York: Paragon Press.

Bushnell, John. 1990. *Moscow Graffiti: Language and Subculture.* Boston: Unwin, Hyman.

Flam, Helena. 1996. "Anxiety and the Successful Construction of Societal Reality: The Case of KOR." *Mobilization* 1: 103–21.

———. 1998. *Mosaic of Fear: Poland and East Germany before 1989.* Boulder, CO: East European Monographs.

Gumperz, John J. 1982. *Discourse Strategies.* Cambridge: Cambridge University Press.

Habermas, Jürgen. 1984. *The Theory of Communicative Action*. Vol. 1 of *Reason and Rationalization of Society*. Trans. Thomas McCarthy. Boston: Beacon Press.

Hirsch, Eric. 1990. *Urban Revolt*. Berkeley: University of California Press.

Hvat, Ivan. 1984. *The Catacomb Ukrainian Catholic Church and Pope John Paul.* Cambridge, MA: Ukrainian Studies Fund.

Johnston, Hank. 1989. "Toward an Explanation of Church Opposition to Authoritarian Regimes." *Journal for the Scientific Study of Religion* 28: 493–508.

———. 1991. *Tales of Nationalism: Catalonia, 1939–1979*. New Brunswick, NJ: Rutgers University Press.

Johnston, Hank, and Aili Aarelaid-Tart. 2000. "Generations, Microchorts, and Long-Term Mobilization: The Estonian National Movement, 1940–1991. *Sociological Perspectives* 43: 671–98.

Johnston, Hank, and Carol Mueller. 2001. "Unobtrusive Practices of Contention in Leninist Regimes." *Sociological Perspectives* 44, no. 3: 351–74.

Johnston, Hank, and David Snow. 1998. "Subcultures of Opposition and Social Movements: The Estonian National Opposition, 1940–1990." *Sociological Perspectives* 41: 473–97.

Joppke, Christian. 1995. *East German Dissidents and the Revolution of 1989*. New York: New York University Press.

Korbonski, Andrzej. 1983. "Dissent in Poland 1956–1976." In *Dissent in Eastern Europe,* ed. Jan Leftwich Curry, 25–47. New York: Praeger.

Krylova, Anna 1999. "'Saying Lenin and Meaning Party': Subversion and Laughter in Late Soviet Society." In *Consuming Russia: Popular Culture, Sex, and Society since Gorbachev,* ed. Adele Marie Barker. Durham, NC: Duke University Press.

Kubik, Jan. 1994. *The Power of Symbols against the Symbols of Power*. University Park: Pennsylvania State University Press.

Kurzman, Charles. 1996. "Structural Opportunity and Perceived Opportunity in Social-Movement Theory: The Iranian Revolution of 1979." *American Sociological Review* 61: 153–70.

Kusin, Vladimir V. 1983. "Dissent in Czechoslovakia after 1968." In *Dissent in Eastern Europe,* ed. Jan Leftwich Curry, 48–59. New York: Praeger.

Laba, Raymond. 1991. *The Roots of Solidarity*. Princeton, NJ: Princeton University Press.

Lipski, Jan Jozef. 1985. *KOR: A History of the Workers' Defense Committee in Poland 1976–1981*. Berkeley: University of California Press.

Medvedev, Roy. 1980. *On Soviet Dissent: Interviews with Peiro Ostellino*. Ed. George Saunders. New York: Columbia University Press.

Misztal, Bronizlaw, and J. Craig Jenkins. 1995. "Starting from Scratch Is Not

Always the Same: The Politics of Post Communist Transitions in Poland and Hungary." In *The Politics of Social Protest: Comparative Perspectives on States and Social Movements,* ed. J. Craig Jenkins and Bert Klandermans, 324–40. Minneapolis: University of Minnesota Press.

Morris, Aldon. 1984. *The Origins of the Civil Rights Movement.* New York: Free Press.

Mucha, Janusz L., and Maciej K. Zaba. 1992. "Religious Revival or Political Substitution: Polish Roman Catholic Movements after World War II." In *Religion and Politics in Comparative Perspective,* ed. Bronislaw Misztal and Anson Shupe, 54–66. Westport, CT: Praeger.

Mueller, Carol. 1994. "Conflict Networks and the Origins of the Women's Movement." In *New Social Movements: From Ideology to Identity,* ed. Enrique Larana, Hank Johnston, and Joseph R. Gusfield. Philadelphia: Temple University Press.

Oliver, Pamela A., and Gerald Marwell. 1993. "Mobilizing Technologies for Collective Action." In *Frontiers in Social Movement Theory,* ed. Aldon d. Morris and Carol McClurg Mueller. New Haven: Yale University Press.

Oliver, Pamela A., and Hank Johnston. 2000. "What a Good Idea! Frames and Ideology in Social Movement Research." *Mobilization: An International Journal* 4: 37–54.

Opp, Karl-Dieter, and Christaine Gern. 1993. "Dissident Groups, Personal Networks and Spontaneous Cooperation: The East German Revolution of 1989." *American Sociological Review* 58: 659–80.

Pesman, Dale. 1995. "Standing Bottles, Washing Deals, and Drinking 'for the Soul' in a Siberian City." *Anthropology of East Europe Review* 13, no. 2: 65–75.

Polletta, Francesca. 1999. "Free Spaces in Collective Action." *Theory and Society* 28: 1–38.

Rasler, Karen. 1996. "Concessions, Repression, and Political Protest in the Iranian Revolution." *American Sociological Review* 61: 132–52.

Rein, Gerhard. 1990. "Die protestantische Revolution 1987–1990." In *Entwürfe für einen anderen Sozialismus,* ed. Gerhard Rein. Berlin: Wichern-Verlag.

Ries, Nancy. 1997. *Russian Talk.* Ithaca, NY: Cornell University Press.

Rupp, Leila J., and Verta Taylor. 1987. *Survival in the Doldrums: The American Womens' Rights Movement 1945 to the 1960s.* New York: Oxford University Press.

Scott, James C. 1985. *Weapons of the Weak.* New Haven: Yale University Press.

———. 1990. *Domination and the Arts of Resistance.* New Haven: Yale University Press.

Searle, John. 1969. *Speech Acts.* Cambridge: Cambridge University Press.

Sharlet, Robert. 1983. "Varieties of Dissent and Regularities of Repression in the European Communist States: An Overview." In *Dissent in Eastern Europe*, ed. Jan Leftwich Curry, 1–19. New York: Praeger.

Shlapentkokh, Vladimir. 1989. *Public and Private Life of the Soviet People*. New York: Oxford University Press.

Smith, Christian. 1996. *Resisting Reagan: The U.S. Central American Peace Movement*. Chicago: University of Chicago Press.

Szajokowski, Bogdon. 1983. *Next to God . . . Poland*. New York: St. Martin's Press.

Taagepera, Rein. 1993. *Estonia: Return to Independence*. Boulder, CO: Westview Press.

Tannen, Deborah. 1986. *That's Not What I Meant*. New York: William Morrow and Co.

Uncensored Poland News Bulletin. 1988a. "Friday 7 October." No. 19/88: 3. London: Information Centre for Polish Affairs.

———. 1988b. "More on the 'Orange Alternative.'" No. 12/88: 22–23. London: Information Centre for Polish Affairs.

White, Robert W., and Terry Falkenberg White. 1995. "Repression and the Liberal State: The Case of Northern Ireland, 1969–1972." *Journal of Conflict Resolution* 39: 330–52.

Yang, Guobin. 2002. "The Internet as Free Space for Collective Action: The Case of China." Paper presented at the ASA Collective Behavior and Social Movements Research Section's Conference, "Authority in Contention: Interdisciplinary Approaches," August 13–15, 2002, University of Notre Dame.

Zaslavsky, Victor. 1979. "The Problem of Legitimation in Soviet Society." In *Conflict and Control*, ed. Arthur J. Vidich and Ronald M. Glassman, 159–202. Beverly Hills, CA: Sage Publications.

**6**

# Soft Repression:
# Ridicule, Stigma, and Silencing in Gender-Based Movements

*Myra Marx Ferree*

Once upon a time, social movement scholars lived in a world in which the only form of social protest that they could recognize was directed against the state. In this state-centered world, political elites wielding formal authority over governments were the only real targets for movement concerns, and the troops protecting the castle of political power were the armies, police forces, and prisons that the authorities could and did send into battle against those who would challenge their authority in general or their policies in specific. As protests in democratic states became more legitimate, ritualized, and nonviolent, the scholarly focus remained on the interaction between states and challengers to their formal political authority. Whether the scholar thought the good guys were in the castle or on the offensive outside the walls made a difference in how the particular strategies of attack or defense were judged, but explaining the rules of engagement was the central task. The way that the castle was defended from attack, violent or not, generally fell under the rubric of repression, particularly if one's sympathies were—often with good reason—on the side of those outside the walls.[1]

Like all fairy tales, there is a good bit of mythical exaggeration in this story. There is also a central and important truth, namely, that the concept of repression is bound up with a state-centered view of social movements. Repression evokes an image of a central political authority using the formal apparatus of the state to put down rebellions, whether overtly or covertly holding the reins and directing the actions being taken in its defense. Repression is what states do, especially bad states that cannot manage dissent in more democratic and disarming ways.

However, for at least the past two decades, social movement scholars have generally been widening their understanding of what protest is and where and how it occurs to encompass a broader and less centralized landscape than the image of the castle under siege would suggest. From so-called new social movement theories through the cultural turn in social movements to the current focus on discourses, the terrain of protest has been reconceptualized to include a variety of nonstate institutional targets and change strategies that depend on cultural subversion as much or more than stone-throwing confrontation. Whether looking at ACT-UP die-ins aimed at directing public attention to the AIDS crisis, student protests against the corporations that produce their university's athletic apparel aimed at changing their reliance on sweatshops, environmentalists relying on recycling, organic foods, and less energy-dependent lifestyles—what Vice President Dick Cheney derided as the politics of personal virtue—or feminists going out and building alternative institutions such as shelters for battered women, rape-crisis centers, and women's studies programs, scholars have recognized and studied a great variety of protest that has been decentralized and directed at institutions other than the state.[2]

My question is whether the concept of repression is useful at all in the wider and more varied landscape of social movement action that has been discovered and studied. Certainly, the state is not directly the target of any of these protest actions, and typically, if the state actively responds to them at all, it does so relatively late in the process, largely to co-opt rather than to quash them. Thus, once public concern has been mobilized by social movements about violence against women, AIDS, sweatshops, or the environment, states may get involved in providing subsidies, regulations, and services that help to institutionalize this new way of seeing the world. But it is the change in values, perspectives, culture, norms, expectations, and behavior in the public at large that is the real goal of the movement, and state action, if any, is one of many means to its end, not an end itself.[3] The castle looks less like a fortress on a hill and more like a service station.

In this view of contentious political action, where the castle of the state is not so much under siege as surrounded by competing demands for services and support, is the idea of repression obsolete or irrelevantly narrow? Might repression only be a useful concept for those truly state-centered conflicts in which protest movements are contending for control over the political system as such or where state dominance is being used to keep contenders off the map? Does a focus on repression necessarily return us to apparently old-fashioned definitions of social movements and their tactics that keep more cultural and decentralized forms of protest out of sight and out of mind?

Clearly, a return to the castle image would be a mistake. The fairy-tale version of social movements, for example, has no room for the princess who smashes the mirror, cuts off her hair, and makes a bolt for the draw-bridge, deciding that happy-ever-after endings are not her style. Women's movements in particular are scarcely to be found in the familiar catalogs of contention over state power. Even though feminist protest is as old as Lysistrata, confronting the state with the expectation of replacing the current elite is not how it is done. Instead, women's movements are, and have been for generations, the very epitome of movements focused on making change in (and experiencing resistance from) civil society.[4]

Although the idea persists that class-based movements are "old" and gender-based social movements are "new," both were actively engaged with each other and with state and social definitions of family, work, and personal freedom in the nineteenth century as well as today. Rather than a chronological difference, the distinction between them is one of focus and strategy—working-class movements were often contenders for state power, and women's movements were not. Women's movements addressed changes in values and norms directly in the institutions of religion, medicine, family, and economy. Women's movements worked in, on, and through civil society as much as or more than on the state as such.[5]

In this sense, women's movements provide a useful, long-term lens on the decentralized and cultural strategies of social protest that have since be-come more familiar among men. Ever more social movements direct them-selves to civil society rather than the state.[6] Especially in modern, industrial democracies with a wide range of formal social institutions outside the state that observe, direct, and sanction behavior, issues of power and autonomy are not only to be found in direct interaction with the state and its minions. Understanding social movements in civil society as being just as important as social movements directed at the state, as most scholars now do, should mean that women's movements take a central place as one of the oldest and most globally widespread forms of such protest.

Alas, research on women's movements has generally not been main-streamed into the study of social protest. Thus the question of when and how women's movements have been repressed is not taken as a significant challenge to conventional state-centered models of repression, but has been of interest only to feminist scholars working on gender issues. But if women's movements are indeed, as I have argued, forerunners and exemplars of how decentralized social movements in civil society operate, then social move-ment theorists are missing an important opportunity to use the history of feminist protest to expand their understanding of movement dynamics in this arena in general.

Looking at repression in relation to feminism and women's mobilizations certainly takes us away from the castle-like, state-centered model of responses to challenge. I offer the term "soft repression" as a consciously gendered image of the forms that repression frequently takes in civil society, in contrast to the more conventional, male-gendered imagery of hard repression in which states more typically engage, even though both soft and hard forms of repression can in principle be used by any agent. Whereas hard repression involves the mobilization of force to control or crush oppositional action through the use or threat of violence, soft repression involves the mobilization of nonviolent means to silence or eradicate oppositional ideas.

Not all forms of nonviolent resistance to challenging ideas merit the label soft repression, either. Normative theories of discursive democracy include the potential for much contentious speech that is not polite or respectful, but also establish criteria of fairness in debate that place sharp limits on any person's or institution's use of power to restrict others' ideas.[7] The distinguishing criterion of soft repression is the collective mobilization of power, albeit in nonviolent forms and often highly informal ways, to limit and exclude ideas and identities from the public forum. Also, although there are continuities between the uses of power for social control over individuals and for silencing and excluding social movements, the concept of soft repression is most usefully applied to the nonviolent uses of power that are specifically directed against movement collective identities and movement ideas that support "cognitive liberation" or "oppositional consciousness."[8]

Although both states and institutions of civil society may engage in either soft or hard repression, it seems likely that some patterns of association between types of actors, opportunity structures, and types of repression may found. After all, unlike states, the institutions of civil society do not have privileged control over the means of violence. Conflicts within civil society should thus be more likely to be expressed in conflicts over naming, speaking, labeling, defining, and knowing, but they may spill over into overt violence if and when state power permits its use. For example, violence against women in the form of rape and spousal abuse has long been permitted by many states, and nonstate paramilitaries from the Ku Klux Klan to Guatemalan landlords, Colombian drug barons, and Hindu nationalists have been allowed to act violently against ethnic minorities and social critics. That states monopolize the means of violence to a greater or lesser degree does not prevent them from also using nonviolent means of censorship and exclusion to repress disturbing ideas, and sometimes civil society endorses and facilitates state use of soft repressive measures (as the McCarthy period in the United States illustrates). However, because the notion of soft repression includes the presumption that there exist some autonomous public forums in which ideas and identities could be formed and articulated, the concept may be limited to situations in which the state does not completely dominate or destroy civil society's institutions.

In the rest of this essay, I offer a few selective examples from studies of gender-based mobilizations in democratic states to consider how soft repression can work in civil society to limit or eliminate collective challenges to dominant forces in a variety of decentralized social institutions. I place each type of example of soft repression directed at movements after discussion of similar, but not identical, processes of social control that are directed at nonorganized members of disempowered groups, in order to draw out both the continuities of means and the differences in targets that distinguish soft repression from these more omnipresent uses of power as social control. The evidence here is eclectic and can only be suggestive. Whether the concept of soft repression is actually fruitful for understanding conflict in civil society awaits examination by studies directly designed to address this.

I organize these examples into three rather loose and possibly overlapping categories—ridicule, stigma, and silencing—roughly corresponding to the micro-, meso- and macrolevels of analysis. All three of these levels must surely interact with one another in practice, a complexity that would require an extended single-case study to explore. Contradictions and disjunctions between them are also certainly points at which we might expect social movements to find cracks in the system of social control where leverage can be exerted. In fact, social movement scholars may be better at recognizing the cultural and discursive strategies that movements adopt in response to soft repression than the operations of soft repression itself.[9] Thus I do not wish to suggest that these processes are a monolithic whole, nor to imply that they are unconnected or alternative strategies, but rather to argue that studying the relationships among them would be a way to begin to understand how soft repression operates and can be overcome.

## Microlevel Ridicule

I begin at the microlevel of ridicule directed at individuals and groups by others in face-to-face interaction, and thus with the sort of use of social power that is rarely associated with social movements at all. The use of ridicule to mock fags and queers and dykes begins even in elementary school to police the boundaries of appropriate gender behavior. Stepping out of line brings interpersonal retaliation in the form of name-calling at any age. Such attacks, more or less vehement or subtle, can be emotionally painful, and learning to pay careful attention to respecting these boundaries and calculating when or how they could be crossed without bringing ridicule is an early form of self-defense. Boundary policing at the interpersonal level can limit the ability of both men and women even to recognize similarities across gender and differences within gender categories.[10]

But ridicule is not only a widespread means of enforcing gender conformity in general and on a routine basis; it is also a tool explicitly put to use to diminish and disarm cultural challengers who are mobilizing or mobilized. Here is where soft repression enters in. Recall, for example, women's early efforts to redirect the energy of the social movements of the 1960s in which they were participating to include their own claims for gender justice. National liberation movements were happening around the world, and the more radical elements of the civil rights movement in the United States spoke of black liberation as well. But when women mobilized and raised the parallel demand for women's liberation, the immediate response was a mocking abbreviation to call this "women's lib." Similarly, the draft-card burners of the anti-Vietnam War movement in the United States inspired feminist demonstrators to throw bras and girdles and high heels into a "freedom trash can" in Atlantic City, earning them the collective media sobriquet of "bra burners." More recently, consider the term *feminazi* that Rush Limbaugh coined to ridicule feminists, and that my students report is widely used on campus to attack any woman who stands up for her rights.

Of course, ridicule as a form of soft repression from civil society is met with resistance on its own terms and on its own ground. Social movements take the language that is used to mock and attempt to intimidate them and turn its meaning around to be a positive self-description. Queer politics reclaims the word *queer* and inverts it to be a proud term, as feminists earlier attempted to do with terms ranging from blue-stocking to dyke and crone.[11] So-called "tree-huggers" and "peaceniks" are no strangers to this strategy. The underlying reality here is that the ability to convey social values through labeling is a valuable political resource in civil society and thus a fiercely contested domain. Contests over meaning often take the form of struggles over the word to be used and the connotation to be attached to that word. The use of the term "politically correct" to ridicule social concerns of various sorts provides a familiar case in which ridicule is being deployed as a strategy of soft repression.[12] It is, not surprisingly, being met with efforts to resist the labeling process and reclaim the label from the connotations of ridicule that are now attached to it.

Although such civil society–based struggles over labels and names are increasingly common today, feminists faced such attacks first and most frequently. Ridicule is a decentralized weapon that is, not coincidentally, rarely deployed by the state. It is used to secure power and privilege in and for a variety of nonstate institutions. Feminists confronting male domination within such institutions were historically at the forefront of facing repression from them and thus the characteristic targets of ridicule. They were mocked more than socialists or black liberation fighters, not because feminism is by nature funnier, but because the civil society terrain on which gender battles are characteristically fought made ridicule a preferred weapon.

## Mesolevel Stigma

Of course, one outcome of ridicule at the interpersonal level is stigma at the group level. But stigma is more than active acts of ridicule, no matter how frequently repeated and widespread they become. Stigma means an impaired collective identity, where connection with the group is a source of discredit and devaluation because that is how the group as a whole is viewed, whether or not anyone makes an issue of it through name-calling or other forms of ridicule. A classic example of stigma attached to a collective identity is found in the sensitive exploration by Richard Sennett and Jonathan Cobb of what they call the "hidden injuries of class."[13] The implied lack of intelligence and initiative attributed to the white men who work with their hands that makes them ashamed to think of themselves as working class has parallels, of course, with more commonly recognized gender and race stigma that attaches to groups such as "welfare moms." Karen Seccombe's study of welfare ideology in the United States provides an example of how such soft repression works to demobilize recipients from asserting their rights.[14] Many women on welfare in the early 1990s, she found, accepted the culturally dominant image of "most women" on welfare as less intelligent and even as less moral, and struggled to differentiate themselves from this image and justify their own need to rely on state support. Not seeing any other way to take care of their children, they took aid, and then feared being seen as just like the other women, who were in fact in similar positions of need.

Back in the 1960s, Betty Friedan skewered the prevalence with which achieving women could accept the most derogatory stereotypes of women while exempting themselves from the implications of their disrespect for women as a group as being a "three-sex theory," namely, that "there's men, there's women, and there's me."[15] Stigma as a form of soft repression is a cultural strategy to prevent collective action by actively discouraging identification with a group that could make claims against an institution. Negative stereotypes of groups that are socially subordinate are the classic means by which civil society represses the formation of a positive collective identity. The social movement literature has often acknowledged the way that mobilization efforts have attempted to defang some of these most pernicious forms of entrenched stigma through such appeals as "Black is beautiful," "woman power," and "gay pride." It has not been so apt to acknowledge the strategic mobilization of stigma as a means of repressing and resisting social movements.

I do not want to minimize the repressive effect of racism and sexism, nor downplay their general usefulness in constructing and feeding into other stereotypes, but not all forms of stigma are as broad, long-standing, and deeply institutionalized. Such existing stigmatization of social groups, however, is a generalized resource that can be used by countermovements to advance their agenda. More narrow and specific uses of stigma can be brought to bear to limit and silence movements and discredit their members and policies, and it is in understanding these strategic uses of stigma that the concept of soft repression is most useful.

For example, stigmatization of affirmative action as an unmerited benefit going to unqualified recipients, rather than a change of the preference structure of a particular institution to reduce the built-in preference for members of dominant groups, can be seen as a political tactic by nonstate forces to defend an institutional status quo in civil society. By setting themselves up as ending the supposed stigma of association with being an unqualified recipient of preference, conservative opponents of affirmative action in fact defined the program in terms of stigma and group association, inviting individuals whose interest was served by the program to be reluctant to step forward and be identified with it.[16] In such skirmishing over the stigma of affirmative action in recent years, I have frequently been reminded of an interview in the *Harvard Crimson* in the early 1970s, when the first woman was appointed as a full professor at the medical school, and the reporter asked whether she thought her being a woman had something to do with receiving this appointment, implicitly suggesting that some illegitimate preference was being exercised. The professor nimbly responded, "I certainly think my being a woman had everything to do with my not having been appointed until now."

Soft repression in the form of stigma, I suggest, also can illuminate the declining proportions of individuals in national surveys who are willing to apply the term "feminist" to themselves, even as the proportion of respondents who say that the women's movement in the United States has made things better for most women and for them remains stable or even increases. At the high point of feminist self-identification (in the late 1980s), approximately one in three American women described herself as feminist or said the term "feminist" fit her "very well." However, the very newspapers and magazines that had commissioned these polls reported their results in stigmatizing terms: "only a third" of all women, they said, called themselves feminist, so where had the women's movement gone wrong?[17] By stressing that feminism was a "minority" point of view and claiming that "most women rejected feminism," while acknowledging that strong majorities favored most of the changes that the movement had brought, the media constructed a division between feminism and its goals. This division then allowed conservative women in notably small groups such as the Independent Women's Forum to create a specter of what they called "victim feminism" and load it with every stereotype available, while approving of the actual changes that the women's movement had brought about.[18] Thus more adults identified themselves as supporters of the women's movement in 1995 (42 percent) than in 1986 (30 percent), even though the percentage of women who call themselves feminist declined (from 33 percent in 1989 to 26 percent in 1999) and the proportion of women who considered the term "feminist" to be an insult increased (from 16 percent in 1992 to 22 percent in 1997).[19]

Both of these examples involve the active and deliberate use of stigma by nonstate groups to undercut group identity and to repress the mobilization potential of a social movement that had achieved some success. Unlike ridicule, using stigma as a means of soft repression does not imply that the movement is trivial or a laughing matter. Directed at a movement that has already achieved some credibility in civil society, stigma as a weapon seeks to limit further gains by making identification with the group more costly. Stigma deliberately used as weapon of resistance to social change in civil society makes use of, bleeds into, and is reinforced by the more widespread and nondeliberate forms of stigma that are prevalent in relations of domination already; thus resistance to affirmative action and welfare rights makes use of stereotypes that already demean African-Americans, and resistance to feminism evokes antisex, antimale stereotypes that are culturally attached to older women and lesbians.[20] But the impossibility of totally separating ordinary forms of stereotyping associated with ongoing relations of domination from the active use of stigma for strategic purposes by certain groups at certain times should not deter us from considering how this type of soft repression operates.

## Macrolevel Silencing

Finally, at the macrolevel, I want to consider silencing as a form of soft repression that can be embedded in the ordinary institutional practices of a social system. Although both ridicule and stigma can accumulate to produce silence at the macrolevel, silence can also be achieved directly through processes that act at the level of the system as a whole. Understanding silence is the other side of the coin to understanding voice. Mobilization processes that are aimed at producing voice for groups in civil society can face soft repression in the form of system processes that specifically block such voices from being heard.

In modern industrial democracies, the main vehicle for voice in the society at large is the mass media, and the proliferation of point-to-point media of communication such as e-mail and the Internet does not change the role of mass media in creating a shared reality that is simultaneously known to be shared. Point-to-point media allow for pluralistic ignorance: everyone may in fact know the same thing, but there is no common knowledge that everyone has this knowledge.[21] The ability to have a voice in the mass media is still, therefore, a powerful influence on creating the collective reality within which civil society's separate institutions function. Similarly, to be silenced or excluded from having a voice in the mass media is a powerful form of repression. States can exercise hard repression on the media in the form of censorship, of course, but my focus here is instead on the soft repression by which civil society, including institutionalized media practice, excludes voices and produces silence, even when there is no direct censorship.[22] The issue is therefore not whether the media is free or not, but what a free media does.

There has been no dearth of media criticism pointing out that making news is a social process and reflects the social interests that underlie the media: the financial concerns of advertisers, for example, may make it seem less significant to cover stories that affect the poor or urban communities of color, if they do not seem to be a market where selling newspapers will also get advertisers the attention they want from the demographic groups they care about. What makes news is also generally understood as a process that reflects the values, expectations, and perspectives of those who construct the stories.[23] Whether from the vantage point of the media consumer, understood as a market, or from the perspective of the workers who produce the media reality that is consumed, it is hard to overlook the selectivity—some would say bias—built into the ordinary operation of mass media in modern society. At the institutional level, therefore, analysts have to assume that silences are what is being produced along with speech.

Producing silences can range from a mere side effect of the ordinary relations of domination in civil society to a more deliberate strategy of exclusion that blocks social movements, and it is to this latter process particularly that I would apply the label of soft repression. Again, women's movements provide examples of contesting the underlying institutional power structure of silencing directly. The strong growth of independent women's media in the 1970s was one marker of the extent to which mainstream media had not included women's voices; a major social movement strategy was to bring women in as journalists, publishers, and filmmakers, positions from which they could in turn create voice for other women. It is almost hard to imagine today the climate in which women were seen as incapable of reading the news on television, relegated to writing for the women's pages of the newspapers, and seen as an inherently apolitical group rather than a significant voting bloc. The 1968 so-called bra-burning incident, for example, was reconstructed as important only in retrospect from alternative media; at the time, the mainstream newspapers and magazines did not waste space on this protest. Were one to rely only on the *New York Times* or *Reader's Guide*, one would have to conclude it never took place at all.[24] What concerned women politically was simply not news, and this has changed. These norms did not change all by themselves, of course, and if such struggle is recognized, it would seem important to acknowledge not only that the women's movement engaged from one side, but also that there was another side engaged in struggle, resisting change.[25]

But recognizing such change also should be a warning sign that the ups and downs of media coverage of social movements are driven by factors other than what events are occurring. The choice of speakers to interpret and give meaning to events is even more at the mercy of media standards of importance, and these are themselves contested values within civil society. These factors also may vary significantly between countries. To draw just one example from the study of abortion discourse in Germany and the United States in which I and several colleagues have been engaged, we find dramatic differences in the extent to which speakers in civil society have a voice at all in the newspapers of these two countries.[26] In Germany, state-based speakers make up 58 percent of all voices quoted or paraphrased as interpreting abortion, compared to 38 percent of U.S. speakers who are state-based actors. Moreover, the civil society voices heard from in Germany on this issue are overwhelmingly the institutionalized voices of the churches. Compared to the United States, the silence of social movements in the German media is deafening: over the twenty-five-year period from 1970 to 1994, speakers associated with social movements account for just about 2 percent of all voices and 6 percent of civil society voices in West Germany, but 23 percent of all and 39 percent of civil society speakers in the United States.[27] By comparison, the churches are 55 percent of German and 17 percent of U.S. civil society speakers.

This is not because there are no feminist or right-to-life mobilizations in Germany, but because the media have a strong preference against giving voice to less institutionalized speakers like these, at least in relation to a gender-based conflict. Individuals not officially associated with any organization or group form 18 percent of the U.S. discourse, but only 8 percent of the German speakers. While fully seven of eight of these German speakers are enlisted as experts into the debate, only half of the noninsitutional speakers in American media are experts, rather than people directly affected by the conflict. Media norms about what deserves coverage and how stories should be told are part of what works to silence less institutional voices. For example, individual women and doctors who are prosecuted for illegal abortion are not sought out to tell their side of the story in Germany, nor are advocates on either side of the issue given space to reflect on why and how they came to have the positions that they do, both of which are relatively common ways of discussing the issue in the United States.[28] In fact, the structure of articles in the United States formally institutionalizes the idea that there are two sides to every story and gives nonstate actors the opportunity to comment on and rebut assertions from state actors in a way that is rarely found in the German media.

I would suggest that, for better or worse, the mobilization potential for social movement mobilization is enhanced in the United States and repressed, softly, in Germany by the institutional forms by which movements relate to civil society in media practices. But the ability of media to reduce movement mobilization potential by withdrawing attention from them is also available as a conscious and deliberate strategy of soft repression. Covering protest events is not equivalent to providing a voice in the media for protesters, and soft repression may be particularly an issue of excluding the perspectives and frames that make sense of the actions of the movement (movement actors as speakers providing their point of view) rather than of trying to ignore the very existence of the movement (event-based coverage).

I draw another example from feminist research in Germany to illustrate this process of soft repression and its potentially demobilizing effects on social movements. Ingrid Miethe followed women involved in dissident politics in the German Democratic Republic (GDR) through the process of unification and into their subsequent political careers (or lack thereof) in the unified, dominantly West German state.[29] She found that quite a few of the women were disconcerted by the lack of response that their demonstrations and protests engendered in the new democratic Germany. In their old state-centered and directly repressive milieu, any protest activity was assessed for its effectiveness by how strongly the state acted against it, and although this yardstick may have been misleading, it provided a standard for evaluation that continued to feed their sense of efficacy and importance. However, they discovered that protest actions in unified Germany did not elicit state responses and typically did not even draw media attention. Their self-doubt as political actors grew, and a substantial proportion withdrew from political activity, despite having just as profound disagreements with the new state as they ever had with the old.

I draw my examples from Germany because it is familiar to me, not because I want to suggest that it has a particularly repressive form of civil society. But I do think that the variation between countries, as well as over time, in the exercise of soft repression against social movements in general or specific subtypes and categories of social movements in particular is an institutional aspect of civil society that deserves more investigation than it has received. Recognizing that states are democratic does not necessarily say much about the degree or focus of the soft repression that may characterize their civil societies. Women's movements, in being particularly attuned to trying to make change in the institutional structure of civil society, may be especially aware of and responsive to such variation. But social movement theory in general might well consider the nature of the media structures and practices that create silences about specific issues or for particular constituencies when attempting to explain the resistance and opposition that movements in civil society confront.[30]

## Conclusions

This essay suggests that the conventional understanding of repression only in terms of violence and state action, or what I have called hard repression, takes us away from the wider and more complex views of social movements as contending in and against institutions of civil society and not just against state. The turn toward more cultural and decentralized views of social movement activity in recent years has brought gains, not least in allowing scholars to recognize the way that women's movements have been ahead of their time in fighting their battles on this postmodern terrain. Studies of feminism thus offer clues to scholars of other movements about how civil society is a different sort of target than the state, and yet also reminds us that resistance to change comes from a variety of sources and takes multiple forms. Soft repression, especially when it arises in and is expressed through the institutions of civil society, will be neither as centralized as state action nor as visible as hard repression, but it can still be powerful and effective in blocking or disarming social movements. Decentralized forms of soft repression can exist at the micro-, meso-, or macrolevels, and I have taken the examples of ridicule, stigma, and silencing to suggest how such soft repression of social movements operates on all three of these levels.

Studies of women's movements may be particularly effective means of seeing how soft repression has operated in the past, but it seems likely that overall tendencies toward movements operating in and on civil society in the postmodern world will make the findings from such research ever more generally applicable. Research on feminism and the reception given to it can offer scholars of all social movements a wide variety of insights into soft repression that will be more useful as we move away from the castle model toward a more complex view of social conflict and protest.

## Notes

1. A classic example of the state-centeredness of even accounts sympathetic to the protesters' agenda is William A. Gamson, *The Strategy of Social Protest* (Homewood, IL: Dorsey Press, 1975; revised edition, New York: Wadsworth, 1990). The issue of cycles of protest related to repressive responses is raised by Sidney Tarrow, *Democracy and Disorder* (New York: Oxford University Press, 1989), and the specific focus on repression as a matter of state/police response to even "new" social movements is exemplified by the studies done by Donatella della Porta (e.g, "Social Movements and the State: Thoughts on the Policing of Protest," in *Comparative Perspectives on Social Movements: Political Opportunities, Mobilizing Structures and Cultural Framings,* ed. Douglas McAdam, John McCarthy, and Mayer Zald, 62–92 [New York: Cambridge University Press, 1996]) and by Clark McPhail (this volume).

2. Paul Lichterman's study of the mix of personal and collective environmental action strategies, *The Search for Political Community: American Activists Reinventing Commitment* (New York: Cambridge University Press, 1996), and Verta Taylor's study of women's self-help groups confronting with the medical establishment (*Rock-a-Bye Baby: Feminism, Self Help, and Postpartum Depression* [New York: Routledge, 1996]) provide excellent, explicit arguments for the widening of this lens, as well as specific cases.

3. This is a perspective shared and well articulated by Hank Johnston and

Bert Klandermans in their important essay "The Cultural Analysis of Social Movements" in the collection they edited, *Social Movements and Culture* (Minneapolis: University of Minnesota Press, 1995), 3–24.

4. Verta Taylor explicitly addresses this civil society focus in *Rock-a-Bye Baby*, but it is also evident in the catalogs of demands raised by feminists from the Seneca Falls declaration forward; cf. the collections of first-wave documents in Alice Rossi, ed., *The Feminist Papers* (New York: Columbia University Press, 1973), and of second-wave documents in Rosalyn Baxandall and Linda Gordon, eds., *Dear Sisters: Dispatches from the Women's Liberation Movement* (New York: Basic Books, 2000).

5. The struggle for suffrage would seem to contradict this view, but although winning the right to vote was an important political milestone, whether, when, and how a focus on gaining the suffrage—or formal equal rights—was a considered a primary goal, a means to an end, or a diversion from other organized efforts to change educational systems, family culture, sexual practices, and other social relations has always been controversial in women's movements. See, for example, Naomi Black, *Social Feminism* (Ithaca, NY: Cornell University Press, 1989). A sense of how peripheral the state was to feminist activists in the early twentieth century in the United States is conveyed by Nancy Cott, *The Grounding of Modern Feminism* (New Haven: Yale University Press, 1987).

6. The discovery of such forms and tactics by relatively privileged men concerned about issues that did not fit a conventional left–right spectrum (e.g., environmentalism, anticolonialism) spawned their conceptualization as being "new," but it seems increasingly evident that such cultural tactics were integral to working-class mobilization in the nineteenth century (see Craig Calhoun, "'New Social Movements' of the Early Nineteenth Century," in *Repertoires and Cycles of Collective Action*, ed. Mark Traugott (Durham, NC: Duke University Press, 1995), 173–215.

7. Amy Gutmann and Dennis Thompson, *Democracy and Disagreement* (New York: University Press, 1996), offer an extensive and inclusive set of rules that creates considerable space for contentious speech, but they still focus attention on the ways that power holders can and do limit speech "unfairly." It is the variety of forms that such unfair silencing can take that I consider under the rubric of soft repression, and I also suggest that the power holding that permits unfair strategies is at least as characteristic of civil society as of states.

8. See Doug McAdam, *Political Process and the Development of Black Insurgency* (Chicago: University of Chicago Press, 1982), and Aldon Morris, *The Origins of the Civil Rights Movement* (New York: Free Press 1984), for the use of these terms initially; Morris expands on this idea in "Political Consciousness and Collective Action," in *Frontiers of Social Movement Theory*, ed. Aldon Morris and Carol McClurg Mueller (New Haven: Yale University Press, 1992).

9. There is often acknowledgment of the significance of movement strategies to re-name themselves or their issues, to find alternative forums in which positive identities can be formed apart from the mainstream, and to produce new media through which to circulate alternative ideas, but studies of these forms of resistance rarely name the repression against which the resistance is being mounted. It is important to recognize that such cultural conflicts involve two sides, both of which can be acting strategically.

10. Barrie Thorne, *Gender Play* (New Brunswick, NJ: Rutgers University Press, 1993), offers a revealing look at the dynamic processes involved among children policing each other's behavior for deviations, and Candace West and Don Zimmerman offer a more general model of how all culturally competent persons are held accountable for gender conformity in "Doing Gender," *Gender and Society* 1, no. 2 (1987): 125–51.

11. Mary Daly is one of the most active feminist exponents of this linguistic strategy among the second wave in the United States. See, for example, her "dictionary" done "in cahoots with" Jane Caputi, *Webster's First New Intergalactic Wickedary of the English Language* (Boston: Beacon Press, 1987).

12. See the discussions of the political uses of "political correctness" language in Katha Pollitt, *Reasonable Creatures: Essays on Women and Feminism* (New York: Alfred A. Knopf, 1994), and in Dorothy Smith, *Writing the Social* (Toronto: University of Toronto Press, 1999).

13. Richard Sennett and Jonathan Cobb, *The Hidden Injuries of Class* (New York: Vintage Books, 1972).

14. Karen Seccombe, *So You Think I Drive a Cadillac? Welfare Recipients' Perspectives on the System and Its Reform* (Boston: Allyn & Bacon, 1999).

15. The idea of the "three-sex theory" first appears in Betty Friedan's introduction to her account of feminist emergence, *It Changed My Life: Writings on the Women's Movement* (New York: Random House, 1976), 19.

16. See discussions of the language and politics of affirmative action by race in the United States in John David Skrentny, *The Ironies of Affirmative Action: Politics, Culture and Justice in America* (Chicago: University of Chicago Press, 1996), and by gender across in various national contexts in Carol Bacchi, *The Politics of Affirmative Action: "Women," Equality, and Category Politics* (Thousand Oaks, CA: Sage, 1996).

17. See the discussion of this process in Elaine J. Hall and Marnie Salupo Rodriguez, "The Myth of Post-Feminism," *Gender and Society* 17, no. 6 (2003): 878–962.

18. See discussions of the Independent Women's Forum (IWF) in Pollitt, *Reasonable Creatures,* and their own web page at www.IWF.org. The membership of the IWF is small but elite, being largely dominated by hard-right politicians and

columnists such as Lynne Cheney, Linda Chavez, and Mona Charren, who have excellent access to conservative media such as the *Wall Street Journal*.

19. Because different questions were asked in different years, it is difficult to be certain about which way and when public opinion changed. For details on time trends, see Hall and Rodriguez, "The Myth of Post-Feminism," and Leonie Huddy, Francis Neely, and Marilyn Lafay, "The Polls: Trends Support for the Women's Movement," *Public Opinion Quarterly* 64, no. 3 (2000): 309–50.

20. See, for example, Kenneth Neubeck and Noel Cazenave, *Welfare Racism* (New York: Routledge, 2001).

21. Elisabeth Noelle-Neumann, *The Spiral of Silence: Public Opinion, Our Social Skin* (Chicago: University of Chicago Press, 1993), specifically analyzes polling data to show the way that pluralistic ignorance can be produced by the media's failure to include certain frames or arguments that are then believed to be idiosyncratic concerns, and focuses on when and how surveys are distorted by this but also can reveal some of the process.

22. The "symbolic annihilation"of women by their utter invisibility in the mass media of the 1950s and 1960s was critiqued in the classic introduction by Gaye Tuchman in Gaye Tuchman, Arlene Kaplan Daniels and James Benét, eds., *Hearth and Home: Images of Women in the Media* (New York: Oxford University Press, 1978), 3–50.

23. The classic analysis of the news-making process is Herbert Gans, *Deciding What's News* (New York: Pantheon Books, 1979). A cross-national analysis along similar lines is offered by Akiba Cohen, Hanna Adoni, and Charles Bentz, *Social Conflict and Television News* (Thousand Oaks, CA: Sage, 1990). See also Pamela Oliver and Gregory Maney, "Political Processes and Local Newspaper Coverage of Protest Events," *American Journal of Sociology* 106, no. 2 (2000): 463–505.

24. This omission from standard media references is something of which I became aware as I attempted to find the original wording used by reporters to cover this protest; for the most part, this event was not covered at all or trivialized. Although no bras were burned, the placing of bras, girdles, and high heels in a "freedom trash can" was covered as a mere curiosity in the back pages of the *New York Times* and hardly mentioned elsewhere.

25. Some women reporters of the period provide first-person accounts of the editorial resistance they faced when trying to get coverage for women's political action. See, for example, Nan Robertson, *The Girls in the Balcony: Women, Men and the New York Times* (New York: Random House, 1992).

26. Myra Marx Ferree, William A. Gamson, Jürgen Gerhards, and Dieter Rucht, *Shaping Abortion Discourse: Democracy and the Public Sphere in Germany and the United States* (New York: Cambridge University Press, 2002).

27. The percentage of all voices applies to all nonjournalists quoted or para-

phrased, whether or not their comments included substantive framing about abortion. Percentages of civil society voices were calculated on a base of nonstate, nonparty speakers other than journalists who were quoted or paraphrased in saying something framing abortion. The former is the widest and the latter the narrowest relevant calculation of the base for comparison.

28. Actual access to abortion is similar in the United States and Germany, although Germany makes abortion in the first trimester "illegal but unpunished" if appropriate counseling is certified and the United States imposes parental consent and counseling rules that make some abortions extralegal, even though in principle women's choice of abortion is supposed to be permitted.

29. Ingrid Miethe, "From Mother of the Revolution to Fathers of Unification: Concepts of politics among Women Activists following German Unification," *Social Politics* 6, no. 1 (1999): 1–22, and more extensively reported in *Frauen in der DDR-Opposition: Lebens- und kollektivgeschichtliche Verläufe in einer Frauenfriedensgruppe* (Opladen: Leske und Budrich, 1999).

30. As *Shaping Abortion Discourse* points out, advocates of violence in the abortion debate get virtually no space in mainstream newspapers to make their case, even though some antiabortion activists, especially in the United States, actively justify bombings and murders of abortion providers within their own media (newsletters and Web pages). There appears to be a deliberate strategy by the newspapers to deny such advocates a voice, presumably in the interest of limiting their effectiveness, which would be a good example of soft repression at work. However, in this instance it may have had the opposite consequence, since such radical appeals could widely circulate in antiabortion circles without becoming obvious or being taken seriously by those outside these circles. When they did surface, after several murders of doctors, they were perceived as very discrediting to the whole antiabortion movement.

# Part III
# Media, Measurement,
# and Contention

# 7

# Repression and the Public Sphere:
# Discursive Opportunities for Repression against
# the Extreme Right in Germany in the 1990s

*Ruud Koopmans*

Repression is an act of strategic communication in the public sphere—that is the argument of this essay. By focusing on the discursive dimension of repression, the approach followed here departs from the mainstream of research on the relationship between repression and dissent. Traditional approaches have analyzed the repression–dissent nexus from the point of view of the direct interaction between repressive agencies and protest participants. In the rational-choice perspective, parties in such interactions influence each other's behavior by altering the other party's balance of costs and benefits, for example, when severe repression stifles protest by making it too risky and costly for most participants (e.g., Muller and Weede 1990; Opp and Roehl 1990). In the social-psychological perspective, the crucial causal mechanism in interactions between repressive agencies and dissenters is emotional states such as frustration and anger, as when repression that is perceived as illegitimate becomes a catalyst for further protest (e.g., Gurr 1969; Brockett 1995).

The contention of this essay is that such direct interactions are less and less the key to understanding contentious politics in modern democracies. Instead, the relationship between repression and dissent is an indirect, *mediated* one in which public discourse and the mass media play a crucial role. Both repression and dissent have increasingly become acts on a public stage, and third parties who watch, comment on, and intervene in the play are crucial to understanding the sequence of events. This is so because political actors in modern democracies increasingly depend on public-sphere resources to achieve their aims. As a result of individualization and the dissolution of traditional milieus, direct communication between political actors and their constituents has eroded dramatically. This is perhaps most clearly visible for political parties, but it is also true for modern social movement organizations such as Amnesty International, Greenpeace, or Médecins sans frontières. Simultaneously, the communication channels of the mass media, from the printed press via radio and television to, most recently, the Internet, have enormously expanded and have emancipated themselves from their formerly (especially in Europe) strong ties to the state or to specific political ideologies and parties. As a result, political communication nowadays typically means communication via the mass media, and political contention increasingly consists of a battle over media attention and legitimacy in the public discourse (Kriesi 2001).

This is easily seen for forms of political contention such as election campaigns, but it is perhaps not so obvious for protest, and even less so for repression (but see Wisler and Giugni 1999). The recent rise of protest event analysis as a methodological tool for social movement studies and related research into the mechanisms of media selection have begun to sensitize researchers to the dependency of protest on media attention. In the age of mass communication, protests that are completely ignored by the media are literally meaningless. Apart from the few onlookers who perhaps happened to be present at the scene of the protest, neither the general public nor those authorities at whom the protesters had addressed their demands will have taken notice of the event and thus there is no way in which such "invisible" protests will ever have a wider impact on public opinion or policies. However, the impact of protests that *do* receive media coverage also depends on the resonance they have in the public sphere, for example, by provoking supportive or dissenting reactions from other actors, or, and here we arrive at the particular topic of this essay, by inviting repression.

My contention is that, in a similar vein, the actions of repressive agencies depend on the dynamics of public discourse as reflected in the mass media. First, rather than simply a reaction to directly observed characteristics of protest (i.e., whether or not it involves lawbreaking from a purely legalistic point of view), repression to a considerable extent responds to protest *as it appears in the public sphere.* This includes not only the question of whether a certain category of protests or protest actors receives media attention at all, but also the extent and nature of other actors' public reactions to these protests. Other things being equal, for example, protests that are widely condemned in the public sphere as illegitimate are more likely to be repressed than protests that receive broad public support. Second, repression is itself a topic of public discourse, and repressive agents are likely to respond to public pressures for more or less repression, as well as to praise and criticism of their handling of protest. Third, the *impacts* of repression too are to a considerable extent mediated by the public discourse. Although repression usually aims at certain direct effects on the repressed target that do not require mediation (e.g., preventing a continuation or repetition of the person's behavior by way of imprisonment), repression always has important deterrence and socialization components that aim not at the repressed subject, but at the wider public, to deter those who might consider committing a similar offense, or to symbolically reward and satisfy those citizens who refrain from breaking the rule. Under modern conditions, such wider deterrence and socialization effects can only be achieved by way of the media. Analogous to the example for protests, acts of repression that are not reported in the media have no meaning beyond their direct impact on the offender and can be considered to not have happened at all from the point of view of their impact on the wider society. Similarly, the deterrent effect of repression is likely to be much more powerful if such repression is highly visible and receives strong support in the public sphere, and may well be counterproductive if it is widely condemned, or inconsequential if the media pay no attention to it.

I contend that the mediating role of public discourse in shaping both the conditions and the consequences of repression goes a long way in explaining the wide variety of effects that students of the repression–dissent nexus have found. From the point of view advanced in this essay, the search for generalizations on the effects of repression on protest or vice versa is futile as long as the crucial mediating role of the public discourse is not recognized. Repression deters protest in some cases, and encourages it in others, not so much because of any inherent characteristics of the repression or the protest, but because of differences in the way in which repression and protest appear in the public sphere, including the kind of reactions they draw from third actors. We can conceive of this mediating role of the public discourse as a set of *discursive opportunities*. This concept will be discussed on a general theoretical level in the next section. The body of the essay is then devoted to an empirical test of the argument through an analysis of the determinants of repression against extreme right and xenophobic violence in Germany in the 1990s.

## Evolutionary Dynamics and Discursive Opportunities: Visibility, Resonance, Legitimacy

The point of departure for my theoretical argument is to conceive of the public sphere as a bounded space for political communication characterized by a high level of competition. To be sure, the boundaries of the public sphere are not fixed, but can expand and contract over time. For instance, the rise of new channels of communication such as the Internet, or the multiplication of existing ones (e.g., through cable and satellite television), may expand the structural boundaries of the public sphere. At the same time, increasing commercialization of the media and a shift toward entertainment and human interest rather than political content may lead to a contraction of the communicative space available for public discourse. In addition to such more structural and long-term trends, the public sphere may also fluctuate importantly within shorter time periods. During close election campaigns or political crises, for instance, the media pay more attention to political issues than during times of routine politics.

These structural and conjunctural shifts and fluctuations imply that the public sphere is a *loosely* bounded space, but at any particular time and place it is a *bounded* space nonetheless. The number of channels of communication (newspapers, magazines, radio stations, television networks, etc.) and the size of their respective news holes (pages, broadcasting time, etc.) are by necessity limited. At the same time, groups and individuals in modern democratic societies make a huge number of attempts to insert messages in the public sphere compared to the available communicative space. On a typical day in a medium-sized democratic society, thousands of press statements are issued by a wide variety of parties, interest groups, and voluntary associations; hundreds of demonstrations, pickets, and other protests are staged; thousands of individuals write letters to the media or call in on radio and television programs; and dozens of press conferences vie for the attention of the public. Almost every conceivable position regarding an extremely wide range of political issues is represented among this daily cacophony of messages. Away from the mainstream of issues that are generally considered important (e.g., unemployment, immigration) and positions on these issues that are considered legitimate at a particular time and place, each democratic society harbors a wide variety of groups and individuals who try to insert issues and positions in the public discourse that are less generally held to be important and legitimate—for example, the interests of pigeon breeders, or the demand to abolish voting rights for women or blacks.

The enormous disproportion between the available space in the public sphere and the number of messages that are potential candidates for inclusion in it implies a high level of competition among groups who aim to get their messages across in the public discourse. To understand the dynamics of this competition, we need to begin by distinguishing two categories of actors: the *gatekeepers* of the public discourse, on the one hand, and the *speakers* of communicative messages, on the other (Neidhardt 1994).[1] The gatekeepers of the public discourse are those who decide which messages to include in the particular communicative channel they are responsible for, and how large and how prominent these messages will be displayed. The selectivity of coverage and the mechanisms of allocating prominence to covered messages are quite well known for the traditional media and include decisions about the size and placement of articles, or the amount and primacy of air time. But even in the relatively nonhierarchical Internet, providers, Internet browsers, and search engines prestructure access to information on the Web in such a way that certain sites are more easily and more frequently accessed than they would have been in the absence of such gatekeeping.

The actions of gatekeepers produce the first and most basic type of discursive opportunity that I distinguish: *visibility*. Visibility depends on the number of communicative channels by which a message is included and the prominence of such inclusion. It ranges from "invisible" messages that are not included in any channel at all, via messages with limited visibility that are, for example, only covered by local media, to "obtrusive" messages that are displayed prominently by most channels. Visibility is a necessary condition for a message to influence the public discourse, and, other things being equal, the amount of visibility that gatekeepers allocate to a message increases its potential to diffuse further in the public sphere.

From communications and media research we know quite a lot about the "news values" that structure the decisions of journalists and editors to assign newsworthiness to "stories" or not. These include, for instance, (geographical) proximity, the prominence and prestige of the speaker, the level of conflict related to the message or the actor, the relevance of an issue, possibilities for dramatization and personalization, and the novelty of a story (Galtung and Ruge 1965; Schulz 1976; Eilders 1997). With the partial exception of the proximity factor, these news values are not given characteristics of events, actors, or messages that exist outside of, and prior to, the discursive realm, but are themselves to an important extent a product of previous rounds of public discourse, from which notions of who is considered to be prominent, and which issues are considered relevant or controversial, have emerged. To be sure, there are also certain inherent characteristics of events that increase the probability of inclusion in the public discourse. Research into media selection bias in coverage of protest events (e.g., McCarthy, McPhail, and Smith 1996; Hocke 1999; Oliver and Myers 1999) has, for instance, shown that events with large numbers of participants (supposedly taken by journalists as an indicator of relevance) are more likely to be covered than small ones, and some studies also find a higher likelihood of coverage for violent events (which indicates a higher level of conflict).

Social movement organizers and other public actors are, of course, not ignorant about these selection mechanisms and try to anticipate them in the ways in which they bring their messages across. Many modern protests, including Greenpeace-style professional direct action, as well as more grassroots forms such as antiglobalization protests at international summits, are to an important extent scripted and staged to maximize the chances of drawing media attention. However, there are clear and usually severe limits to the degree to which actors such as social movements can influence the amount of visibility that is allocated to their messages. This is so first of all because of their fierce competition with other speakers, some of whom may have found even better ways of attracting media attention. Second, only a small number of aspects of newsworthiness can be manipulated by speakers, and much depends on how news values such as prominence or relevance have come to be defined in past public discourse. As a result, statements by "important" politicians tend to get covered to a large extent regardless of their substantive content or original presentation, whereas less prominent actors have to go to great lengths to realize their slight chances of access to the public discourse.

This brings us to the role of other speakers in shaping the discursive opportunities of any particular actor or action in the public sphere. Public actors know they are in competition with each other and their strategies are directed toward outdoing, neutralizing, convincing, or otherwise influencing their competitors and opponents. Beyond the competition for media visibility, other speakers are the main source of two additional types of discursive opportunity: resonance and legitimacy. Although gaining visibility is a necessary condition for communicative impact, the career of a discursive message is likely to remain stillborn if it does not succeed in provoking reactions from other actors in the public sphere. The degree to which a message provokes such reactions I call *resonance*.[2] Resonance is important for at least two reasons. First, messages that resonate travel further. Through the reactions of other actors, the message of the original speaker is at least partially reproduced and may reach new audiences. For instance, actors such as social movements who themselves lack prominence and other discursive resources may receive an enormous boost if established political actors express sympathy for their demands. Such support carries the message to the constituency of the established ally in question, and allows the message to profit from that actor's prominence and prestige. This form of supportive resonance I will call *consonance*.

However, even negative resonance, or *dissonance,* may be helpful to the diffusion of the original message.[3] The maxim that "any publicity is good publicity" is also relevant for political messages: even the rejection of a demand has to reproduce that demand and thereby diffuses it further in the public sphere. Of course, the reproduction of messages by way of resonance is always imperfect. Even in the case of consonance, allies are likely to support or emphasize only certain aspects of the original speaker's message; for example, in the case at hand, xenophobic violence found consonance in the public discourse regarding its aim to limit immigration, while simultaneously the violent means by which extreme right groups sought to advance this aim were rejected by other speakers. The distortion of the original message is, of course, likely to be even stronger in the case of dissonant reactions. Nevertheless, even a strongly negative public reaction to a message has to reproduce the original message to at least some extent and thereby always runs the risk of providing potential imitators of the original message with a model for successful public action (see, e.g., Holden 1986 for the case of airplane hijackings).

The second reason why resonance is important is that it increases the actor's chances to reproduce the desired message in the public sphere. Messages that resonate, whether negatively or positively, become more "relevant" in the eyes of journalists and editors and the actors behind them more "prominent," which increases the speaker's chances to achieve a high level of visibility for similar messages in the future.

Although to some extent we can treat consonance and dissonance as having similar effects on the discursive opportunities of a message, in other respects it certainly matters what the balance is between negative and positive responses in the public sphere. The degree to which, on average, reactions by third actors in the public sphere support or reject an actor or her claims I call *legitimacy.* Defined in such a way, legitimacy is independent of resonance. Highly legitimate messages may have no resonance at all because they are uncontroversial, whereas highly illegitimate messages may have enormous resonance (e.g., anti-Semitic violence in Germany). The relation between legitimacy and a speaker's discursive opportunities is a complicated one. All other things being equal, one might expect legitimacy to have a positive effect on the diffusion chances of a message, but because of the complex relation of legitimacy to resonance and visibility, other things will rarely be equal. Ideally, the speaker would like high resonance and high legitimacy, but will usually have to settle for less because normally high resonance is only achieved at the cost of an increase in controversiality, and thereby a net decrease in legitimacy. All in all, then, we may perhaps expect a curvilinear reaction between a message's chances of diffusion and its legitimacy, with messages whose legitimacy is controversial generally better placed than either highly legitimate or highly illegitimate messages.

Summing up, what I have presented here are the rough contours of an evolutionary model of the development of public discourse. In it, the public sphere is seen as a (loosely) bounded communicative space in which a variety of organizations, groups, and individuals compete for public attention. The model starts from the assumption of a wide variety of messages that become available for inclusion in the public discourse every day. Given the restricted communicative space available, only a small proportion of these messages will be included (visibility), of these only some will be further diffused through the reactions of other actors (resonance), and of these in turn only some will achieve the status of legitimacy. The reproduction of the original message thus achieved is, however, usually imperfect for reasons already explained. This explains why there is no long-term tendency toward an increasingly uniform public discourse: if successful messages were reproduced unaltered, discursive opportunities would cumulate over time and the public discourse would soon converge on uniform standards of who and what is relevant and legitimate, and cease to be a discourse in the true sense of the word. Of course, even in democracies there is a high degree of self-reproduction in the public discourse: what was prominent, relevant, and legitimate yesterday is usually a good predictor of today's parameters. The argument is, however, that ultimately the public discourse is kept alive by the perhaps small minority of "distortions" or "mutations" rather than by the perfect reproduction of messages.

It is important to realize that the selective pressures exerted by the mechanisms of visibility, resonance, and legitimacy are not external to the discursive process, nor are they opportunity *structures* in the true sense of the term. What we are dealing with is an interactive, coevolutionary process in which discursive opportunities are constituted by strategic actions of other actors in the public sphere. Thus, the communicative actions of actors B and C constitute the set of discursive opportunities for actor A, but A and B do so also for C, and C and A for B. However, I certainly do not want to argue that everything is discourse and that the public sphere is a completely self-referential system. Political opportunity *structures* in the true sense of the word, such as the institutional structure of the political system or the configuration of power (see Kriesi et al. 1995), remain important, because they set general parameters for the public discourse and influence the distribution of discursive resources among actors.[4] For instance, in highly centralized countries such as France, local actors will find it difficult to be considered important and legitimate enough for their opinions to play a major role in public discourse. The syndrome of Paris, then a long time nothing, and finally "la province" is not just a feature of the French institutional structure, but is reflected in French public discourse and in the centralized nature of its media system. Likewise, structural facts of political power such as a change in the composition of government will have strong effects on the public discourse. For instance, left-wing media, politicians, and parties are likely to provide left-wing social movements with visibility, resonance, and legitimacy as long as they are in the opposition, but their support for extraparliamentary action is often much more lukewarm once they are in government and have nothing to gain from stirring up a critical public debate.

Neither would I want to argue that "real" events and social problems do not play a role in structuring the public discourse. One important factor that informs speakers' strategies is their anticipation of what the general public, the media gatekeepers, and other speakers want to hear. Extra-discursive developments are often used as indicators for such expectations about other actors. For example, if unemployment or immigration levels rise, politicians may anticipate an increased demand for messages whose aim is to combat unemployment or to curb immigration. It sometimes does not even matter whether the underlying theory about the relation between objective events and public opinion was correct or not. If enough politicians assume that high immigration creates a demand among their constituents for tough statements on immigrants, immigration may indeed become a hot issue in the public debate and the rise in anti-immigrant statements may produce or reinforce the very sentiments that were anticipated among the wider public.

## Data and Hypotheses

I will now apply the preceding argument to an analysis of repression against extreme right and xenophobic groups and individuals in Germany in the 1990s. In the context of the project Mobilization on Ethnic Relations, Citizenship and Immigration (MERCI), data were collected on the public discourse on immigration and ethnic relations issues, including all claims by, against, or on behalf of extreme right and ethnic minority groups.[5] The units of analysis are instances of political claims making, defined as "the collective and public articulation of political demands, calls to action, proposals, criticisms, or physical attacks, which, actually or potentially, affect the interests or integrity of the claimants and/or other collective actors."[6] Claims were included irrespective of their form and include not only public statements but, among other things, also political decisions, judicial actions, demonstrations and other protests, and violence.[7] Important for the purpose of this essay, the data also include repressive measures by state agencies against the extreme right or xenophobic groups. The latter include political repression such as bans of organizations, judicial repression such as trials and convictions, as well as police repression such as arrests or house searches. All in all, the data set includes more than 11,000 instances of claims making during the period 1990–99, including 931 instances of extreme right and xenophobic violence, and 1,043 instances of repression against the extreme right.

The data were coded from all Monday, Wednesday, and Friday issues of the national quality newspaper *Frankfurter Rundschau*. This newspaper was chosen because pretests indicated that it paid much more attention to the topic of interest than alternative sources. For shorter periods of time, samples were drawn from other newspaper sources to check the representativeness of the primary source for the wider media landscape. These other newspapers were the national tabloid newspaper *Bild-Zeitung*, the Turkish immigrant daily *Hürriyet*, and three East German local newspapers. Comparisons of these newspapers displayed a consistent pattern.[8] First, in any paired comparison, the *Frankfurter Rundschau* was by far the most inclusive source in terms of the number of claims reported. Second, these quantitative differences had only very small qualitative consequences. For instance, although the *Rundschau* reported more than four times as many claims as *Bild*, the distributions of claims across actors, issues, positions with regard to issues, as well as temporal units were almost the same.[9] This indicates that the *Frankfurter Rundschau* can be considered representative for the wider German media landscape, at least regarding the type of information that was coded for the project.[10]

For the analysis reported here, the data were aggregated by year and by federal state to construct a cross-sectional time series data set with 160 cases (ten years, sixteen federal states), and variables consisting of counts of claims of a specific type (e.g., repression) per year–state combination. The estimation procedure used for the analysis was the XTGEE routine in STATA. Because of the fact that the variables consist of nonnegative counts with overdispersion, a negative binomial distribution for the dependent variable was modeled, as well as a first-order autoregressive correlation structure, which is typical for time series (see King 1989 for a discussion of event count data).[11]

Regarding repression, I excluded police action that was directly linked to extreme right events—that is, arrests or police violence during xenophobic riots (I have earlier called this "situational" repression). The main reason for this is that these events are inextricably linked to the occurrence of violence and therefore lead to a confounding of dependent and independent variables. The dependent variable therefore consists of independent instances of what I have called "institutional" repression of the types already indicated.[12]

At this point it is important to point at a major caveat to which I will come back in the conclusions. The dependent variable in my analysis is *repression as it appears in the public sphere* and as measured by the number of repressive events mentioned in my newspaper source. Ideally, I would have liked to include the full number of repressive acts against the extreme right that have actually occurred. Unfortunately, such data are not available. This is because in official statistics on police and judicial activity, extreme right and xenophobic violence is not listed as a separate category. Instead, these statistics are organized along the lines of types of offenses in terms of the sections and paragraphs of the penal code. As a result, repressive actions against extreme right violence can be classified under various headings (murder, disturbance of the public peace, arson, etc.) and each of these categories of course also includes crimes that have nothing to do with the extreme right or xenophobia.

In the absence of such extra-media data, we cannot know how representative my media data are of the actual population of repressive events. I want to emphasize, however, that my argument *does not* rest on the assumption of such representativeness. On the contrary, I expect that at any particular time and place there will be a certain noncorrespondence between the repression that actually occurs and the repression that appears in the media; otherwise my whole argument about discursive opportunities would not make any sense. Still, the lack of extra-media data on repression implies that I can only draw firm conclusions regarding the public dimension of repression. It is my contention that if a rise in discursive opportunities increases the diffusion chances of repression in the public sphere, this will also positively affect the real number of repressive acts. However, this part of my argument I cannot prove with the data at hand.

The zero hypothesis against which I want to test my argument about the relevance of public discourse is that the level of repression is merely a function of the level of extreme right violence (present and/or lagged one year to allow for a delayed reaction of repressive agencies to violence), the past level of repression (the dependent variable lagged one year), and a number of crucial extra-discursive control variables:

- The number of police and judicial personnel per thousand inhabitants in 1999, the assumption being that a larger number of personnel resources enhances the state's repressive capacity;
- The composition of the state government for each year, with a value of 1 for a right-wing government, and 0 otherwise.[13] Right-wing governments may either be expected to repress the extreme right more, because they favor law-and-order policies in other domains, or to repress it less, because they stand ideologically closer to the extreme right than left-wing governments;
- The trend variable "year," which could have a positive effect on repression because the right-wing violence of the 1990s was a qualitatively as well as quantitatively new phenomenon in Germany, especially in the East, and therefore it may have taken some time before the state and its repressive agencies developed adequate responses;
- The dummy variable "East." Former East and West Germany are still very different in many respects. This variable measures whether there is a difference in the level of repression between the East and the West that cannot be explained by any of the other variables. On the basis of the existing literature on the German extreme right, one might expect a negative East effect on levels of repression, which results from the ill-preparedness of the East German police and judiciary for dealing with the extreme right. In addition, some commentators claim that the authorities in the eastern states sometimes sympathize with the extreme right and may therefore not be as inclined to intervene as their western colleagues (e.g., Bürgerrechte und Polizei, CILIPS, and Diederichs 1995).
- The logarithm of the state population in thousands. Because the dependent variable is a count of instances of repression, it is of course likely to depend on the size of a state.

Although these variables may indeed be relevant, my argument is that we will be able to significantly improve our understanding of repression by including discursive opportunities in the analysis. An adequate model of the discursive opportunities for repression should include not only indicators of repression and extreme right violence, but also the public reactions of other actors to both types of claims. In addition, we have to take into account the targets of extreme right violence, who were, in the vast majority of cases, immigrants and ethnic minorities. Therefore, I also include statements about immigration and immigrants in the analysis. Thus, the relevant discursive space consists of five types of public claims:[14]

- Repression against extreme right and xenophobic groups and individuals;
- Extreme right and xenophobic violence;
- Claims regarding repression;
- Claims regarding the extreme right and xenophobia;
- Claims regarding immigration and immigrants.

My first hypothesis is that repression reacts more strongly to extreme right violence as it appears in the public discourse than to the real level of violence (hypothesis 1). This hypothesis can be tested by comparing the predictive power of two different measures of extreme right and xenophobic violence:

- The number of extreme right and xenophobic events reported in our media source;
- The number of extreme right and xenophobic events as registered by the Federal Office for the Protection of the Constitution, which in turn is based on police data from the different federal states. The number of violent events registered by the police is about ten times as high as the number of events captured in the newspaper sample. It is used here as an indicator of the extra-media reality regarding right-wing violence.

My second hypothesis is that the level of repression at any given time and place depends on the direct discursive opportunities of repressive claims:

- The visibility of repression, measured as the percentage of repressive events per year–state combination that is reported on the front page of the newspaper. Ideally, one would instead or additionally have the number of reported events as a percentage of all repressive acts against the extreme right that actually take place. However, as already indicated, such data are not available. A high degree of visibility indicates favorable conditions for the diffusion of a particular type of message and should be associated with a higher number of repressive events (hypothesis 2.1). Note that this is not a tautology because visibility is measured by the percentage and not by the absolute number of front-page events;
- The resonance of repression, measured as the number of statements on repression of the extreme right by actors other than the police and judiciary. A high degree of resonance indicates favorable conditions for the diffusion of repression and should therefore be associated with higher levels of repression (hypothesis 2.2);
- The legitimacy of repression, measured as the average valence of claims

on repression as specified earlier. Claims were scored −1 if they were against repression, 0 if they were neutral or ambivalent, and 1 if they were in favor of repression of the extreme right. Generally, I expect legitimacy to increase the diffusion chances of repression, but for the reasons explained, this relationship may be not so outspoken or have a curvilinear shape (hypothesis 2.3). Because of too many cases where the number of events was zero or too few to compute a meaningful average valence score, this variable is only included in the analysis as the average valence per year, and is therefore constant across federal states.

A third cluster of hypotheses states that the level of repression additionally depends on the degree to which it resonates with and is legitimated by evaluations of the target of repression, that is, extreme right and xenophobic groups. Generally, I expect that the more the extreme right is problematized in the public discourse, the more this increases the diffusion chances of repression. To test this hypothesis, the following variables are used in the analysis:

- The number of claims on the extreme right and xenophobia (excluding, of course, those that are directly related to repression, for these are already included). I hypothesize that the more the extreme right becomes an issue in the public debate, the more this increases the diffusion chances of repression (hypothesis 3.1);
- The visibility of claims against the extreme right, measured by the percentage of such claims that were reported on the front page of the newspaper. The greater the visibility of the extreme right as an issue of public debate, the greater the diffusion chances of repression (hypothesis 3.2);
- The legitimacy of the extreme right in the public debate, measured by the average valence of claims on the extreme right, with −1 indicating rejection, 0 ambivalent or neutral claims, and +1 claims supportive of the extreme right. Not surprisingly, the extreme right as an actor found little support in the German public discourse, with almost 90 percent of claims evaluating it negatively, and less than 5 percent being supportive. However, to the extent that there were fluctuations in the level of legitimacy of the extreme right, I expect the chances of diffusion of repression to be negatively related to the legitimacy of the extreme right in the public discourse (hypothesis 3.3). As in the case of the legitimacy of claims on repression, this variable is included only as the average yearly score across federal states, because there were too many

empty or nearly empty year–state combinations to allow the meaning-ful computation of averages for each case.

A final set of hypotheses states that repression also depends on the public discourse regarding the extreme right's favored targets, namely, immigrants and ethnic minorities. Of all acts of extreme right violence, 74 percent were directed against these groups, and within that category especially against asylum seekers (37 percent of all violence). I hypothesize that the more the public discourse problematizes or delegitimates immigration and im-migrants, and thus legitimates and resonates with the aims of the extreme right, the more this limits the diffusion chances of repression against the extreme right. Again, I test this hypothesis by way of three variables:

- The number of public claims on immigrants and ethnic minorities. I hypothesize that the more immigrants and minorities become prob-lematized and contested in the public discourse, the more this creates a conducive environment for extreme right violence against these groups, and lowers the diffusion chances of repression against the extreme right (hypothesis 4.1);
- The visibility of public claims on immigrants and ethnic minorities, indicated by the percentage of such claims that were reported on the front page of the newspaper. The greater the visibility of the immigra-tion and minorities debate, the lower the diffusion chances of repres-sion (hypothesis 4.2);
- The legitimacy of immigrants and minorities in the public discourse, measured by the average valence of claims on them, with –1 indicating a negative position with regard to immigrants and their rights, 0 stand-ing for ambivalent or neutral positions, and +1 for claims supportive of immigrants and their rights. I expect that the greater the legitimacy of immigrants and minorities in the public discourse, the more this enhances the diffusion chances of repression against the right-wing groups that attack immigrants and minorities (hypothesis 4.3). Again, this variable is included only as the average yearly score across federal states, because there were too many empty or nearly empty year–state combinations to allow the meaningful computation of averages for each case.

## Results

To give the reader an idea of the temporal patterning of the actions of the two main protagonists, Figure 7.1 shows the yearly development of repres-sion (left axis), as well as of extreme right violence in all federal states taken together. For extreme right violence, the figure gives both the data from the Federal Office for the Protection of the Constitution (right axis) and the numbers based on the newspaper sample (left axis).

The figure shows that repression and violence were temporally closely linked and that repression developed as a reaction to violence, as indicated by the one-year lag that is apparent especially in the first half of the 1990s. Low levels of repression in the first three years of the decade may have contributed to the steep rise in the number of violent events in these years. That, however, is a topic for another paper; here we are concerned with the determinants of repression. The question to be answered is to what extent repression was indeed a straightforward reaction to rising levels of violence, or whether it was more complexly embedded in a discursive setting that made repression, its targets, and its targets' targets more or less visible, resonant, and legitimate.

Regarding the comparison of the two sources for data on violence, we can note that both show us roughly the same pattern. Beyond these similarities, the number of newspaper-reported compared to police-registered

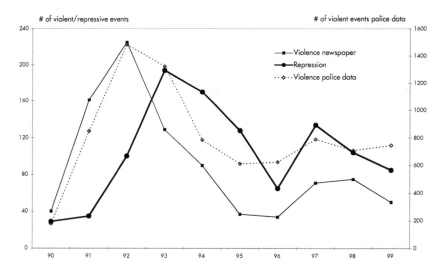

Based on data from the Federal Office for the Protection of the Constitution in the first column, on the media data in the other columns. Because of the use of lagged variables for repression and violence, the first year in the series (1990; sixteen cases) is excluded from the analysis.

*Figure 7.1. Development of extreme right and xenophobic violence (police and media data) and repression against the extreme right, all federal states, 1990–99*

events seems to have been relatively high in the initial years and relatively low later in the decade. This might indicate a decline in media attention for extreme right violence over the course of the decade as such violence became part of business as usual. However, just as plausibly, one can argue that it was the attentiveness of the police and other security agencies that increased over the course of the decade. Widespread criticism of the authorities' dealing with the extreme right in the early 1990s actually led to a broadening of the official definition of "extreme right and xenophobic violence," and to collaborative data gathering by the federal police and the Federal Office for the Protection of the Constitution, who initially had separate statistics of violence. Although the data for the earlier years were subsequently corrected according to the new definition, it is easily possible that such corrections were imperfect and that the police data remained less than complete for the early years of the decade. For the purpose of this essay, however, it is irrelevant which of these readings is correct. What interests us here is whether the repressive activities of state agencies such as the police and the judiciary depended on the extreme right violence as they themselves registered it, or on the violence as it appeared in the media, as the theoretical approach advocated here would suggest.

This and other questions I will address by way of cross-sectional time series analyses of the determinants of repression, the results of which are displayed in Table 7.1. In addition to temporal differences such as those displayed in Figure 7.1, this analysis also takes into account the considerable variations between the sixteen federal states. The first column of Table 7.1 gives the results of the model according to the zero hypothesis that repression is a function only of past repression, past and present levels of extreme right violence as indicated by the extra-media data of the Federal Office for the Protection of the Constitution, the number of police and judiciary personnel as an indicator of resources available for repression, the composition of government as an indicator of the political opportunity structure, as well as controls for temporal trends, the East–West difference, and the size of a state's population.

First and most obviously, we find a strong effect of population size on the count of repressive events. In addition, repression responds to the development of extreme right violence, but, as expected on the basis of Figure 7.1, it does so with a certain time lag in that only last year's and not the present level of violence has an impact on the level of repression. This is partly a result of the fact that I excluded direct police interventions from the analysis, and partly it reflects that many types of repressive reactions take time to unfold their full potential (e.g., the judicial response of putting on trial and

**Table 7.1. Results of cross-sectional time series regressions with the level of repression as the dependent variable**

| | Model 1 B | Model 1 p | Model 2 B | Model 2 p | Model 3 B | Model 3 p | Model 4 B | Model 4 p | Model 5 B | Model 5 p | Model 6 B | Model 6 p | Model 7 B | Model 7 p |
|---|---|---|---|---|---|---|---|---|---|---|---|---|---|---|
| Repression t-1 | .003 | .705 | .019 | .013 | .012 | .153 | .025 | .001 | .024 | .000 | .018 | .008 | .017 | .015 |
| Log of population | .577 | .002 | .677 | .000 | .646 | .000 | .527 | .001 | .776 | .000 | .732 | .000 | .744 | .000 |
| East | .882 | .000 | .564 | .008 | .508 | .037 | .544 | .013 | .651 | .002 | .505 | .026 | .480 | .039 |
| Year | .003 | .877 | .034 | .125 | .112 | .075 | .112 | .019 | .010 | .678 | .086 | .257 | .113 | .039 |
| Police and judiciary personnel | .136 | .016 | .106 | .049 | .120 | .021 | .059 | .249 | .148 | .001 | .151 | .010 | .154 | .008 |
| Right-wing government | -.193 | .120 | -.380 | .004 | -.329 | .009 | -.253 | .059 | -.294 | .007 | -.161 | .125 | -.197 | .080 |
| Extreme right violence t0[a] | -.000 | .859 | .014 | .068 | .020 | .019 | .006 | .521 | .028 | .000 | .026 | .007 | .027 | .005 |
| Extreme right violence t-1 | .008 | .000 | .043 | .000 | .034 | .000 | .045 | .000 | .010 | .089 | .012 | .106 | .014 | .035 |
| Claims on repression | | | | | .049 | .004 | – | – | – | – | .043 | .032 | .040 | .039 |
| Visibility of repression | | | | | .093 | .000 | – | – | – | – | .075 | .000 | .071 | .000 |
| Legitimacy of repression | | | | | .596 | .480 | – | – | – | – | -.379 | .727 | – | – |
| Claims on extreme right | | | | | | | .019 | .002 | – | – | .009 | .243 | .007 | .301 |
| Visibility of claims on extreme right | | | | | | | -.188 | .606 | – | – | -.349 | .254 | – | – |
| Legitimacy of extreme right | | | | | | | -2.948 | .029 | – | – | -2.977 | .026 | -2.751 | .045 |
| Claims on immigration | | | | | | | | | -.003 | .443 | -.007 | .219 | -.007 | .188 |
| Visibility of claims on immigration | | | | | | | | | -.838 | .068 | -.980 | .008 | -.936 | .008 |
| Legitimacy of immigrants | | | | | | | | | 3.185 | .000 | 2.297 | .000 | 2.295 | .001 |
| X² (denominator) | 175 | .000 | 344 (8) | .000 | 1682 (11) | .000 | 1002 (11) | .000 | 1230 (11) | .000 | 1695 (14) | .000 | 4743 (14) | .000 |
| F-statistic | 22 | | 43 | | 153 | | 91 | | 112 | | 121 | | 339 | |
| N | 144[b] | | 144 | | 144 | | 144 | | 144 | | 144 | | 144 | |

[a] Based on data from the Federal Office for the Protection of the Constitution in the first column, on the media data in the other columns.

[b] Because of the use of lagged variables for repression and violence, the first year in the series (1990, sixteen cases) is excluded from the analysis.

convicting extreme right activists). In line with the expectations, we also find a positive effect of the available resources for repression, in the form of the number of police and judiciary personnel. A surprising finding is that, contrary to the widely shared assumption of a badly prepared and sometimes ideologically sympathetic police and judiciary in the East, the level of repression is significantly higher in the East than in the West. I cannot presently give a convincing explanation for this finding.[15]

Comparison of these results to the model in the second column of the table allows for a test of my first hypothesis that repression responds more to extreme right violence as it appears in the media than to the extra-media reality. Instead of the official violence data, model 2 uses the newspaper data on violence as a predictor of repression. In all other respects, models 1 and 2 are exactly the same. As the more than doubled chi-square indicates, the model with the newspaper violence fits the data much better. Moreover, the coefficients of the effect of violence on repression are much stronger now, and the coefficient of the present level of violence now becomes significant at the 10 percent level, although the effect of last year's violence is still much stronger. In addition, two effects of the other variables now attain significance. First, we now see that repression is partly self-reproductive, as indicated by the positive effect of past on present levels of repression. Second, we now find that repression of the extreme right is significantly lower under right-wing governments. Although this is what a political opportunity structure perspective would lead us to expect, it contradicts the law-and-order image that is normally associated with the political right. This image is probably correct when it comes to fighting nonpolitical crime or left-wing protest. In the case of ideologically closer right-wing protests, there has been a tendency on the right to downplay the seriousness of the problem—for instance, by denying the racist motivations behind attacks and treating them as normal street fights—which may explain the lower priority that right-wing governments have given to repression. Hypothesis 1 has thus found strong confirmation. Repression, at least insofar as it becomes publicly visible, reacts much more strongly to extreme right violence as it appears in the media than to the extra-media reality—"reality" insofar as we can trust the police data, of course.

Turning to the second set of hypotheses, in model 3, I added the direct discursive opportunities of repression: its visibility in the form of the percentage of front-page stories on repression, its resonance in terms of statements on repression by third actors, and its legitimacy measured by the average valence of claims on repression. Introducing these discursive opportunities again leads to a strong improvement in the model's fit and two of the three new variables are highly significant and in the expected direction. Claims by third actors on repression were for the most part criticisms of the authorities' dealing with the extreme right and calls for increased or more efficient repression. The prevalence of such resonant claims, even if they were critical, provided a favorable environment for repression. Media attention for repression likewise has the expected positive effect on the level of repression. The legitimacy of repression, on the contrary, has no significant impact, nor could such an impact be detected by additionally including a squared term (not displayed in the table) to capture a possible curvilinear relation to the level of repression. This may be owing to the fact that there was very little disagreement about the need for a stronger approach by the control agencies against the extreme right.[16] The debate was more about whether this required new legislation or not, or whether repression alone would be enough.

Of course, in interpreting the effects of repression's visibility and resonance on the level of repression, we must allow for the possibility of a reciprocal relation between the two. Claims by third actors on repression might be little more than a reaction to repression and the coefficient we find in the present model may just be an artifact of this reverse effect. The fact that most claims by third actors on repression criticized the *lack of* sufficient repression does not point in this direction. On the other hand, the nature of my argument about each actor's actions in the public sphere conditioning those of others, *and vice versa,* leads us to expect that the reverse causal chain may also have been important. For reasons of space, I cannot here display the full analysis of the determinants of third actors' statements on repression. However, such an analysis shows that indeed third actors' claims on repression partly depended on a high level of (present, not past) repression. However, the analysis also shows that third actors' statements on repression were far from reducible to a mere reaction to repression. They responded much more strongly still to other discursive opportunities, most importantly the number of statements on the extreme right, as well as the number and valence of statements on immigration. In other words, third actors tended to increase their calls for repression in response to both a higher degree of problematization of the extreme right in the public discourse and an increase in debate about the victims of extreme right violence, especially if such debate signaled a high degree of legitimacy of immigrants.

For the visibility of repression, one might argue that media are inclined to react disproportionately to increases and decreases in repression, which would imply that when repression is high, not only the absolute number but also the percentage of front-page stories increases. An analysis with the percentage of front-page stories on repression as the dependent variable shows that this was indeed, to some extent, the case. Again, however, we find that visibility is by no means reducible to this. Two other variables have stronger effects, the (lack of) legitimacy of the extreme right, on the one hand, and the legitimacy of immigrants, on the other. In other words, the media tended to give repression higher visibility when the public discourse displayed a strong rejection of the extreme right, and when it was relatively positive with regard to immigration and immigrants.

We now turn to the third set of hypotheses and investigate if and how the public discourse on the extreme right influenced the level of repression. Because of the kind of interdependencies among different types of claims in the public sphere that I just discussed, I will first assess the effects of each set of discursive opportunities separately, before trying to bring them together in one model. Model 4 in Table 7.1 shows that the inclusion of the variables relating to the discourse on the extreme right also leads to a significant improvement of the model vis-à-vis the baseline models 1 and 2. However, model 4 does not fit as well as model 3, which is not unexpected because the discursive opportunities in model 3 are more directly linked to repression than is the public discourse on the extreme right. Again, two of the three variables are significant. According to the expectations, a high level of public debate about the extreme right and a low degree of legitimacy of the extreme right tended to improve the opportunities for the diffusion of repression in the public sphere. The visibility of claims about the extreme right, on the contrary, did not have a noticeable effect on repression.

The fourth and final set of hypotheses says that repression also depends on the public discourse regarding the main victims of the extreme right, immigrants and ethnic minorities. Model 5 provides strong support for this idea. The fit of the model, although again not as good as model 3, is better than that of model 4, even though arguably the discursive opportunities related to the immigration discourse are "further away" from the dependent variable than those in model 4. The public discourse about the direct object of repression—the extreme right—was a less important determinant of repression than the public discourse about immigrants, to whom repressive agents had no direct relation. Even though in a direct sense the extreme right as an actor had little legitimacy, it seems to have been legitimated indirectly by the delegitimation of its victims, and the results show that this has partly shielded the extreme right from repression. Again, two effects are significant and in the expected direction. First, there is a very strong effect of the legitimacy of immigrants on the level of repression: the more positive the public discourse about immigration and immigrants, the more likely are the control agencies to step up repression against xenophobia and the extreme right. Second, there is also an effect of the visibility of claims on immigration regardless of their valence, indicating that a strong focusing of media attention on the immigration issue was detrimental to the diffusion chances of repression. The absolute number of statements on immigration, however, has no significant independent effect.

In the next column of the table, model 6 brings together all the variables from models 2–5. With one exception, the number of statements on the extreme right, all discursive variables that were significant in the separate analyses remain so in the full model, and no new effects that run counter to the expectations appear. Closer inspection reveals that the disappearance of the effect of claims on the extreme right is caused by its high correlation with the claims on repression variable. Although the two variables have been operationalized in such a way that they do not overlap, both are actually subsets of a larger category of claims on the extreme right and how to combat it. Apparently, beyond the effect of the more specific claims on repression variable, the claims on the extreme right variable as it is defined here does not have any additional predictive power for the level of repression. The effects of two other variables now also drop slightly below a significant level, namely, those of the composition of government and the lagged level of extreme right violence.

The fit of the model as a whole, however, is not impressive. In spite of the larger number of predictors (with concomitant losses in the degrees of freedom), the chi-square is only marginally above the one for model 3, which includes only the direct discursive opportunities for repression. This is probably the result of the fact that with seventeen predictors, the model has become too complex and contains redundancy owing to the interdependencies among the predictors. Therefore, I eliminated the variable that had the lowest level of significance—namely, the legitimacy of repression—from the model, which resulted in a large increase in the chi-square. From the resulting model, I again removed the least significant variable—namely, the visibility of claims on the extreme right—which again led to a substantial increase in the chi-square. Removal of any further variables from this model caused the chi-square to drop substantially.

The final and best-fitting model 7 is displayed in the last column of the table. Compared to model 6, the composition of government and lagged violence reappear as predictors of repression. A weak positive time trend, which was already visible in some of the earlier models, also appears, and indicates that, controlled for all other factors repression, increased over the course of the decade as the security agencies gradually redirected their attention from the radical left to the radical right and developed more adequate responses to extreme right violence. Apart from these minor changes, all the effects that were significant in earlier models, again with the exception of claims regarding the extreme right, remain significant and of a similar magnitude in the final model.

All in all, the analysis provides considerable support for the relevance of discursive opportunities. Far from being a simple reaction to extreme right violence, repression depended strongly on the discursive environment, an environment that was made up not only of reactions to, and evaluations of, repression itself, but also of the public discourse on repression's target, the extreme right, and the main victims of extreme right violence, immigrants, and ethnic minorities. Six of the ten hypotheses that I derived from the model were consistently confirmed by the data, namely:

- Repression depended more strongly on violence as it appeared in the public sphere than on the violence registered by the security agencies themselves (hypothesis 1);
- Resonant statements by third actors on repression had a positive impact on levels of repression (hypothesis 2.1);
- A high visibility of repression in the public sphere likewise had a positive impact on levels of repression (hypothesis 2.2);
- The lower the legitimacy of the extreme right in the public discourse, the higher the level of repression (hypothesis 3.3);
- A strong focus of media attention on the immigration issue lowered the level of repression (hypothesis 4.2);
- The higher the legitimacy of immigrants in the public discourse, the higher the level of repression against those who attack immigrants and ethnic minorities (hypothesis 4.3).

In addition, hypothesis 3.1, which states that repression is higher when the number of claims about the extreme right is high, received partial support. The remaining three hypotheses could not be confirmed, but we did not find any significant effects regarding them that went contrary to the expectations, either. Partly, the lack of confirmation for some of the hypotheses is a result of interdependencies among the different discursive opportunities. Statements on the extreme right correlate strongly (.64) with statements on repression, and once the latter variable is introduced, the additional explanatory power of statements on the extreme right is no longer sufficient to attain significance. Something similar holds for the number of claims on immigration and immigrants, which in all equations had the correct sign but remained insignificant. The final model can in fact be significantly improved (chi-square 7603) by adding the number of statements on immigrants lagged by one year, which then is highly significant (p = .000) and in the expected direction. Nothing much else changes in that model, apart from the fact that the effect of the legitimacy of the extreme right ceases to be significant.

The introduction of discursive opportunity variables did not, however, lead to the disappearance of the effects of the control variables. The positive effect on repression levels of eastern location and the state's repressive capacity in the form of the number of police and judiciary personnel, as well as the negative effect of right-wing government incumbency, remain relevant. However, the magnitudes of the eastern location and right-wing incumbency effects decline considerably (compare the B's in models 1 and 2 to those in model 7) after we introduce the discursive variables. This suggests that while right-wing incumbency partly affects repression directly (e.g., because right-wing governments make fewer resources available for such repression), partly the causal relation is mediated via the effect right-wing incumbency has on patterns of public discourse surrounding repression, the extreme right, and immigrants. Similarly, we can at least partly attribute the difference between eastern and western Germany to a different structure of the public discourse in the two parts of the country, creating generally more favorable conditions for repression in the East.

## Conclusions

In this essay, I have presented an evolutionary model of the development of repression that treats repression as a form of strategic communication in the public sphere. Departing from the assumption of strong competition among communicative messages for—by necessity limited—public attention, I have introduced three elements of "discursive opportunities" that can explain why some messages are able to diffuse and reproduce in this competitive environment and others are not. These reproduction chances depend on the degree to which messages are made visible by the gatekeepers of the channels of communication, most importantly the mass media (visibility); the extent to which third actors or speakers react to a message and thereby diffuse it further in the public sphere (resonance); and finally the degree to which other speakers positively evaluate a message (legitimacy).

In addition to such direct discursive opportunities, communicative messages always operate in a discursive environment where there are other types of messages that either serve to add to, or to substract from, the visibility, resonance, and legitimacy of any particular type of message. In the example at hand, the relevant discursive context for repressive "messages" consisted of four other types of messages: extreme right violence, of course, but not necessarily as what it "really" is, but as it appears in the public sphere; claims by other speakers on repression, such as calls for more repression or criticisms of the police; claims on the extreme right and xenophobia; and claims on immigration and immigrants, the primary victims of extreme right violence.

The four main hypotheses—that repression reacts to violence as it appears in the public sphere; that media visibility and supportive reactions by third actors increase the level of repression; that the problematization and delegitimation of the extreme right enhance the diffusion chances of repression; and that the problematization and delegitimation of immigrants make such diffusion less likely—were all confirmed. Out of the ten more specific hypotheses that I formulated, which I will not reiterate here, six received full, and another two partial, confirmation, while none of the models analyzed contained any effects that ran counter to the expectations.

Although the results offer strong support for the role of discursive opportunities in explaining the dynamics of repression in the public sphere, it remains to be seen if the model will stand the test for other types of discourse. The specific nature of repression gives us reason both to be confident and to be skeptical in this respect. Even if I have taken repression as a form of strategic communication in the public sphere, it is clear that it is quite a special form of communication, and, importantly, it has a life of its own *outside* the public sphere. Communicative messages such as public statements on immigrants or the extreme right do not really have such an outside life, at least not one that is knowable by, and consequential for, anybody, apart from the unsuccessful speaker herself. The fact that the discursive approach developed here has proven its use for the explanation of an atypical form of communicative action such as repression that does have such an extra-discursive life may give us confidence that the model will also apply to more standard forms of discourse, for which its relevance is much more obvious. However, the atypical nature of repression can also mean that the results found here cannot be generalized. The following question would then have to be answered: why, if the assumption of repression as a form of communicative action is misconceived, is it so strongly embedded in the dynamics of public discourse?

The fact that repression has an extra-media existence further leads to the question what the extra-media implications are of our findings on the public dimension of repression. Unfortunately, in the absence of reliable data on repression that are independent of media sources, I cannot answer this question here. I can only repeat the supposition that in modern societies, repression against forms of collective contention such as extreme right violence that is unable to achieve public visibility, resonance, and legitimacy is unlikely to sustain itself, and will not be very effective in the longer run.[17] As we have seen in the analysis, I have both media and extra-media data for another form of claims making, which also has a strong extra-media component, namely, the direct, physical violence of extreme right groups against immigrants and other minority groups. Analyzing the discursive dynamics behind the genesis of extreme right violence allows us to go one step further and to answer the question whether discursive dynamics such as those analyzed here are epiphenomena or in another sense irrelevant for what goes on in the real world, or whether my contention is correct that nowadays the more consequential—and in these consequences "real"—world is the one we watch on the public stage.[18]

## Notes

1. As will become clear, the notion of "speaker" is here meant in a broad sense, and includes those who "speak" through nonverbal messages, such as violence against immigrants or the making of arrests.

2. In developing these concepts, I have been inspired by the work on collective action frames of David Snow and his colleagues (e.g., Snow et al. 1986; Snow and Benford 1992; see also Gamson and Modigliani 1989). My approach differs in that I do not focus on a particular actor's (here: the state's repressive agencies) own discursive mobilization strategies, but on the—largely strategically unanticipated— reactions that actors encounter once they enter the public sphere. Thus, I emphasize the effects of the discursive context, whereas Snow and his colleagues emphasize the internal perspective of the discursive strategies of social movement activists and organizers. These two perspectives are obviously complementary rather than mutually exclusive.

3. I thank Thom Duyvené de Wit for suggesting to me this distinction between consonance and dissonance as two types of resonance.

4. For the necessity of distinguishing opportunities from opportunity structures, and political opportunity from other types of opportunity (e.g., discursive), see Koopmans 1999.

5. As indicated by its name, this project investigates a wider range of questions pertaining to the politics of immigration, migrant integration, and ethnic relations. In addition to Germany, this project is carried out in Great Britain, France, the Netherlands, and Switzerland, with collaborators at the Universities of Leeds

(Paul Statham), Lausanne (Florence Passy), Amsterdam (Thom Duyvené de Wit), and Geneva (Marco Giugni).

6. This definition is close to Charles Tilly's definition of contentious gatherings (1995, 63). However, my definition includes a much broader range of discursive forms, and is not limited to the physical mobilization of people in a public place. Tilly's notion of the public sphere, in other words, is much narrower in that he largely ignores the media in their various forms—even though he uses them as his main source—and focuses heavily on material public places as the locus of contentious interaction.

7. For further details on the method of political claims analysis, see Koopmans and Statham 1999b.

8. See Koopmans and Statham 1999a for more details on these comparisons.

9. Of course, there were qualitative differences between the *Rundschau* and the Turkish and local newspapers. However, these differences were related to biases of these alternative sources rather than the *Rundschau*. Thus, *Hürriyet* obviously reported more claims by Turkish organizations, and the regional papers more about their own region.

10. An additional coding of editorials for the different newspapers did reveal enormous qualitative differences, with, for instance, the *Bild* editorials much more in favor of restricting immigration than those of the *Rundschau*. However, because we systematically disregarded editors' and journalists' "own voice," such differences do not enter into our data.

11. This way of modeling the data has been developed in cooperation with Susan Olzak, and was also used in a paper coauthored with her, focusing on the explanation of extreme right-wing violence (Koopmans and Olzak 2004).

12. For this distinction and an early analysis of the effects of these two types of repression on extreme right violence in Germany, see Koopmans 1997.

13. Right-wing are governments composed of either the Christian Democrats alone (Christian Democratic Union [CDU] or Christian Social Union [CSU]) or in coalition with the Liberals (Free Democratic Party [FDP]).

14. The different claims categories were defined as much as possible independently from one another. Thus, claims by extreme right and xenophobic groups were, where relevant, excluded from all other categories, and claims by the police and judiciary were excluded from claims regarding repression.

15. I did check whether the East effect resulted from the fact that on average the per capita level of violence in the East is much higher than in the West (about two times as high according to the official data, about four times as high according to the newspaper data). Perhaps this intensity created a higher sensibility among the authorities in the East to step up their efforts to combat the extreme right.

However, the inclusion of squared terms for past and present violence in the analysis did not result in significant coefficients; moreover, the sign of these coefficients was negative rather than positive.

16. With an average valence score of .75 and 76 percent of all claims in favor of repression, the legitimacy of repression was very high during most of the period in most states.

17. I grant that this does not hold to the same extent for repression directed at regular, individualized crime, in which much of the purpose is achieved by catching and punishing the individual culprit. However, the notorious ineffectiveness of such individualized crime prevention—after all, most convicts continue their criminal careers—suggests that if there is a rationale behind repression in such cases, it may lie in its effects on the wider public, and for these, the argument developed here applies with full force.

18. In an article together with Susan Olzak (Koopmans and Olzak 2004), we have applied the model of evolutionary dynamics and discursive opportunities to the explanation of extreme right violence. There we use the police figures on extreme right violence as the dependent variable and find that the magnitude as well as the targets of violence are strongly affected by discursive opportunities. These results suggest that, indeed, public discourse surrounding contentious political action can have important material consequences.

## Works Cited

Brockett, Charles D. 1995. "A Protest-Cycle Resolution of the Repression/Popular-Protest Paradox." In M. Traugott, ed. *Repertoires and Cycles of Contention*, 117–44. Durham, NC: Duke University Press.

Bürgerrechte und Polizei, CILIP, and Otto Diederichs, eds. 1995. *Hilfe, Polizei. Fremdenfeindlichkeit bei Deutschlands Ordnungshütern*. Berlin: Elefanten Press.

Eilders, Christiane. 1997. *Nachrichtenfaktoren und Rezeption. Eine empirische Analyse zur Auswahl und Verarbeitung politischer Information*. Opladen: Westdeutscher Verlag.

Galtung, Johan, and Marie Homboe Ruge. 1965. "The Structure of Foreign News: The Presentation of the Congo, Cuba and Cyprus Crises in Four Norwegian Newspapers." *Journal of Peace Research*, no. 2: 64–91.

Gamson, William, and Andre Modigliani. 1989. "Media Discourse on Nuclear Power: A Constructionist Approach." *American Journal of Sociology* 95: 1–37.

Gurr, Ted Robert. 1969. *Why Men Rebel*. Princeton, NJ: Princeton University Press.

Hocke, Peter. 1999. "Determining the Selection Bias in Local and National Newspaper Reports on Protest Events." In Dieter Rucht, Ruud Koopmans, and Fridehelm Neidhardt, eds., *Acts of Dissent: New Developments in the Study of Protest,* 131–163. Lanham, MD: Rowman and Littlefield.

Holden, Robert T. 1986. "The Contagiousness of Aircraft Hijacking." *American Journal of Sociology* 91: 874–904.

King, Gary. 1989. *Unifying Political Methodology: The Likelihood Theory of Statistical Inference.* Cambridge: Cambridge University Press.

Koopmans, Ruud. 1997. "Dynamics of Repression and Mobilization: The German Extreme Right in the 1990s." *Mobilization* 2, no. 2: 149–65.

———. 1999. "Political. Opportunity. Structure. Some Splitting to Balance the Lumping." *Sociological Forum* 14, no. 1: 93–106.

Koopmans, Ruud, and Susan Olzak. 2004. "Discursive Opportunities and the Evolution of Right-Wing Violence in Germany." *American Journal of Sociology* 110, no. 1.

Koopmans, Ruud, and Paul Statham. 1999a. "Challenging the Liberal Nation-State? Postnationalism, Multiculturalism, and the Collective Claims-Making of Migrants and Ethnic Minorities in Britain and Germany." *American Journal of Sociology* 105, no. 3: 652–96.

———. 1999b. "Political Claims Analysis: Integrating Protest Event and Political Discourse Approaches." *Mobilization* 4, no. 1: 40–51.

Kriesi, Hanspeter. 2001. *Die Rolle der Öffentlichkeit im politischen Entscheidungsprozess.* WZB: Research Unit Political Communication and Mobilization, paper P 01-701.

Kriesi, Hanspeter, Ruud Koopmans, Jan Willem Duyvendak, and Marco G. Giugni. 1995. *New Social Movements in Western Europe: A Comparative Analysis.* Minneapolis: University of Minnesota Press.

McCarthy, John D., Clark McPhail, and Jackie Smith. 1996. "Images of Protest: Estimating Selection Bias in Media Coverage of Washington Demonstrations, 1982, 1991." *American Sociological Review* 61, no. 3: 478–99.

Muller, Edward N., and Erich Weede. 1990. "Cross-National Variation in Political Violence: A Rational Action Approach." *Journal of Conflict Resolution* 34: 624–51.

Neidhardt, Friedhelm. 1994. "Öffentlichkeit, öffentliche Meinung, soziale Bewegungen," special issue *Kölner Zeitschrift für Soziologie und Sozialpsychologie* 34: 7–41.

Oliver, Pamela E., and Daniel J. Myers. 1999. "How Events Enter the Public Sphere: Conflict, Location, and Sponsorship in Local Newspaper Coverage of Public Events." *American Journal of Sociology* 105: 38–87.

Opp, Karl-Dieter, and Wolfgang Roehl. 1990. "Repression, Micromobilization, and Political Protest." *Social Forces* 69: 521–47.

Schulz, Winfried. 1976. *Die Konstruktion von Realität in den Nachrichtenmedien: Analyse der aktuellen Berichterstattung.* Freiburg: Alber.

Snow, David A., and Robert D. Benford. 1992. "Master Frames and Cycles of Protest." In Aldon D. Morris and Carol McClurg Mueller, eds., *Frontiers in Social Movement Theory,* 133–55. New Haven: Yale University Press.

Snow, David A., E. Burke Rochford Jr., Steven K. Worden, and Robert D. Benford. 1986. "Frame Alignment Processes, Micromobilization, and Movement Participation." *American Sociological Review* 51: 464–81.

Tilly, Charles. 1995. *Popular Contention in Great Britain, 1758–1834.* Cambridge: Harvard University Press.

Wisler, Dominique, and Marco Giugni. 1999. "Under the Spotlight: The Impact of Media Attention on Protest Policing." *Mobilization* 4, no. 2: 203–22.

# 8

# On the Quantification of Horror: Notes from the Field

*Patrick Ball*

During the conflict between NATO and Yugoslavia between March and June of 1999, the parties offered sharply differing explanations for the ethnic Albanians' migration out of Kosovo. NATO spokespeople claimed that Serb forces were committing ethnic cleansing, including, in a chilling echo of Srebrenica, the claim that a hundred thousand Kosovar Albanian men were missing. The Yugoslav Ministry of Information responded that the Kosovars' mass exodus was motivated by their attempts to avoid the NATO bombing campaign.

Contending political claims sometimes turn on arguments about who committed what (and how much) political violence against whom. For example, the NATO and Yugoslav explanations are so different, that if data had been available, it would have been possible to conduct what Arthur Stinchcomb called a "critical test" (Stinchcombe 1968). Adequate data would have shown migration flows consistent with either the bombing motivation argument or the ethnic cleansing argument.[1] Many human rights arguments require scientifically defensible data analysis.

The data needed for human rights work are similar to what students of contentious politics call frequency measures of events data (Schrodt 1994; Olzak 1989; Franzosi 2000). This essay discusses how similar analysis is done for human rights documentation projects. For this essay, the unit of analysis is a political killing. Which killings are "political" is debated in different projects, but in all human rights data projects, the objective is to create massive, undeniable, and intersubjectively reliable documentation of some human rights atrocity. The broader purpose of these projects is to advance a political goal, such as the establishment of historical memory, the clarification of institutional responsibility for the violations, or, in rare cases, the prosecution of individual perpetrators.

Human rights arguments face intense adversarial criticism. Quantitative analysis in the service of such arguments must use data that are valid as well as estimates that are measurably reliable and precise. By validity, I mean that that data truly represent the social phenomenon of interest. Reliability refers to the measuring process: reliable measurement is one that yields the same value regardless of who does the measuring, usually defined as measurable intersubjective agreement among data coders. Precision describes how close the estimate comes to the true population parameter.

In this essay, event counts based on the coding of thirteen Guatemalan newspapers from 1960 to 1996 are compared to counts of the same kinds of events coded from approximately twenty thousand interviews done in three separate human rights projects. The quantitative press data turn out to be sparse and wildly different from the interview and documentary data. Using a technique called "capture-tag-recapture," techniques for controlling bias and estimating magnitude are illustrated using the interview data, providing a further critique of the raw event counts from press sources. The essay concludes by arguing that in most studies of severe state violence, press sources are likely to be weak at best, and in some cases, press sources may negatively correlate with actual patterns of violence. Other sources—especially contemporaneous reporting by human rights organizations—are suggested as more adequate measures of state violence.

## Note about Terms

The academic literature on events coding uses the term "event" for the unit of action being coded. In human rights, the unit of analysis is the *violation*. There are various types of violations, and each is defined by its core content, boundary conditions distinguishing it from other violation types, counting rules, and examples.

Violations have victims and perpetrators, both of which may be individuals or institutions. A particular victim (or perpetrator) may be a victim or a perpetrator in another violation. *Events* are broad constructs that link conceptually related sets of violations. Some projects consider violations that occur in the same time and place as a single event, whereas other projects have more complicated definitions of events. There have been several efforts to articulate the data structure that adequately represents the components of human rights violations (Ball et al. 1994, 1996; Dueck, Guzman, and Verstappen 2001). To confuse this a bit, the "violation" is similar to what

Franzosi (2000, 6) calls an event. What is common between Franzosi's formulation and the human rights usage is the sense of a consistently scaled, countable unit defined by "who did what to whom." This unit is usually the core of a densely multidimensional recursive structure represented in an object-oriented or relational database.

In this essay, *events* will refer to the academic literature on events coding. I will use *violations* to describe units of interest in human rights that can be subject to quantitative analysis.

## Events Data and Social Reality

Event coding begins with a record, that is, some body of documentation that can be converted into units of common scale and attributes. For example, a run of a newspaper between two dates could be read so that all the political killings described therein could be enumerated according to the victims' names, ages, sexes, time and place of death, and so on. The enumeration is called "data coding," and the process and its pitfalls have been thoroughly examined (Schrodt 1994; Olzak 1989).

How a killing comes to appear in a newspaper has received relatively less quantitative attention, with exceptions (Tilly, Tilly, and Tilly 1975). Debates about which newspapers provide less biased measures rarely address whether or not it is possible at all for newspapers to provide quantitatively valid measures of political violence. Instead, newspapers are often recommended as providing broad coverage across type of event, time, and space. (Olzak 1989, see also Tilly, Tilly, and Tilly 1975). Some analysts go further, arguing that local newspapers are "superior to regional and global ones in terms of the extent of coverage and richness of detail on protest" (Aditjondro, Kowalewski, and Peterson 2000, 121). These claims notwithstanding, when media event counts are compared to "authoritative" baseline indices, the media counts inevitably turn out to exclude many (if not most) of the events.

Scholars who use event data note that newspaper information is "censored," by which they mean that not all events are reported. In some contexts, the claim is made that all "important" events are reported. The proportion of all events that are reported may be as small as "a few percent" (Schrodt 1994) or as much as one-third (Woolley 2000). Despite the low proportion of coverage, the reported events are used as valid measures. This may be because, for some kinds of public events, although few events are reported, most of the large events probably are (Rucht and Neidhardt 1998). This opens the question about the stability of an "event" as a unit of analysis when it varies so widely in scale (McPhail and Schweingruber 1998).

But censoring may be a more serious problem than has been understood. The proportion of all violations $N$ reported in the record $n$ is denoted $C = \frac{n}{N}$ and is called the coverage rate. If $C$ varies as a function of the underlying social conditions related to what is being measured, then the quantity of violations reported in the record $n$ may reflect changes in the reporting process more directly than changes in the social phenomenon being studied (Poe et al. 2000). Reported violations are measured directly, but the population total and coverage rate are unknown.[2] Note that $N = \frac{n}{C}$ and so conjectures about $N$ are related to $C$, as well as to $n$. If the data had been collected by a probability sample, $C$ would be the sampling probabilities.

Unlike sample surveys, most human rights data are collected via convenience or judgment samples. The sampling probabilities are therefore unknown, but many analysts assume that $C$ is constant with respect to the strata of interest. Typically, this assumption is untested, but without knowing how $C$ varies, data analysis based on $n$ can be misleading. In the context of political violence, the most obvious example is to take censoring at its synonym: when political repression increases, the number of political killings may rise. But if the state simultaneously increases pressure on media not to report bad news embarrassing to the regime, the number of *reported* political killings may fall as *real* political killings increase.

For example, in Guatemala some critics linked to the state claimed that the various large-scale human rights data projects had focused intensively on gathering evidence about violations committed by the state, but that the human rights projects had paid relatively little attention to violations allegedly committed by guerrilla forces; that is, investigators tracked down every witness whom they thought might have something to say about state violations, but they ignored witnesses who might have given evidence about guerrilla atrocities. Essentially the claim is that $C_{state} > C_{guerilla}$, and consequently the observation that $n_{state} > n_{guerilla}$ does not necessarily mean that $N_{state} > N_{guerilla}$.[3] When nonquantitative critics allege that a human rights project is biased, this is often what they mean.

If an analyst has only one source, this pattern may be difficult to detect. With multiple sources of the same type, such as data collected from multiple newspapers covering the same region over the same period, there are ways to detect changes in the coverage rate $C$. Multiple sources enable the analyst to describe changes in the relationship between what happens and what is reported. Tilly, Tilly, and Tilly (1975, 315) note that large events documented in newspapers also always appear in supplementary sources, while smaller events more frequently are omitted from the newspapers or the secondary sources. From this they conclude that their data are biased in favor of larger events. An analogous conclusion would be that the coverage rate for larger events is higher than for smaller events.

Looking simultaneously at multiple sources, violations may be reported in zero, one, or more newspapers. Violations reported zero times are censored, and violations reported only once are the simple case. But a violation may be reported in several or all of the newspapers being coded. The number of newspapers in which a violation is reported is the violation's reporting density, denoted $d$. Statisticians have noted that reporting density $d$ tends to be correlated with coverage rate $C$; that is, strata in which violations have a higher mean reporting density probably have a higher proportion of violations appearing in the record (as opposed to violations that are undocumented).

Without controlling for variation in $C$, analysis based on $n$ is vulnerable to criticism on the grounds that unmeasured changes in $C$ are biasing $n$ with respect to $N$. An example of a problem of this kind is presented later. I argue that, like all sources, press sources are incomplete (i.e., $C < 1$). But the extent of press sources' "incompleteness" varies drastically according to social conditions. Unfortunately for analysts, some of the social conditions that influence the level of press sources' completeness are the very conditions analysts hope to measure.

There is a way around the completeness problem. By looking at how much multiple press sources report the same events, inferences can be drawn about changing levels of completeness; that is, observations about $d$ give information about $C$. Under certain circumstances, information about $d$ can enable estimation of $N$.[4] With sufficient information, these estimates can be made for several strata simultaneously (e.g., by period or across regions).

## Detecting Shifting Bias

The coverage rate $C$ may vary across the same strata that the analyst wants to compare. As suggested earlier, the coverage of political killings in the newspaper may decline just when political violence escalates. Looking exclusively at newspaper data, two clues that coverage rates may be changing are *(a)* implausible relationships between the quantity of media coverage and the content of qualitative reporting, and *(b)* changes in the mean reporting density. Examples of both are presented here.

In Guatemala, political violence increased substantially during the late 1970s under the government of General Romeo Lucas García, and the army's terror became literally genocidal under the regime of General Efraín Ríos Montt. Qualitative reports by social movement activists and human rights observers indicated that there were many killings and disappearances, from thousands in the late 1970s to tens of thousands in the early 1980s (Americas Watch 1982, 1983; CDHG 1982), but press reports did not reflect the increasing violence. A small Guatemalan human rights NGO (the International Center for Human Rights Research, CIIDH) coded thirteen newspapers' reports of political violence for the years 1960–96 (Ball, Kobrak, and Spirer 1999). The CIIDH database shows that the annual number of killings documented in the Guatemalan press during the period 1973 to 1987 varied between less than a dozen to a few hundred.

Figure 8.1 shows the number of press reports by year covering rural and urban areas. Urban killings vary from a minimum of four in 1978 to a maximum of 296 in 1983. The relatively high years (1979, 1980, 1983) correspond roughly to anecdotal reports of periods of extraordinary violence. Urban killings vary from one report in 1978 to 181 reports in 1973. The years during which anecdotal reports of rural massacres number in the hundreds (1979 through 1982) there are five to thirty-one deaths reported in the newspapers annually, with no reports at all in 1980.

The press finding is so inconsistent with other sources of information about Guatemala that it cannot be taken as valid. But even in the absence of alternative sources, looking at the newspaper data alone there are hints that the coverage may have fundamentally changed around 1979. Returning to the CIIDH database (see Figure 8.2), the overall annual mean reporting

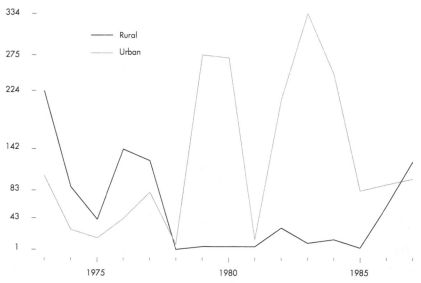

*Figure 8.1. Number of press reports of political killings, by region*

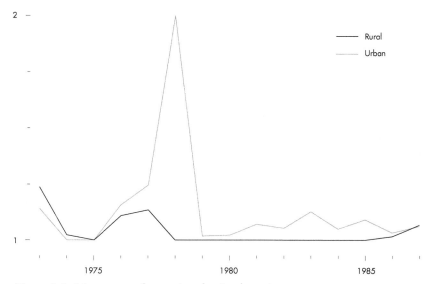

*Figure 8.2. Mean annual reporting density, by region*

density of violations *d* is usually near one, with a small number of high-profile violations being reported more frequently. However, in 1978 the few urban cases reported are all reported twice. Rural cases—when reported at all—were reported only once.

The difference in the pattern of reporting density of over time compared for rural and urban political killings signals that how political killings came to be reported was different in rural and urban areas. The observation that the reporting density of rural violations during the worst period of violence equaled one implies that the newspapers covered only a very small fraction of violence in that area. Higher coverage rates are usually associated with higher reporting density. Conversely, finding reporting density $d = 1$ suggests a very low coverage rate, *C*. With additional types of sources, the validity of newspaper reports can be more thoroughly evaluated.

### Comparing Patterns across Source Types

Human rights organizations gather most of their information through interviews with witnesses of human rights violations. In the CIIDH database, there are three types of sources of information about human rights violations: newspapers (described earlier), documentary materials coded from other human rights groups' published reports, and original interviews conducted by the CIIDH.[5] All the data were matched internally, that is,

multiple reports of the same violations were linked. The matching information was preserved so that the analysis can be done on the dataset as a whole
or on parallel subsets.

The purpose of comparisons among multiple types of sources is to
consider whether the patterns and tendencies evident in one source type are
consistent with those in other sources (McCarthy et al. 1998). Figure 8.3
shows the number of political killings reported in each of the three sources:
newspaper reports, documentary materials, and interviews. Whereas the
number of violations reported in the documentary and interview accounts
increases into the tens of thousands in 1980–82 (indicated by the cutoff
peaks in those series for those years), press reports suggest annual counts
varying between zero and three hundred. Between the documentary and
interview series, on the one hand, and the press series, on the other, there
is little relationship. The press series reflects neither the same annual variation nor the scale of the documentary and interview series, though the press
reports document more violations than other sources before and after the
massive killings in the early 1980s.

The estimated coverage rate $\hat{C}$ in the press data on political killings for
Guatemala in the early 1980s is on the order of 0.01, and so therefore can-

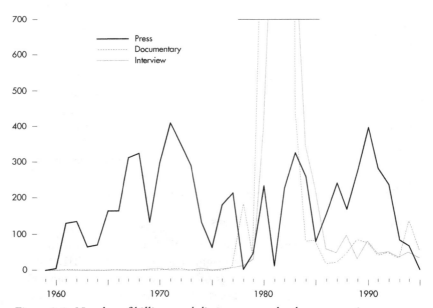

*Figure 8.3. Number of killings and disappearances by three sources in
Guatemala, by year*

not be relied on for estimates of magnitude.[6] The press series' variation over time during this period also seems implausible given the comparison with the interview and documentary data. Looking at the regional concentration of killings reported in the press compared to killings reported in the other sources, another major difference emerges. In Figure 8.4, the proportion of all killings occurring in rural areas is compared between press and other sources.

Whereas nonpress sources see three-quarters or more of all reported killings occurring in rural areas, from 1978 to 1985, press sources report almost no rural killings during the same period. The Guatemalan Commission for Historical Clarification found that during the same period massive acts of genocide were committed in four rural areas from 1981 to 1983. As shown in Figure 8.3, this violence went unreported in the popular media. This may be why some event-based indices rated Central American countries as "freer" than these statistics imply (Brockett 1992).

With multiple, independent enumerations of the events in question, and with approximate estimate coverage rates of 0.36, it is possible to estimate $N$ directly. Such estimates avoid the problems described here.

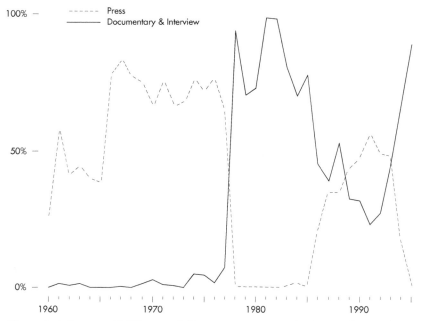

*Figure 8.4. Percent of killings and disappearances occurring in rural areas, by year and source*

## Capture-Recapture Techniques

While originally developed to estimate wildlife populations, capture-recapture (sometimes called capture-tag-recapture [CTR]) techniques have been adapted by demographic, public health, and human rights researchers for a variety of projects. Among other things, capture-recapture techniques have been used to estimate the prevalence of drug use (Doscher and Woodward 1983; Mastro et al. 1994), HIV infection (Drucker and Vermund 1989; Perucci et al. 1992), and prostitution (McKeganey et al. 1994). This technique has also been used extensively to evaluate the level of undercount in the decennial census of the United States (Cowan and Malec 1986). In the area of human rights, capture-recapture techniques have been applied to analyze the number of killings during violence in Guatemala between 1960 and 1996 (Ball 2000a), and in Kosovo for the period March to June 1999 (American Bar Association and American Association for the Advancement of Science 2000).

Underlying capture-recapture techniques is basic probability theory. If $A$ and $B$ are two independent events, then the probability of the two events jointly occurring is equal to the probability of $A$ occurring times the probability of $B$ occurring.

$$p(AB) = p(A) \cdot p(B) \text{ where } p(A) = \frac{A}{N}$$

$A$ and $B$ jointly contain a known number of violations $M$, and so

$$p(AB) = p(M) = \frac{M}{N} = \frac{A}{N} \cdot \frac{B}{N} \text{ and thus } \hat{N} = \frac{AB}{M}$$

Thus, in the two-system notation, $n_{11}$ is the number of violations documented by both sources; $n_{10}$ is the number of violations in system $A$ but not in $B$; and $n_{01}$ is the number of violations in $B$ but not in $A$. Therefore,

$$\hat{N} = n_{11} + n_{10} + \hat{n}_{00} \text{ where } \frac{n_{10} \cdot n_{01}}{n_{11}}$$

This solution generalizes to three systems (Marks, Seltzer, and Krotki 1974) and to $n$-systems (Bishop, Fienberg, and Holland 1975). Returning to event count applications, $A$ and $B$ might be two records that cover a similar set of events. To make an estimate of $\hat{N}$ in a given stratum, the coverage of $A$ and $B$ must be homogeneous within the stratum, which means that the estimate of $\hat{N}$ must be made by stratum. There are several assumptions that must be tested, and sources of potential bias that must be evaluated; these have been described in detail elsewhere (Cowan and Malec 1986; Hook and Regal

1993). Similarly there are a variety of variance estimators (Bishop, Fienberg, and Holland 1975; Marks, Seltzer, and Krotki 1974).

## Using CTR in Human Rights Arguments

Many of the problems with press data stem from its sparseness—with $C \approx 0.01$, variation in $N$ is only accidentally reflected in $n$. Most authors note that in the low range of $C$, more data are better: by increasing $C$, $n$ becomes a better approximation of $N$. But even with a larger $C$, how much better is the approximation? Getting more data by adding sources (and types of sources) may improve coverage sufficiently to permit a CTR estimate of N. The $\hat{N}$ is an unbiased estimate of magnitude. By estimating $\hat{N}$ for each stratum (e.g., for the state and the guerrilla), unbiased comparisons can be made. In an adversarial human rights context, it can be more important to examine the structure of the bias than to make unbiased estimates. Part of the CTR method disaggregates the data into project-specific components ($n_{111}$, $n_{110}$, etc.). Comparing these components shows how some projects may have focused coverage in some strata at the expense of other strata. The Commission for Historical Clarification (CEH) was concerned that its statistical findings be transparently unbiased, and CTR provided a means to this goal.

The CEH was established to "clarify with objectivity, equity, and impartiality the human rights violations and acts of violence connected with the armed confrontation that caused suffering among the Guatemalan people. The Commission was established . . . to clarify the history of the events of more than three decades of fratricidal conflict" (Commission for Historical Clarification 1999, 11). Two aspects of this mandate require population-level estimates. First, the analysis must be evenhanded with respect to the institutions that committed political violence: $C_{state}$ must approximate $C_{guerilla}$. Second, if the magnitude of the killing were high enough, the CEH might make the claim that genocide had been committed. Under international law, genocide cannot be amnestied (though Guatemala has amnestied its military officers and troops many times), and many countries claim universal jurisdiction over crimes against humanity. A genocide finding could open the door to the prosecution of some senior Guatemalan military officials anywhere in the world.

CTR provides the capability to control bias and to estimate total magnitude. At the CEH, three systems were used for the CTR estimate, each of which attempted to enumerate the complete universe of victims of gross human rights violations in Guatemala.[8] First, the CIIDH project, described earlier, contributed its interview material to this estimation (the direct interviews contained about one-quarter of the total CIIDH data). Second, the project for the recuperation of historical memory of the Catholic church (REMHI) contributed material. Third, the CEH used its own list developed from more than seven thousand interviews.

Random samples of approximately fifteen hundred were drawn from each list and matched to the other two lists. Multiple coders did sections of each sample and their results were compared to assure high levels of inter-rater reliability. The samples were stratified by region because not all projects covered all the regions equally. In each sample, a certain number of records matched neither, one, or both of the other two lists. By merging and averaging the matched samples, rates of overlap for each list were determined. The list counts were estimated from the rates, denoted $n_{111}$ for the count of killings in all three lists, $n_{110}$ for the count of killings in the first and second lists, $n_{100}$ for the count of killings in the first list, and so on. The sum of these seven components is $n_k$, and its standard error (computed by jackknifing the original samples) is the result of the sampling. Using methods described in Marks, Seltzer, and Krotki (1974), the violations omitted from the three $\hat{n}_{000}$ were estimated from the components; $\hat{N}$ is the sum of $\hat{n}_{000}$ and the list overlap counts. These estimates are presented by region in Figure 8.5.

In Figure 8.5, the effect of controlling for varying coverage becomes clear. Taking $\hat{C} = \frac{n_k}{\hat{N}}$ for the most regions $\hat{C} \approx 0.3$. For Regions II and IX, however, $\hat{C}$ is closer to 0.5, and for Region X, 0.16. Relative to $n$, the analysis done on $\hat{N}$ does not change in its fundamentals: Regions 0 and I are the big ones, followed by III, IX, VI, and V. Some of the relative spacings change a little: for example, VI and IX seem farther apart in $n_k$ than in $\hat{N}$. Among the smaller regions, there is more change, with X becoming greater than VII and II in $\hat{N}$. Given the large coefficient of variation in Region X, this may be an artifact. With $\hat{C} \approx 0.36$, there are fewer hidden biases in the combined interview data than there were in the newspaper data.

Another approach to testing that coverage is equitable among strata is to compare the proportion of the number overlapping cases relative to all cases:

$$r = \frac{n_{111} + n_{110} + n_{011}}{\hat{N}}$$

The idea here is that $r$ will vary directly with $C$. The values of $r_{state}$ and $r_{guerilla}$ (and their standard errors) are shown in Figure 8.6. The values are not significantly different at the 0.05 level. Note that the projects individually may have been biased—the CIIDH, for example, explicitly notes that

| Estimate | 0 | I | II | III | IV | V | VI | VII | VIII | IX | X | Total |
|---|---|---|---|---|---|---|---|---|---|---|---|---|
| $n_{111}$ | 67 | 141 | 15 | 146 | 0 | 0 | 17 | 2 | 0 | 2 | 2 | 391 |
| $n_{110}$ | 378 | 406 | 8 | 98 | 5 | 0 | 67 | 3 | 0 | 16 | 2 | 983 |
| $n_{101}$ | 1,358 | 1,010 | 204 | 170 | 13 | 206 | 336 | 24 | 43 | 681 | 13 | 4,059 |
| $n_{011}$ | 133 | 419 | 16 | 122 | 0 | 0 | 0 | 0 | 0 | 0 | 0 | 690 |
| $n_{100}$ | 8,260 | 3,187 | 221 | 1,028 | 1,325 | 1,597 | 1,642 | 226 | 156 | 1,720 | 182 | 19,545 |
| $n_{010}$ | 2,256 | 2,708 | 85 | 836 | 16 | 1 | 195 | 15 | 41 | 30 | 91 | 6,274 |
| $n_{001}$ | 5,228 | 3,999 | 295 | 926 | 59 | 765 | 1,166 | 77 | 1,099 | 2,054 | 106 | 15,773 |
| $n_k$ | 17,696 | 11,870 | 844 | 3,328 | 1,418 | 2,569 | 3,416 | 347 | 1,339 | 4,501 | 396 | 47,706 |
| $SE(n_k)$ | 110 | 135 | 24 | 79 | 11 | 44 | 76 | 9 | 26 | 77 | 5 | 228 |
| $\hat{n}_{000}$ | 38,856 | 17,397 | 466 | 6,467 | 0 | 5,548 | 5,836 | 561 | 2,265 | 5,052 | 2,019 | 84,468 |
| $SE(\hat{n}_{nn})$ | 3,809 | 2,045 | 105 | 1,152 | 0 | 1,826 | 1,890 | 350 | 3,062 | 995 | 1,840 | 6,388 |
| $\hat{N}$ | 56,535 | 29,267 | 1,310 | 9,795 | 1,418 | 8,117 | 9,252 | 908 | 3,604 | 9,553 | 2,415 | 132,174 |
| $SE(\hat{N})$ | 3,918 | 2,175 | 127 | 1,218 | 11 | 1,870 | 1,964 | 357 | 3,087 | 1,072 | 1,844 | 6,568 |

Figure 8.5. Estimated number of killings for three projects, by region

its project covers *state* terror, and not violence committed by the guerrillas of URNG (Guatemalan National Revolutionary Unity). The proportion of killings with known perpetrators attributed to the state varied from 94.3 percent (REMHI) to 98.2 percent (CIIDH). The overall CTR estimate is 95.4 percent (Commission for Historical Clarification 1999, vol. 12, 262, nn. 23–25). Together, the projects produce unbiased estimates of the relative proportions of responsibility between the perpetrators.

With estimates that are reasonably free of bias by region and perpetrator, analysis can be disaggregated further to compare ethnicities in Regions I–VI during the period 1981–83. This analysis includes only those killings committed by the state. Estimates of total deaths by ethnicity were converted to population rates using the 1981 census, and the results are presented in Figure 8.7. The enormous difference in the killing rates between indigenous and nonindigenous victims—in most regions a factor of eight—is not by itself proof that perpetrators targeted indigenous communities and avoided non-indigenous communities. However, this finding is consistent with the argument that state forces committed acts of genocide. Along with documentary evidence, findings from forensic exhumations, subjective narratives, and other materials, the CEH finding on genocide was based on the magnitude and ethnic differences in killing rates in Regions I, III, IV, and VI.

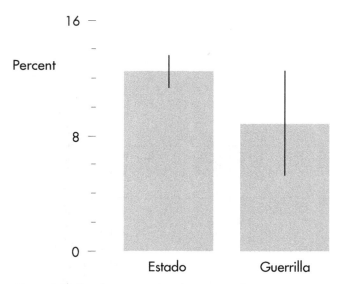

*Figure 8.6. Overlap proportion, by perpetrating party*

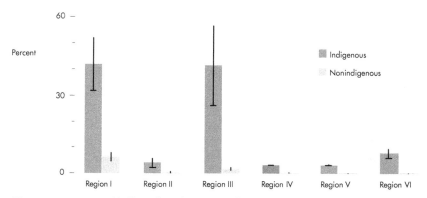

*Figure 8.7. Rates of killing, by ethnicity and region*

## Conclusion

Human rights arguments require methods and data that can withstand adversarial criticism by nonquantitative critics—few of whom are social scientists. Quantitative claims need to be based on analysis that controls the biases that are certain to be present in the data. The methods must explore the structure of the bias in order to make transparent the process of control.

The issues with human rights data are similar to those described by scholars of contentious politics. I agree with the first conclusion of Tilly, Tilly, and Tilly 1975, 16): all data are censored. But they go on to conclude that a continuous run of a big newspaper is the best possible source for data of this kind. If the events occurred long in the past, few alternatives may exist. Furthermore, for events in which the actors are intentionally trying to gain public attention, such as protest, and strikes, or when the events are international and important to elites in contending countries, newspaper coverage may be a plausible source. In contrast, state violence often occurs in private, and the state itself may have a substantial interest in repressing coverage of its embarrassing atrocities. Whatever the reasons, the press clearly did not cover political violence in Guatemala very well. I suspect that media sources—local and global—are equally unrepresentative of the quantitative patterns and magnitude during other countries' periods of severe state terror.

Similar to Davenport's conference presentation, these results imply that newspapers must be understood as part of the society in which they are located. Indeed, my claim is stronger than Davenport's: while he links coverage to the development of the conflict cycle, I suggest that press coverage may be negatively correlated with state violence. Extreme state violence itself conditions what newspapers are able to do (journalists may stop covering conflict when they could be killed for doing so); censorship (self- or otherwise) limits the validity of quantitative patterns of reporting on violence derived from the news. The effect of the censorship spreads through the society, because media coverage in turn influences what media consumers understand about social processes. Guatemalan newspapers' inattentiveness certainly influenced what Guatemalan newspaper readers would have understood about state violence in the period 1980–83. Figure 8.1 shows that reported urban killings (with which the urban newspaper readers might have had personal experience) declined from the 1979–80 peak; rural killings, meanwhile, had been absent from the Guatemalan press since the mid-1970s. When human rights organizations began to report massive, literally genocidal killings of Mayan people in the early 1980s, the newspaper-reading urban elites simply refused to believe them. Someone who used press sources to analyze political violence would encode as scholarship this metropolitan naïveté about the periphery.

Claims about state violence are necessarily controversial because the accused have strong interests in denying the claim. Such claims may be more a part of contentious politics than a part of the study of contentious politics, and sociologists and political scientists sometimes argue that newspapers are in some way more objective than are social movement organizations. This essay makes the opposite claim. The anecdotal work done by activist human rights groups turns out to be far more representative of quantitative trends than newspaper reporting, at least in Guatemala. Informally, from my experience, I would add, El Salvador, Haiti, South Africa, Sierra Leone, and Kosovo to places where domestic and international media coverage is uncorrelated with the quantity of political violence. This is likely to be truer when examining events that are more usually private than public. One implication of these observations is that, under some circumstances, scholars should treat activists' documentation as a more adequate representation of quantitative reality than the press.

Future research in this area might compare the various indices and Likert-like scales and global press event counts to activists' documentation. I hypothesize that the global press would show the same lack of variance and insensitivity to scale as the local press in Guatemala. Further, I believe that even when they are prima facie plausible when compared to anecdotal reporting, ordinal index measures will evidence so much compression (i.e., so little variance) at the top end of the scales that they are not particularly useful for a study of terror. However, such indices may still be useful for comparisons among many countries, most of which are not suffering state terror.

Grassroots human rights activists monitor and document human rights violations on a permanent, continuous basis. Their work is published and available as a rich source of data for going beyond ordinal scales to estimating total numbers of events. Many such groups crave scientific assistance in managing their data and making defensible quantitative claims. This is a massive, valid data source awaiting academic attention, but scholars who want to undertake such work will need to be willing to build long-term partnerships with the social movement organizations collecting raw information.

## Notes

I want to thank Matt Zimmerman for help with the design of the graphs, and Michelle Dukich for secretarial and document layout assistance.

1. The data are consistent with the ethnic cleansing argument, but inconsistent with the other claims; see Ball 2000, 6. These data were presented as evidence in the trial of Slobodan Milovsevic at the International Criminal Tribunal for Former Yugoslavia. See http://hrdata.aaas.org/kosovo/icty_report.pdf for a full discussion.

2. So-called authoritative sources to which media counts can be compared are, of course, simply alternative records subject to censoring. Some events will be excluded from all records, even from relatively complete records.

3. See Figure 8.6, which considers the relationship between coverage rate of documented violations versus the inferred violation frequencies for the case of Guatemala, 1980–96.

4. Schrodt (1994) notes that this can be done, but he does not provide examples. He asserts that the sources must be randomly selected, which is not strictly correct. In the statistical literature, this problem is known as "heterogeneous catchability" (Hook and Regal 1993). By isolating heterogeneous coverage rates in district strata, and by using data that attempt the complete enumeration of some portion of the universe, "list" data are adequate for estimation.

5. For a full discussion of this project, see Ball, Kobrak, and Spirer 1999, Part I. The data are available at http://hrdata.aaas.org/ciidh/data.html.

6. See Commission for Historical Clarification (1999) to compute this estimate. On p. 84, note numbers of disappearances and executions documented by the commission $(n)$ by year and compare to the total estimate $(N)$ on p. 17, paragraph 2.

7. See Ball (2000a) for a complete discussion in English. See also Commission for Historical Clarification (1999, vol. 12).

## Works Cited

Aditjondro, G., D. Kowalewski, and S. Peterson. 2000. "Protest Targeting and Repression: Campaigns against Water Projects in Indonesia. In C. Davenport, ed., *Paths to State Repression*. Oxford, UK: Rowman and Littlefield.

American Bar Association and American Association for the Advancement of Science. 2000. *Political Killings in Kosova/Kosovo, March–June 1999*. American Bar Association.

Americas Watch. 1982. *Human Rights in Guatemala: No Neutrals Allowed*. New York: Americas Watch.

———. 1983. *Creating a Desolation and Calling It Peace*. New York: Americas Watch.

Amnesty International. 1980. *Los derechos humanos en Guatemala*. London: Amnesty International.

———. 1981. *Guatemala: A Government Program of Political Murder*. London: Amnesty International.

———. 1982. *Guatemala: Massive Extrajudicial Executions in Rural Areas under the Goverment of Efraín Ríos Montt*. London: Amnesty International.

Ball, P. 1996. *Who Did What to Whom?: Planning and Implementing a Large-Scale Human Rights Data Project*. Washington, DC: American Association for the Advancement of Science.

———. 2000a. "The Guatemalan Commission for Historical Clarification: Generating Analytic Reports." In P. Ball, H. Spirer, and L. Spirer, eds., *Making the Case: Investigating Large-Scale Human Rights Violations Using Information Systems and Data Analysis,* chapter 11, 259–83. Washington, DC: American Association for the Advancement of Science.

———. 2000b. *Policy or Panic: The Flight of Ethnic Albanians from Kosovo, March–May 1999*. Washington, DC: American Association for the Advancement of Science. Online at http://shr.aaas.org/kosovo/policyorpanic/toc.html (May 9, 2004).

Ball, P., R. Cifuentes, J. Dueck, R. Gregory, D. Salcedo, and C. Saldarriaga. 1994. *A Definition of Database Design Standards for Human Rights Agencies*. Technical report. Washington, DC: American Association for the Advancement of Science.

Ball, P., P. Kobrak, and H. Spirer. 1999. *State Violence in Guatemala, 1960–1996: A Quantitative Reflection*. Washington, DC: American Association for the Advancement of Science.

Bishop, Y., S. Fienberg, and P. Holland. 1975. *Discrete Multivariate Analysis: Theory and Practice*. Cambridge: MIT Press.

Brockett, C. 1992. "Measuring Political Violence and Land Inequality in Central America." *American Political Science Review* 86, no. 1: 169–76.

CDHG. 1982. *Cien días de masacre, genocidio y terror en Guatemala (Carta a Ríos Montt)*. Mexico City: Comisión de Derechos Humanos de Guatemala.

Commission for Historical Clarification. 1999. *Guatemala: Memoria del Silencio*. Guatemala City: United Nations Office of Project Services.

Cowan, C., and D. Malec. 1986. "Capture-Recapture Models when Both Sources Have Clustered Observations." *Journal of the American Statistical Association* 81, no. 394, 461–66.

Doscher, M., and J. Woodward. 1983. "Estimating the Size of Subpopulations of Heroin Users: Applications of Log-Linear Models to Capture-Recapture Sampling." *International Journal of Addiction* 18: 167–82.

Drucker, E., and S. Vermund. 1989. "Estimating Population Prevalence of HIV Infection in Urban Areas with High Rates of Intravenous Drug Use." *American Journal of Epidemiology* 130, no. 1: 131–42.

Dueck, J., M. Guzman, and B. Verstappen. 2001. *HURIDOCS Events Standard Formats*. 2d ed. Versoix, Switzerland: HURIDOCS Advice and Support Unit.

Franzosi, R. 2000. "From Words to Numbers." Unpublished manuscript.

Hook, E., and R. Regal. 1993. "Effect of Variation in Probability of Ascertainment by Sources (Variable Catchability) upon 'Capture-Recapture' Estimates of Prevalence." *American Journal of Epidemiology* 137: 1148–66.

Marks, E., W. Seltzer, and K. Krotki. 1974. *Population Growth Estimation: A Handbook of Vital Statistics Measurement*. New York: Population Council.

Mastro, T., D. Kitayaporn, B. Weniger, S. Vanichseni, V. Laosunthorn, T. Uneklabh, C. Uneklabh, K. Choopanya, and K. Limpakarnjanarat. 1994. "Estimating the Number of HIV-Infected Injection Drug Users in Bangkok: A Capture-Recapture Method." *American Journal of Public Health* 84, no. 7: 1094–99.

McCarthy, J., C. McPhail, J. Smith, and L. Crishock. 1998. "Electronic and Print Media Representations of Washington, DC, Demonstrations, 1982 and 1991: A Demography of Description Bias." In D. Rucht, R. Koopmans, and F. Neidhardt, ed., *Acts of Dissent*. Berlin: Die Deutsche Bibliothek.

McKeganey, N., M. Bernard, A. Leyland, I. Coote, and E. Follet. 1994. "Female Streetworking Prostitution in Glasgow." *British Medical Journal* 308, no. 6920: 27–30.

McPhail, C. and D. Schweingruber. 1998. "Unpacking Protest Events: A Description Bias Analysis of Media Records with Systematic Direct Observations of Collective Action—the 1995 March for Life in Washington, DC." In D. Rucht, R. Koopmans, and F. Neidhardt, eds., *Acts of Dissent,* Berlin: Die–Deutsche Bibliothek.

Oficina de Derechos Humanos del Arzobispado de Guatemala. 1998. *Guatemala*

*Nunca Más: Informe Proyecto Interdiocesano de Recuperación de la Memoria Histórica.* Guatemala City: ODHAG.

Olzak, S. 1989. "Analysis of Events in the Study of Collective Action," *Annual Review of Sociology* 15: 119–41.

Perucci, C., F. Forastiere, E. Rapiti, M. Davoli, and D. Abeni. 1992. "The Impact of Intravenous Drug Users on Mortality of Young Adults in Rome, Italy." *British Journal of Addiction* 81, no. 12: 1637–41.

Poe, S. C., C. N. Tate, L. C. Keith, and D. Lanier. 2000. "Domestic Threats: The Abuse of Personal Integrity." In C. Davenport, ed., *Paths to State Repression.* Oxford, UK: Rowman and Littlefield.

Rucht, D., and F. Neidhardt. 1998. "Methodological Issues in Collection Protest Event Data: Units of Analysis, Sources, and Sampling, Coding Problems." In D. Rucht, R. Koopmans, and F. Neidhardt, eds., *Acts of Dissent.* Berlin: Die Deutsche Bibliothek.

Schrodt, P. A. 1994. "The Statistical Characteristics of Event Data." *International Interactions* 20, no. 1–2: 35–53.

Spirer, H. F., and L. Spirer. 2003. *Intermediate Data Analaysis for Human Rights.* Vol. in draft. Washington, DC: American Association for the Advancement of Science.

Stinchcomb, A. 1968. *Constructing Social Theories.* New York: Harcourt Brace & World.

Tilly, C., L. Tilly, and R. Tilly. 1975. *The Rebellious Century 1830–1930.* Cambridge: Harvard University Press.

Woolley, J. T. 2000. "Using Media-Based Data in Studies of Politics." *American Journal of Political Science* 44, vol. 1: 156–73.

# Part IV
# Reflections and Future Directions

# 9

# Repression, Mobilization, and Explanation

*Charles Tilly*

Political analysts can take at least three views of mutual relations between repression and mobilization:

1. that they are locally variable, irregular, or even incoherent, and therefore not amenable to systematic description and explanation
2. that, once we clear away conceptual and empirical debris, they conform to general laws
3. that they apply names to classes of episodes for which coherent explanations are possible—but not in the form of general laws at the levels of episodes or classes of episodes

Given the inconsistencies and contradictions among accounts of the repression–mobilization nexus offered in this volume, we might forgive readers for adopting prudent position 1. In his Introduction to this volume, Christian Davenport holds out a distant hope for position 2, but contends that debris clearing will meanwhile take an enormous effort. In this coda, let me give reasons for thinking that position 3 deserves serious attention. Visualized intelligently, I argue, violent interactions provide opportunities for identification of robust mechanisms and processes that explain variable aggregate relations between repression and mobilization.

My arguments extend and apply the Dynamics of Contention (DOC) program of theory and research in contentious politics (McAdam, Tarrow, and Tilly 2001). The DOC program calls for explanation across a wide range of contentious interactions by grouping them into episodes, decomposing those episodes into combinations of recognizable, recurrent processes, then identifying the invariant causal mechanisms that enter those processes. In reverse order, here are the relevant definitions:

*Mechanisms* are a delimited class of events that alter relations among specified sets of elements in identical or closely similar ways over a variety of situations. (We know a relevant event is occurring when a transfer of energy across a set of elements changes subsequent interactions between at least one pair of elements.) Within contentious politics, the elements in question are usually social sites: loci in which organized human action occurs. They include individuals, aspects of individuals, relations among individuals, organizations, networks, and places. The mechanism of boundary activation, for example, lends increasing salience to an us–them distinction that was previously orienting little political interaction.

*Processes* are regular sequences and combinations of such mechanisms that produce similar transformations of those elements. The process of identity formation, for instance, brings into public political life a combination of recognized boundary, social relations on each side of the boundary, and social relations across the boundary. (Because closer examination almost always reveals smaller-scale mechanisms within any particular mechanism, the distinction between mechanisms and processes always remains relative to the current scale of observation.)

*Episodes* are continuous streams of contention including collective claim making that bears on other parties' interests. Episodes of ethnic conflict, to mention an obvious case in point, involve organized claim making across well-defined us–them boundaries.

The DOC empirical program calls for meticulous snipping of streams of contention into episodes of comparable scope, followed by close comparison of those episodes for identification of their similarities and differences (Tilly 2002). It treats empirical regularities as objects of explanation, not as explanations in themselves. It does *not*, however, call for summing of whole classes of episodes (e.g., revolutions, strikes, ethnic conflicts, and social movements) in pursuit of their common properties. It aims at explaining change and variation, not at discovering uniformity.

The DOC explanatory program rests on the assumption that episodes and classes of episodes as such do not conform to general laws, but that small-scale causes within them do operate similarly across a wide range of episodes and political phenomena. The secret of explanation, in this view, lies in showing how robust mechanisms and processes combine under varying initial conditions to produce contrasting but coherent aggregate outcomes. Similar mechanisms and processes, goes the argument, appear at the small scale in revolutions, strikes, ethnic conflicts, social movements, and many other contentious episodes, but their varying combinations, sequences, and initial conditions cause dramatically different processes and outcomes at the large scale. Explanations of whole episodes therefore passes through five steps: (1) identification of the episodes' problematic and distinctive features; (2) comparison with other episodes for similarities and differences in those regards; (3) identification of processes that produce those problematic and distinctive features; (4) decomposition of those processes into component mechanisms; (5) development of account concerning how the relevant mechanisms combine, interact, and produce their aggregate effects given specified initial conditions.

## Collective Violence

DOC proposes to search out explanations for all sorts of contentious phenomena, but this brief introduction to the program focuses on *collective violence,* episodic social interaction that

- immediately inflicts physical damage on persons and/or objects ("damage" includes forcible seizure of persons or objects over restraint or resistance)
- involves at least two perpetrators of damage
- results at least in part from coordination among persons who perform the damaging acts

Collective violence, by such a definition, excludes purely individual action, nonmaterial damage, accidents, and long-term or indirect effects of such damaging processes as dumping of toxic waste. But it still includes a vast range of social interactions. I focus on collective violence here for strong reasons: because such a restriction focuses the discussion on phenomena having some claim to causal coherence, and because the bulk of the work on repression and mobilization cited in this volume actually deals with violent episodes.

Violent interaction often involves efforts of authorities to inhibit or suppress activity by potential or actual opponents (repression), often involves increases in collective direction of pooled resources to shared interests (mobilization), and often involves cause–effect relations in both directions: repression shaping mobilization, mobilization shaping repression. The study of collective violence therefore provides ample opportunity to clarify repression–mobilization connections.

Let us work with the taxonomy of violent episodes displayed in Figure 9.1. Call the horizontal dimension of the scheme *salience of short-run damage.* We look at interactions among the parties, asking to what extent

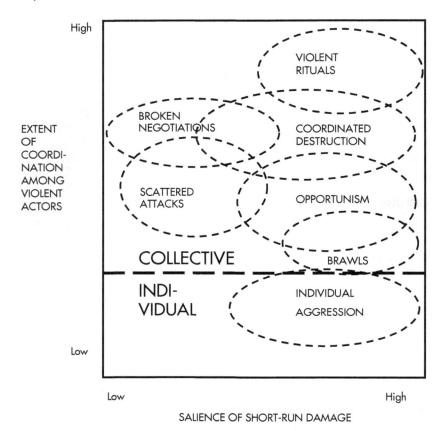

*Figure 9.1. A typology of interpersonal violence*

infliction and reception of damage dominate those interactions. At the Low extreme, damage occurs only intermittently or secondarily in the course of transactions that remain predominantly nonviolent. At the High extreme, almost every transaction inflicts damage, as the infliction and reception of damage dominate the interaction. Routine bureaucratic encounters that occasionally lead to fisticuffs stand toward the Low end of the range, lynching parties toward the High end.

The vertical dimension represents *extent of coordination among violent actors*. The definition of collective violence offered earlier incorporated a minimum position on this dimension: it insisted on at least two perpetrators of damage and some coordination among perpetrators. Below that threshold, we call violence individual. Nevertheless, collective coordination can run from no more than improvised signaling and/or common culture (Low) to involvement of centralized organizations whose leaders follow shared scripts as they deliberately guide followers into violence-generating interactions with others (High). At the Low end we find such events as scuffles between drunken sailors and military police, at the High end pitched battles between opposing armies.

Here is how the classification works: First, we locate a clump of violent episodes in the salience-coordination space—for example, in the upper-left-hand corner, where high coordination among violent actors and relatively low salience of damage doing in all interactions among the parties coincide. Then, we name the location for the most common kind of episode in that location. The upper-left-hand corner gets the name "broken negotiations" because of the frequency with which longer-term nonviolent bargaining processes that go awry result in low-salience, high-coordination collective violence. Proceeding in approximately clockwise order from the upper-right-hand corner, the types include the following:

- *violent ritual:* At least one relatively well-defined and coordinated group follows a known interaction script entailing the infliction of damage on itself or others as it competes for priority within a recognized arena; examples include shaming ceremonies, lynchings, public executions, gang rivalries, contact sports, some election battles, and some struggles among supporters of sporting teams or entertainment stars.
- *coordinated destruction:* Persons or organizations that specialize in the deployment of coercive means undertake a program of damage to persons and/or objects; examples include war, collective self-immolation, some kinds of terrorism, genocide, and politicide—the programmed annihilation of a political category's members.
- *opportunism:* As a consequence of shielding from routine surveillance and repression, individuals or clusters of individuals use immediately damaging means to pursue generally forbidden ends; examples include looting, gang rape, piracy, revenge killing, and some sorts of military pillage.
- *brawls:* Within a previously nonviolent gathering, two or more persons begin attacking each other or each other's property; examples include barroom free-for-alls, small-scale battles at sporting events, and many street fights.
- *individual aggression:* A single actor (or several unconnected actors) engage(s) in immediately and predominantly destructive interaction with another actor; examples include single-author rapes, assaults, robberies, and vandalism.
- *scattered attacks:* In the course of widespread small-scale and generally nonviolent interaction, a number of participants respond to obstacles,

challenges, or restraints by means of damaging acts; examples include sabotage, clandestine attacks on symbolic objects or places, assaults of governmental agents, and arson.

- *broken negotiations:* Various forms of collective action generate resistance or rivalry to which one or more parties respond by actions that damage persons and/or objects; examples include demonstrations, protection rackets, governmental repression, and military coups, all of which frequently occur with no more than threats of violence, but sometimes produce physical damage.

Figure 9.1 shows these types as overlapping ovals to emphasize that the concrete episodes involved necessarily have imprecise boundaries. Violent rituals such as sporting events, for example, sometimes convert into broken negotiations (ushers' attempts to expel rowdy spectators produce attacks on ushers and the stadium) or opportunism (spectators or players take private revenge on their enemies). But an even larger share of violent ritual overlaps with coordinated destruction—feuds, gang fights, and similar contests that look much like war except for their smaller scale and greater containment.

The typology names each segment of the coordination-salience space for the most common process that produces its particular combination of coordination and salience. Most often, for example, extremely high levels of coordination and salience result from activation of a familiar script by parties already specializing in doing damage with monitors who contain their interaction; *violent ritual* describes that sort of process. Now and then, however, two armies at war—and therefore engaged mainly in coordinated destruction—move into the zone of extremely high coordination and salience, stylizing and containing their interaction. The low-coordination but relatively high-salience territory near the individual-collective boundary receives the name *brawls* not because every interaction in the territory actually begins with a nonviolent gathering within which pairs of people begin to fight, but because such a sequence does regularly result in low-coordination, high-salience violence. The typology provides a handy reminder of on-the-average differences in dominant social processes occurring at different locations within the coordination-salience space.

DOC denies that each type of violence conforms to its own covering law, much less that all types of collective violence obey the same general covering law. The closest it comes to generalization at a large scale is in asserting that some clusters of mechanisms regularly raise or lower the level of coordination among violent actors, whereas other clusters of mechanisms regularly increase or decrease the salience of violence among all interactions.

Thus, across a wide range of circumstances, brokerage raises the level of coordination, while, across another wide range of circumstances, activation of organized specialists in coercion increases the salience of violent interactions. (Although not all mechanisms reverse neatly, in these two cases the dissolution of brokerage ties generally does lower the level of coordination and the departure of violent specialists usually does reduce the salience of violent interactions.)

Collective violence therefore presents an interesting, substantial challenge to the DOC program. As visualized here, that challenge has three components:

1. explaining change and variation among the major types of collective violence—for example, how and why scattered resistance sometimes turns into coordinated destruction or vice versa
2. demonstrating that similar clusters of mechanisms producing similar small-scale effects (despite widely varying aggregate outcomes) concentrate at each location within the two-dimensional space—for example, by showing that opportunism repeatedly results from the same array of mechanisms and processes, even though some opportunists achieve state power and others retreat into peaceful acquiescence
3. providing an inventory of the processes that most regularly cause changes in salience and in coordination, and thus deserve close examination for the individual mechanisms that concatenate into those processes

Although an attempt to meet the three challenges might proceed through close study of collective violence, it could also proceed fruitfully through a search for analogies elsewhere, identifying mechanisms and processes that reliably alter salience and coordination in nonviolent forms of contention in order to see whether they operate similarly within the realm of violent encounters.

## Scattered Attacks and Broken Negotiations

Let me illustrate the DOC response to these three challenges by closing in on a comparison of *scattered attacks* and *broken negotiations*. The two types of collective violence differ by definition with respect to levels of coordination. In both, the salience of violent interactions remains low; a large share of all interactions among the parties occur without interpersonal damage. But in broken negotiations relatively high levels of coordination among and within the major parties prevail; for example, governmental tax collection incites large gatherings in the course of which local leaders offer peaceful objections and threaten mass refusal to pay, but troops eventually break up the gatherings by shooting and beating members of crowds. Scattered attacks resemble broken negotiations, except that levels of coordination within and among the major actors remain significantly lower. Comparison of scattered attacks and broken negotiations therefore focuses attention on mechanisms that raise or lower levels of coordination among violent actors.

In both varieties of collective violence, repression and mobilization regularly interact. Both broken negotiations and scattered attacks quite commonly involve efforts of authorities to inhibit or suppress activity by dissidents (repression), almost always involve increases in collective direction of pooled resources to shared interests (mobilization), and normally involve cause–effect relations in both directions: repression shaping mobilization, mobilization shaping repression. But those interactions do not conform to covering laws; at the most general level, for example, repression sometimes flattens resistance, but sometimes magnifies it. How and why?

Much governmental repression does dampen collective claim making by raising the costs of claim making across the board or for particular actors: seizing the media, restricting public assembly, and intensifying surveillance generally reduce overall levels of claim making. But, under some circumstances, increased repression has the opposite effect, actually generating increased collective action (Bernstein and Lü 2002; Khawaja 1993; Lichbach 1987; Mason 1989; Mason and Krane 1989; Moore 1979; O'Brien 1996; Olivier 1991; Schneider 1995). Three processes seem to favor resistance rather than compliance: (1) hesitation, faltering, or visible division on the part of repressive authorities; (2) defensive intervention of powerful allies; and (3) direct attacks by repressive forces on persons, objects, and activities that sustain a population's collective survival. These processes increase the scope and intensity of scattered attacks.

The same processes—especially attacks on persons, objects, and activities that are crucial to collective survival—help produce self-sacrifice on the part of persons who under other circumstances act more egoistically. When valued others will clearly benefit from the sacrifice; when not to sacrifice would betray weakness, fear, or disloyalty; when visible suffering has a chance of attracting third-party intervention; and when inconspicuous exit is difficult, people become more willing to engage in risky, costly actions, including violent actions (Tilly 2001).

Some characteristics of the political setting affect the frequency of scattered attacks. Scattered attacks concentrate in undemocratic regimes. They do so because oppressed parties have fewer alternatives and potential allies than in democratic regimes. They also occur more frequently when regime capacity—the extent to which governmental agents control populations, activities, and resources within the government's territory—is changing rapidly, either increasing or decreasing. Rapid changes in capacity promote scattered attacks by shifting the threats and opportunities that bear on oppressed populations. Rapid capacity increases often threaten group survival, as governments start intruding on previous areas of protected autonomy; states that mobilize for war often meet just such resistance (Levi 1988, 1997). Rapid decreases in capacity signal the vulnerability of authorities to forms of resistance that previously would have been hopeless; defeated states often face that sort of resistance as their wars end (Bearman 1991; Lagrange 1989; Tilly 1992). Under some conditions, then, changes in governmental repressive capacity—up or down—raise the levels of violent mobilization.

More precisely, in particular combinations, mechanisms that occur widely elsewhere—otherwise combined and sequenced—play prominent parts in the generation of scattered attacks. They include the following:

- *network-based escalation:* Networks of mutual aid segregate on either side of a categorical boundary, and a dispute pits people on the two sides against each other for whatever reason; the dispute leads the opponents to seek support from their fellows, which redefines the dispute as categorical.
- *setting-based activation:* Political identities connect people with certain social settings and not with others; drawing them into those settings activates the identities.
- *signaling spirals:* These communicate the current feasibility and effectiveness of generally risky practices, and thereby alter the readiness of participants to face the risks in question.
- *polyvalent performance:* Individual or collective presentation of gestures simultaneously to two or more audiences in ways that code differently within the audiences induces simultaneous but different actions by the audiences.
- *selective retaliation:* Retaliation for previously experienced wrongs occurs in the course of mobilization.

All of these mechanisms facilitate action on a small scale without extensive top-down communication and planning. They build on locally available social structure rather than depending on the creation of new organizational connections. In scattered attacks, these mechanisms and processes combine into more complex processes that convert routine nonviolent contention into small-scale, segmented collective violence. Sometimes they also initiate shifts from scattered attacks into opportunism and coordinated destruction. But here we concentrate on what differentiates scattered attacks from broken negotiations, and what converts one into the other.

## How Negotiations Break

What of broken negotiations? Broken negotiations matter because a significant share of public violence occurs in the course of organized social processes that are not in themselves intrinsically violent. That is notably the case in collective political struggle. Political regimes differ dramatically in the scope they allow for nonviolent collective making of claims—for example, by petitioning, shaming, marching, voting, boycotting, striking, forming special-interest associations, and issuing public messages. On the whole, democratic regimes tolerate such claim making more readily than do undemocratic ones; that is one way we recognize a regime as democratic. Even in democratic regimes, nevertheless, such forms of collective claim making occasionally generate open violence. That occurs for three main reasons:

First, every regime empowers agents—police, troops, headmen, posses, sheriffs, and others—to monitor, contain, and on occasion repress collective claim making. Some of the agents are violent specialists, and most others have violent specialists under their command. Those agents always have some means of collective coercion at their disposal, and always enjoy some discretion in the use of those means. In one common sequence, claimants challenge repressive agents, occupy forbidden premises, attack symbolically significant objects, or seize property, and then agents reply with force. Because variants on that sequence frequently occur, when repressive agents are at hand they actually perform the great bulk of the killing and wounding that occurs in public violence.

Second, collective claim making often concerns issues that sharply divide claimants from regimes, from powerful groups allied with regimes, or from rival groups; examples are campaigns to stop current wars, outlaw abortion, or expel immigrants. In these circumstances, offended parties often respond with counterclaims backed by force, whether governmental or nongovernmental.

Third, in relatively democratic regimes an important share of collective action centers not on specific programs but on identity claims: the public assertion that a group or a constituency it represents is worthy, united, numerous, and committed (WUNC). Assertions of WUNC include marches, demonstrations, mass meetings, occupations of plants or public buildings, vigils, and hunger strikes. Even when the means they adopt are currently legal, all such assertions entail implicit threats to direct WUNC energy toward disruptive action, implicit claims to recognition as valid political actors, and implicit devaluation of other political actors within the same issue area. These features sometimes stimulate counteraction by rivals, objects of claims, or authorities, with public violence the outcome.

Broken negotiations also include some encounters that do *not* begin with concerted collective making of claims. Border guards, tax collectors, military recruiters, census takers, and other governmental agents, for example, sometimes generate intense resistance on the part of whole communities as they attempt to impose an unpopular measure. Similarly, audiences at theatrical performances, public ceremonies, or executions occasionally respond collectively to actions of the central figures by attacking those figures, unpopular persons who happen to be present, or symbolically charged objects. By and large, broken negotiations connect with issues over which groups are also currently contending in nonviolent ways.

One subclass of broken negotiation, however, displays a rather different pattern. Some organizations specialize in controlling coercive means, threatening to use those means if necessary, but seeking compliance without violence if possible. Examples include not only established agents of repression but also mafiosi, racketeers, extortionists, paramilitary forces, and perpetrators of military coups. When such specialists in coercive means encounter or anticipate resistance, they commonly mount ostentatious but selective displays of violence. Their strategy resembles that of many old-regime European rulers, who lacked the capacity for continuous surveillance and control of their subject populations, but often responded to popular rebellion with exemplary punishment—rounding up a few supposed ringleaders, subjecting them to hideous public executions, and thus warning other potential rebels of what might befall them. The strategy is most successful, ironically, when specialists in coercion never actually have to deploy their violent means.

Broken negotiations, then, cover a diverse, interesting array of collective encounters that vary systematically as a function of regime type. They have in common relatively low salience of damage and relatively high coordination among damage-doers. Recurrent mechanisms and processes causing violent breaks in negotiations include the following:

- *brokerage:* linking of two or more previously unconnected social sites by a unit that mediates their relations with one another and/or with yet other sites

- *certification and decertification:* validation (or invalidation) of actors, their performances, and their claims by external authorities
- *network activation:* drawing of previously existing social ties into joint effort
- *object shift:* alteration in relations between claimants and objects of claims; although object shift can reduce the scale of interaction between the parties (as when mass demonstrations against a regime fragment into faction fights between old enemies), the object shifts that promote broken negotiations frequently *increase* that scale—for example, by aligning workers from many different firms against the grouped managers of a whole city
- *polarization:* a more complex process that involves widening of political and social space between claimants in a contentious episode and gravitation of previously uncommitted or moderate actors toward one, the other, or both extremes; polarization combines mechanisms of opportunity/threat spirals, competition, category formation, and brokerage

Unlike the mechanisms and processes behind scattered attacks, these mechanisms and processes, on the average, create or activate two sorts of connections: among previously segmented actors, and between local actors and actors at a relatively large scale. Thus certification of local squatters as part of a national movement for land occupations in itself extends that movement's scope. Similarly, analysts of ethnic mobilization repeatedly notice the powerful influence of brokerage, as patrons and political entrepreneurs form links among aggrieved people who had not previously identified themselves as members of wronged nationalities.

Notice two important implications of the argument so far for the analysis of relations between mobilization and repression. First, all of these mechanisms involve social interaction rather than solo performances. As a consequence, it makes little sense to treat mobilization as something that dissidents do by themselves and repression as something that authorities do by themselves; looked at more closely, those phenomena resemble complex dances. Second, all the various forms of collective violence we have surveyed—not just scattered attacks and broken negotiations, but the rest as well—qualify as mobilization in some sense of the term. Yet quite different causal configurations produce the different types of collective violence. On the face of it, therefore, it would be astonishing to discover that all of them conformed to a single law governing the relationship of mobilization to repression.

*Scattered attacks*                *Broken negotiations*
network-based escalation          brokerage
setting-based activation          certification/decertification
signaling spirals                 network activation
polyvalent performance            object shift
selective retaliation             polarization

*Figure 9.2. Prominent mechanisms and processes in scattered attacks and broken negotiations[o]*

Consider the differences between mechanisms commonly activated in scattered attacks and broken negotiations. Figure 9.2 lays out the contrast. On the average, as promised, the mechanisms listed under scattered attacks promote segmented, small-scale joint action—mobilization and collective action of various sorts—rather than centralized, large-scale efforts. They rely heavily on everyday understandings and networks instead of depending on specialized organizations and political entrepreneurs. In that sense, they resemble the mechanisms underlying Europe's parochial, bifurcated, and particular seventeenth- and eighteenth-century repertoires of claim-making routines (Tarrow 1998, 31–37). They produce relatively low levels of coordination among violent actors.

The mechanisms of broken negotiations—again, as promised—promote relatively high levels of coordination. Brokerage does so by connecting previously segmented clusters of potential actors, certification by giving external validation to certain properties and claims shared by dispersed actors, object shift, polarization, and (less certainly) network activation by orienting all actors more strongly to previously blurred or suppressed boundaries. In that sense, they resemble the more recent repertoires that Tarrow dubs modular—easily transferable claim-making routines such as strikes, boycotts, electoral campaigns, demonstrations, and public meetings (Tarrow 1998, 37–41). Although they need not occur on a regional or national scale, the mechanisms of broken negotiations facilitate the spanning of multiple social sites rather than depending closely on the day-to-day organization of existing social sites.

Precisely because of that partial detachment from existing social sites, however, we might expect the mechanisms of broken negotiations to embody different repression–mobilization relations, on the average, than those of scattered attacks. If repression impinges on brokered alliances among multiple clusters, it is likely to hurt the brokers, damage the alliances, and thus diminish the overall levels of coordination among violent actors, pushing them either toward scattered attacks or toward inaction. It is also likely to encourage them to seek new forms of organization rather than defending the old coalitions. Thus repression would produce demobilization, at least in the short run. The embedding of scattered attacks in established social sites, in contrast, is likely to promote a different reaction to repression: dogged defense of existing solidarities. Of course, these are conjectures, not yet backed by systematic research. But these conjectures have several virtues. They follow fairly directly from the DOC analysis of mechanisms and processes. They focus the analysis of repression–mobilization connections on specific mechanisms rather than broad empirical regularities. And they show how causal regularities could exist in the absence of covering laws at the scale of whole classes of episodes.

Figure 9.3 accordingly sketches a revised approach to the repression–mobilization nexus. It lays out four causal scenarios: (1) repression decreases mobilization, (2) repression increases mobilization, (3) mobilization decreases repression, and (4) mobilization increases repression. Scenarios 1 and 4 represent the classic cost-benefit conception of the nexus: dissidents rationally reduce their efforts when authorities raise their costs, authorities rationally beat down opposition that will impede their programs. Scenarios 2 and 3, however, recur throughout this volume. I have represented only two vastly simplified causal configurations:

- Repression of dissidents (consistent with the earlier discussion of scattered attacks) threatens the survival of dissidents, thereby splits elites, and thus spurs dissident mobilization.
- Dissident mobilization offers allies to elite segments, thereby facilitating alliances between "ins" and "outs," and thus promotes protection of dissidents.

The mechanisms and processes we have been reviewing have, of course, disappeared into the figure's featureless arrows. Inside the arrow running from elite division to in–out alliance in the third scenario, for example, we will discover brokerage, certification, and object shift, perhaps network activation and polarization as well. My aim here is not to lay out a compelling, comprehensive theory of interactions between repression and mobilization, but to show that a mechanisms-processes view of explanation promises to ease the way past problems that otherwise seem intractable.

In writing *From Mobilization to Revolution* (Tilly 1978) a quarter-century ago, I thought that scenarios 1 and 4 expressed something like general laws. I no longer think so. Other people's work (prominently including fellow authors in this volume), criticism of my own work from some of the same people, and my investigations of political processes pushed me toward

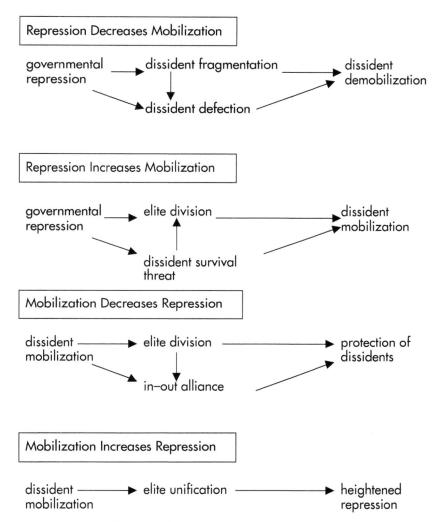

*Figure 9.3. Exemplary causal paths between repression and mobilization*

the recognition that the order in such processes does not lie in one-size-fits-all rules, but in the interplay of mechanisms, processes, and initial conditions. Mechanisms do, indeed, conform to covering laws. But to recognize their regularities, we must also recognize the scales at which they operate. Episodes and classes of episodes do not conform to covering laws. Nor do the big abstractions we call repression and mobilization. Students of repression and mobilization need not despair. They need only shift their angles of vision.

## Works Cited

Bearman, Peter S. 1991. "Desertion as Localism: Army Unit Solidarity and Group Norms in the U.S. Civil War." *Social Forces* 70: 321–42.

Bernstein, Thomas P., and Xiaobo Lü. 2002. *Taxation without Representation in Contemporary Rural China.* Cambridge: Cambridge University Press.

Khawaja, Marwan. 1993. "Repression and Popular Collective Action: Evidence from the West Bank." *Sociological Forum* 8: 47–71.

Lagrange, Hugues. 1989. "Strikes and the War." In Leopold Haimson and Charles Tilly, eds., *Strikes, Wars, and Revolutions in an International Perspective,* 473–79. Cambridge: Cambridge University Press.

Lichbach, Mark Irving. 1987. "Deterrence or Escalation? The Puzzle of Aggregate Studies of Repression and Dissent." *Journal of Conflict Resolution* 31: 266–97.

Mason, T. David. 1989. "Nonelite Response to State-Sanctioned Terror." *Western Political Quarterly* 42: 467–92.

Mason, T. David, and Dale A. Krane. 1989. "The Political Economy of Death Squads: Toward a Theory of the Impact of State-Sanctioned Terror." *International Studies Quarterly* 33: 175–98.

McAdam, Doug, Sidney Tarrow, and Charles Tilly. 2001. *Dynamics of Contention.* Cambridge: Cambridge University Press.

Moore, Barrington, Jr. 1979. *Injustice: The Social Bases of Obedience and Revolt.* White Plains, NY: M. E. Sharpe.

O'Brien, Kevin. 1996. "Rightful Resistance." *World Politics* 49: 31–55.

Olivier, Johan. 1991. "State Repression and Collective Action in South Africa, 1970–84." *South African Journal of Sociology* 22: 109–17.

Schneider, Cathy Lisa. 1995. *Shantytown Protest in Pinochet's Chile.* Philadelphia: Temple University Press.

Tarrow, Sidney. 1998. *Power in Movement: Social Movements and Contentious Politics.* 2d ed. Cambridge: Cambridge University Press.

Tilly, Charles. 1978. *From Mobilization to Revolution.* Reading, MA: Addison-Wesley.

———. 1992. "Conclusions." In Leopold Haimson and Giulio Sapelli, eds., *Strikes, Social Conflict and the First World War: An International Perspective,* 587–98. Milan: Feltrinelli. Fondazione Giangiacomo Feltrinelli, *Annali* 1990/1991.

———. 2001. "Do unto Others." In Marco Giugni and Florence Passy, eds., *Political Altruism? The Solidarity Movement in International Perspective,* 27–50. Lanham, MD: Rowman and Littlefield.

———. 2002. "Event Catalogs as Theories." *Sociological Theory* 20: 248–54.

## 10

# How to Organize Your Mechanisms:
# Research Programs, Stylized Facts, and Historical Narratives

*Mark Lichbach*

## Mechanisms

In *Constructing Social Theories,* Arthur Stinchcombe wrote:

> I usually assign students in a theory class the following task: Choose
> any relation between two or more variables which you are interested in;
> invent at least three theories, not now known to be false, which might
> explain these relations; choosing appropriate indicators, derive at least
> three different empirical consequences from each theory, such that the
> factual consequences distinguish among the theories. This I take to be
> the model of social theorizing as a practical scientific activity. (1968, 13)

Because I find it a useful antidote to the semantic and syntactic theories of science that I learned in graduate school during the 1970s, I often
give Stinchcombe's challenge to my students.

More than three decades after the appearance of Stinchcombe's 1968
classic, the positivism that I learned is out and postpositivism, in its many
equally relevant varieties, is in. Hempel's deductive-nomological theory has
given way, for instance, to Elster's (1989) nuts and bolts. Many philosophers
of science thus advocate a view of theory that aims to uncover the causal
mechanisms, following Stinchcombe, connecting independent and dependent variables, or following Elster, connecting micro- and macrolevels of
analysis. Whereas Kuhn (1970) sees paradigms as heuristic devices based
on exemplars and Lakatos (1970) views research programs as cores generating hypotheses in peripheries, realist philosophy of science (Miller 1987),

an alternative to Kuhn and Lakatos preferred by many philosophers, claims that scientists supply descriptions of relevant causal mechanisms:

> When the search for hidden mechanisms is successful, the result is often to reveal a small number of basic mechanisms that underlie wide ranges [and diverse types] of phenomena. The explanation of diverse phenomena in terms of the same mechanism constitutes theoretical unification. For instance, the kinetic-molecular theory of gases unified thermodynamic phenomena with Newtonian particle mechanics. The discovery of the double-helical structure of DNA, for another example, produced a major unification of biology and chemistry. (Salmon et al. 1992, 34)

According to realists, science achieves theoretical leverage when it can explain diverse outcomes as a function of the same basic processes. Unobserved causal mechanisms can thus explain observed correlations between events. Because they stand between an input/explanans and an output/explanandum, perhaps even those at different levels of analysis, mechanisms tell a deep story that unlocks the black-box correlation between observables.

Many social scientists also view theory as a set of explanatory devices or model types (Kitcher 1993, 18). Merton's (1959, 1968, chap. 2) problem-oriented "middle-range" theorizing, for example, clarifies and rethinks existing theoretical puzzles by providing a small number of heuristic tools or concepts that further empirical investigations (also see Elster 1989, 1999, chap. 1). The latest book from the most prominent students of contentious politics—McTeam—is all about mechanisms (McAdam, Tarrow, and Tilly 2002). Tilly has written extensively on the problem of mechanisms in conflict research (see this volume).

While the postpositivist choruses in science, social science, and conflict studies sing the praises of mechanisms, I raise an important problem in their use: multiplicity. The antidote is to embed causal mechanisms in theories called research programs and evaluate them using empirical materials called stylized facts and historical narratives.

## The Multiplicity of Mechanisms: An Example

After three weeks of bombing in Afghanistan, news sources reported that the Taliban were digging in. Editorialists, with their typical long-range understanding of complex developments, hoped for light at the end of the tunnel and openly wondered whether the United States was in a quagmire. After the United States quickly toppled the Taliban regime, news sources once again thirsted for immediate gratification. They reported that the

Taliban's leadership, as well as Osama bin Laden, were probably still alive; that their forces seemed to be regrouping; and that they had definitely carried out new terrorist attacks. Why should a country that won the Cold War against the Soviet Union, columnists wondered, struggle so hard and take so long to defeat a band of terrorists without a land to call their own?

The United States can adopt two basic strategies toward the terrorist assaults on the World Trade Center in New York and the Pentagon in Washington (Lichbach 1987). The first is repression: attack, with violent and nonviolent means, the terrorists and their supporters. The second is appeasement: make policy changes, such as end sanctions toward Iraq, remove troops from Saudi Arabia, and shift position in the Israeli–Palestinian conflict, that accommodate the underlying grievances, demands, or claims of the terrorists and their supporters.

The terrorists struck the United States before September 11, and one of America's principal concerns is to prevent them from striking us after September 11. To grasp the key difficulty with mechanisms, I therefore begin as Machiavelli began: as a realist aiming to end the string of terrorist attacks from bin Laden and his supporters and thereby prevent more American deaths. What are the attractions of repression as seen by its hypothetical proponents in the U.S. Department of Defense?

Before the appeals of a military response (as seen in Figure 10.1) capture our imagination, we should pause to consider its drawbacks as seen in Figure 10.2 and portrayed by the military's hypothetical critics in the State Department.

At this point, the United States might well give up on the military option as hopelessly entangled in the fog of war. The alternative, hidden deep in the hearts of Foggy Bottom, is presumably appeasement (as seen in Figure 10.3).

If all of this sounds too good to be true, you (and the Department of Defense) guessed it . . .

The complications in Figures 10.1 through 10.4 display the familiar impotence of the intellectual: he or she has an array of ideas but no way to deploy them. The complexities also reveal the familiar worldview of the liberal: skeptical and uncertain. And the figures demonstrate the tragic sense of postmodernity: losses inevitably accompany gains and there is no real and compelling solution to the human condition.

I focus here, however, on the implications for social-scientific explanation. The struggle against terrorism is long and hard because multiple

Because regimes wish to stay in power, repression will stop rogue regimes from serving as the patrons of terrorism.

If the United States attacks the terrorists' leadership, entrepreneurs will be prevented from organizing more terrorism.

By attacking terrorist leaders, repression has a symbolic effect: all terrorists and all of their supporters are shown to be vulnerable.

When the United States increases its efforts to detect, capture, convict, and punish (imprison, injure, kill) terrorists, the costs of engaging in terrorism rise; threats that are convincing also raise costs.

Because military attacks demonstrate the United States' overwhelming power and the futility of the terrorists' position, terrorists will decrease their estimates of the probability of their success.

U.S. military action degrades the resources of the terrorists.

Because repression puts terrorists on the defensive, they will shift resources to protecting themselves rather than to attacking us.

Military action forces terrorists to change their location and hence to engage in open battles with superior forces.

By restricting the mobility of the terrorists to defensive maneuvers, the attacks limit their ability to act.

By resettling terrorists and their supporters, military attacks destroy the preexisting organizational base—the social infrastructure—of the terrorists.

By employing infiltrators and spies, the United States will be better able to detect and monitor the terrorists and hence better able to preempt their actions.

By offering a bounty for each terrorist killed or captured, or a booty to those who distinguish themselves in combat against the terrorists, the supporters of terrorism will be co-opted to our side.

The terrorists and their supporters will shift tactics to more legal and conventional forms of participation, influence, and negotiation.

*Figure 10.1. The top reasons why military action will deter future terrorism*

mechanisms appear as intervening variables between U.S. responses to terrorism and terrorism itself. The simple solutions—pure strategies of repression and appeasement—produce unintended consequences that usually outweigh the intended ones. Each type of U.S. response to terrorism opens a Pandora's box: because second-order problems overwhelm first-order problems and side effects become more significant than direct effects, the solution quickly becomes the problem.

The multiplicity of mechanisms thus explains why each policy the United

The repressive policy itself will be a source of new grievances and hence turn the allies of the terrorists into more terrorists.

By creating martyrs, heroes, and role models, repression engenders permanent hostility to the United States and thus ensures a permanent supply of future terrorists.

Repression increases the illegitimacy of the United States: by showing the real basis of U.S. power, it violates the sense of justice held by allies of the terrorists.

Military attacks increase nationalism and internationalism directed against the United States: the terrorists will gain allies willing to unite against a common enemy.

Repression increases the collective action problem of the allies, coalition partners, and supporters of the United States: international cooperation against terrorism is especially hard to organize and repression splits the U.S. allies, with some going over to the side of the terrorists.

As repression becomes a new grievance, it increases the radicalism of the terrorists' demands.

Repression increases the power of the radicals, who can offer physical protection to people we bomb; it also decreases the power of the moderates, whose ability to interact and negotiate with the United States is diminished.

Military action leads to substitution (displacement) effects—the tactical, temporal, and spatial diffusion of terrorism: terrorists will shift to another form of terrorism that is not being repressed; terrorists will go underground so as to be able to attack at a later time; and terrorists will be displaced from places where repression is high to places where it is low.

In a fight to the death, terrorists will have to fight to the death—which of course prolongs the conflict.

Terrorists will become better organized—smaller, more secretive, more decentralized, and more deadly—but will not go away.

In the short run, repression is not a credible strategy; the yawning gap between repressive words and actual deeds will cost the United States credibility.

In the intermediate run, repression is not a credible strategy: it is a blunt instrument, necessarily inconsistent and incoherent, and subject to poor timing and execution. In particular, repression that becomes arbitrary, indiscriminate, sporadic, and erratic, perhaps because it is unlimited and unrestrained, perhaps because it targets collectivities rather than individuals, perhaps because it is random and unpredictable, creates a public bad that the entire population of terrorists and their supporters would like to remove; and because people are just as likely to be repressed if they were terrorists than if they were not, those who are not terrorists have an incentive to join the terrorists in order to seek protection.

In the long run, repression is not a credible strategy either: it might be the start of a policy, but surely not the end, because the will and resources to implement repression will eventually weaken; states, as Napoleon recognized, cannot rule by force indefinitely: "One can do everything with bayonnettes except sit on them."

*Figure 10.2. The top reasons why military action will promote future terrorism*

When you've got nothing, you've got nothing to lose; if the root causes of terrorism are addressed, terrorists will stop being terrorists.

Appeasement increases the legitimacy of the United States: if we can solve the terrorists' problems, tackle their grievances, and satisfy their demands, the terrorists lose their reason to terrorize us and will become our allies.

Appeasement is a divide-and-conquer strategy that promotes splits among the terrorists and their supporters, encouraging reformists to defect from the radicals.

Appeasement provides selective incentives for terrorists and their supporters to defect to our side; the United States can create ties to replace the terrorists' hold over the populations they control.

By co-opting local and regional power holders, appeasement will turn preexisting organizations away from terrorism.

By offering rewards and amnesty, appeasement will create informants, strikebreakers, and agent provocateurs to join our fight against the terrorists.

*Figure 10.3. The top reasons why appeasing the terrorists' demands will cure terrorism*

States pursues is inevitably followed by damage control: a public-relations campaign to clarify its goals. Spokespeople—the sorcerer's apprentices—for the White House, State Department, and Defense Department tell us what the sorcerer really meant to do.

The plethora of mechanisms also explains why George W. Bush ignored the extremists on both sides who urged the United States to devote all of its resources to either repression or appeasement, in essence advocating what economists call a "corner solution." His absolutist advisers never realized that their favorite strategy would not have unlimited, direct, and linear effects, or that even American hegemony cannot control the uncontrollable. The United States thus plays bad cop and bombs Afghanistan and good cop and makes demands on Israel. And, to balance the balance, we drop food for the people of Afghanistan and claim that Israelis have no better friend than the United States.

However, as we move from either/or to both/and, as we grope for the optimal policy combination, contradictions, incoherences, paradoxes, and hypocrisies emerge from each of our practical syntheses. Pragmatism is a great idea that often fails in practice. Bush's policy choices therefore always involve judgment, the balancing of certain basic maxims for deterring terrorism. Some good advice that Machiavelli can offer the Prince is thus to choose wisely. Even better advice is to appear wise: look resolute while bringing out the experts in damage control. Perhaps they can explain to edi-

By showing that it is a paper tiger, appeasement signals the weakness of the United States: caving in to terrorist demands increases the terrorists' estimates of the probability that future terrorism will be successful.

Appeasement shows that terrorism is effective, increasing the terrorists' estimates of the probability that their own contribution to terrorism can make a difference.

The terrorists' demands are poorly defined: because the specific policy measures that will satisfy their grievances are unclear, any changes in U.S. policy will be inadequate and lead to further demands.

Policy benefits are a public good, and terrorists care about the private benefits that follow from their actions.

Appeasement factionalizes those who appease, increasing the terrorists' estimates of their probability of success.

In the short run, appeasement is not a credible strategy because the United States has limited ability to accommodate terrorist demands: if promises are made today that are not fulfilled tomorrow, appeasement raises expectations and generates more terrorism.

In the intermediate run, appeasement is not a credible strategy: it is a blunt instrument, necessarily inconsistent and incoherent, hypocritical and contradictory, and subject to poor timing and execution.

In particular, after terrorism occurs, it is too late to appease the terrorists, while reformists might be satisfied, radicals will advance new grievances and make endless demands; appeasement thus merely politicizes demands and, even worse, encourages the wrong people (the radicals) at the wrong time (the heat of battle); and because piecemeal reforms are inadequate and total reforms impossible, appeasement will be executed in fits and starts that make everyone angry.

In the long run, appeasement creates new enemies—the opponents of the group being appeased—who also can become terrorists.

*Figure 10.4. The top reasons why appeasing the terrorists' demands will encourage more terrorism*

torialists, columnists, and ultimately the American people why the struggle against terrorism is so long and difficult.

## The General Problem with Causal Mechanisms

The social-scientific points are these: *Generating mechanisms—micro or macro intervening variables that explain a correlation between observables—is easy; locating the mechanisms—factors and forces linking repression or accommodation with terrorism—is an interminable make-work project; and the breathless search for mechanisms substitutes an endless positivist list of hypotheses with an endless postpositivist inventory of mechanisms.*

The world is more than a jumble of nuts and bolts and a grab bag of causal mechanisms. Reality is patterned and ordered in many overlapping ways; the parts stand in relation to one another in interrelated sets of natural systems. These patterns, moreover, have a historical dimension in that they are relatively stable and fixed. Focusing only on the bits and pieces—the pragmatist's dream of a book of proverbs, epigrams, and aphorisms, or the empiricist's dream of a book of anecdotes, stories, and tales—produces disconnected snapshots of reality, with nothing belonging anywhere, and with each part in solitary confinement. The result is convulsion and not consequence, contingency and not causality, simultaneity and not sequence, chaos and not complexity, arbitrariness and not wholeness. Everything is deconstructed and nothing is ever added up. Given the human and scientific need to comprehend the entire order of things and events, a science of only nuts and bolts and causal mechanisms is no science at all. Scientists who work only with mechanisms are like my son playing with his clock: he is bright enough to rip the clock apart and reveal all the cogs and wheels that make it tick, but he cannot put it back together and make the thing work.

Obsessing on mechanisms, in short, multiplies and thus ultimately cheapens them. The end of this social-scientific game is despair.

The real and creative social-scientific challenge is this: *to embed mechanisms in larger and more organized structures of knowledge so as to deepen our understanding of interesting and important causal processes.* Although scientists need a logically consistent combination of mechanisms called a research program, the combination would still constitute a guess about what is interesting and important. Aesthetics alone will never constrain the current euphoria for mechanisms. How can scientists judge whether they are multiplying mechanisms past the point of diminishing marginal utility?

Redescribing the world in terms of mechanisms reproduces the complexity of the world in a new (postpositivist) language game. Because mechanisms overdetermine reality, science must impose two types of empirical constraints: *mechanisms should produce stylized facts that dominate a domain and they should yield chronological narratives that contain time sequences.* After I demonstrate how the logical organization of mechanisms helps satisfy the scientist, I will show how he or she is even more pleased when mechanisms are organized empirically.

## Research Programs: Nuts, Bolts, and Order

Members of the three principal research communities in social science have advocated a nuts-and-bolts or mechanism view of theory (Lichbach 2003).

*Rationality.* Robinson (1933, 1) views economics as a "box of tools." Schumpeter (1954, 15) says that "it is the sum total of such gadgets . . . which constitutes economic theory."

This view is represented in mainstream economics by the books on problems in microeconomics (e.g., Miller, Benjamin, and North 1998) that usually accompany microeconomic textbooks. These texts address a set of historically concrete issues—taxi medallions in New York City, rent control during wartime, or the OPEC oil cartel. By putting the nuts and bolts, causal mechanisms, and ultimately the models of economics to work in different problem areas, these texts help students understand the relevance and scope of microeconomic theory.

*Culture.* Swidler (1973) argues that a culture is a "tool kit" for its members. For students of culture, the tool kit contains the nuts and bolts that can be used to create the subplots of larger narratives that allow understanding of action. Aminzade (1992, 458) thus indicates that "analytic narratives—theoretically structured stories about coherent sequences of motivated actions"—are basic to social science.

*Structure.* Structuralists study how long-term processes and trajectories unfold and combine in different cases. For example, Moore (1966) works with a set of neo-Marxist nuts and bolts that produces causal propositions about development: specific modes of labor repression are behind the bourgeois, fascist, and communist coalitions that forged the historical paths of the commercialization of agriculture and the industrial development of a country. Structuralists often draw on his insight that each historical case can be examined as a potential combination of three modes, coalitions, or paths (e.g., the United States could have become authoritarian had its budding fascist coalition not been destroyed by the Civil War).

Scientists have thus reacted to the multiplicity of mechanisms, their unlimited quantity and infinitely variable qualities, by employing a research program, theory, or model—at least some idea!—to stand behind their mechanisms. The structuring and ordering power of well-articulated scientific programs gives nuts and bolts significance and coherence: programs show how causal mechanisms associate and combine with one another to form characteristic bridges and links that permit larger causal explanations and narrative understandings.

For example, well-developed research programs in contentious politics, first, classify their mechanisms. Structuralists (McAdam, Tarrow, and Tilly 2002) work with political opportunities (PO), mobilizing structures (MS), and cultural frames (CF), and rationalists (Lichbach 1995) with market, community, contract, and hierarchy. Unless scientists classify their mechanisms—and classification can only come from larger structures of understanding called research programs—the search for mechanisms is incomplete.

More important, research programs in conflict studies tell deep stories about social order. Rationalist nuts and bolts in Bates (1989) are connected by hidden hands that produce unintended consequences; culturalist nuts and bolts in Scott (1985) hold together because of the meaning and significance of a society's collective values and beliefs; and structuralist causal mechanisms in Skocpol (1979) are tied together because of deep structures of political power and social causation. Rationalists thus produce analytic narratives of unintended but realized, and intended but unrealized, goals; culturalists, interpretations of meaning in which interests, identities, and ideas are constitutive of social life; and structuralists, studies of kinds or regimes of political domination and social control. Their stories embody different understandings of social order. Rationalists focus on the ongoing bargaining and negotiation in which human wisdom, and hence its ironies and tragedies, become manifest. Culturalists focus on the socially constructed nature of action—its meaning and significance. And structuralists explore the structuring power and causal necessity of hierarchies. Unless the search for mechanisms leads to a dialogue about hidden hands, constitutive meanings, and power structures, mechanisms do not enrich explanation and understanding.

## Stylized Facts: Nuts, Bolts, and Statistics

I now turn from the logical question of what ideas mechanisms derive from to the empirical question of what things they account for. I begin with a realist ontology. Bhaskar (1997, 51) argues that "the world consists of things, not events. Most things are complex objects, in virtue of which they possess an ensemble of tendencies, liabilities and powers. It is by reference to the exercise of their tendencies, liabilities and powers that the phenomena of the world are explained." Realists understand the structure of things by classifying them into characteristic "natural" types. Bhaskar (1997, 210) writes that "the justification of our systems of taxonomy, of the ways we classify things, of the nominal essences of things in science thus lies in our belief in their fruitfulness in leading us to explanations in terms of the generative mechanisms contained in their real essences." For example, democratic states contain voting systems and patrimonial states contain patron–client ties.

The nuts and bolts of things, the "generative mechanisms of nature" (Bhaskar 1997, 14), combine to produce the actual flux of phenomena (outcomes or events) in the world. Hence, "this is the arduous task of science: the production of the knowledge of those enduring and continually active mechanisms of nature that produce the phenomena of our world." Bhaskar (1997, 46, emphasis in original) thus indicates that "there is a distinction between the *real* structures and mechanisms of the world and the *actual* patterns of events that they generate." Hence, "the world consists of mechanisms not events. Such mechanisms combine to generate the flux of phenomena that constitute the actual states and happenings of the world." Because outcomes are conjunctures of a multiplicity of radically different kinds of mechanisms, "science consists in a continuing dialectic between taxonomic and explanatory knowledge; between knowledge of what kinds of things there are and knowledge of how the things there are behave." Whereas pure or abstract theory locates the structures and mechanisms, empirical work studies the outcomes they generate.

The basic problem of empirical work, according to realists, is that events in the world are only weakly related to the nuts and bolts or causal mechanisms of generative structures. Electoral rules only weakly structure electoral behavior in democracies and patron–client ties only weakly structure clientelistic behavior in patrimonial states. Lots of factors confound the linkages between electoral rules and elections and patron–client ties and clientelism. Lawson (1994, 276–77, emphasis in original) thus writes:

> I have argued that universal constant conjunctions of events are rare even in natural science and more so in the social realm. But if this is so how can economic mechanisms be identified? This is the question that is bound to be asked. The point that warrants emphasis is that just because universal constant conjunctions of the form "whenever event $x$ then event $y$" are unlikely to be pervasive it does not follow that the only alternative is an inchoate random flux. These two possibilities—strict event regularities or a completely non-systematic flux exist—merely constitute the polar extremes of a potential continuum. Although the social world is open, certain mechanisms can come to dominate others over restricted regions of time-space, giving rise to rough-and-ready generalities or partial regularities, holding to such a degree that *prima facie* an explanation is called for. Thus, just as autumn leaves do still fall to the ground *much* of the time, so women are *concentrated* in secondary sectors of labor markets, and productive growth in the UK over the last century has *frequently* been slower than that of other comparable industrial countries. Such "stylized facts" can serve both to *initiate* investigation and also in the assessment of the relative *explanatory* powers—the relative abilities to illuminate a range of empirical findings—of competing hypotheses that may, in due course, be constructed.

Empirical work thus demonstrates how universal causal mechanisms that inhere in structures come to dominate outcomes in specific space-time domains. This could involve a comparative analysis of the contexts that activate and deactivate mechanisms (Lichbach 1995, 192–93).

Empirical analysis in contentious politics could show, for example, the types of democracies in which certain electoral rules influence certain electoral outcomes, which in turn influence protest activity; and it could show the types of patrimonial states in which certain patron–client ties influence certain clientelistic outcomes, which in turn influence dissent. One could therefore investigate laws of the following form: given democracies of type D, electoral rules R influence electoral results E and protest outcomes O; and given patrimonial states of type S, patron–client ties P influence clientelism C and terrorism T. The study of mechanisms therefore leads to statistical attempts to establish stylized facts (regression equations) in particular domains (samples of data). Social scientists have thus discovered that in the United States nowadays blacks vote Democratic, the young protest, and economists are paid more than sociologists. My students who take Stinchcombe's challenge are looking for the social, political, and economic mechanisms that dominate domains and thereby generate statistical regularities.

This explanatory modesty with respect to data analysis addresses some postpositivist critiques of the aggregate data and survey research traditions in conflict studies. More important, recognizing that the mechanism world and the variable world do not represent different ontologies, but rather share a realist ontology, allows quantitative and qualitative researchers to collaborate.

## Historical Narratives: Nuts, Bolts, and Stories

No doubt about it: good mechanisms tell good stories. Hartmann (1999, 344) indeed writes that "there is no good model without a story that goes with it." He considers storytelling essential to physics:

> A story is a narrative told *around* the formalism of the model. It is neither a deductive consequence of the model nor of the underlying theory. It is, however, *inspired* by the underlying theory (if there is one). This is because the story takes advantage of the vocabulary of the theory . . . and refers to some of its features. . . . Using more general terms, the story fits the model in a larger framework (a "world picture") in a non-deductive way. A story is, therefore, an integral part of a model: it complements the

formalisms. To put it in a slogan: *a model is an (interpreted) formalism + a story.* (Ibid., emphasis in original)

Similarly, Cartwright (1999, 36–38) suggests that "fables transform the abstract into the concrete, and in so doing, I claim, they function like models in physics. . . . the relationship between the moral and the fable is like that between a scientific law and a model. . . . it is [this] picture of the relationship between the moral as a purely abstract claim and the fable as its more concrete manifestation that mirror what I think is going on in physics." Joined to the use of a major foil, models/stories have an oppositional and critical style that can be quite compelling.

Given the current state of social science, it is trite to argue that structuralist and culturalist nuts and bolts can yield historical narratives. I will therefore show how rationalist nuts and bolts can yield what might be called *rationalist narratives*: historical and comparative analysis of strategic decision-making situations (Bates, et al. 1998). Such efforts can have six components.

1. One begins with a single concrete case (e.g., nation, city, international organization). The motivation for selecting the new case is that, from a rationalist point of view, it is either paradigmatic or deviant.

2. Out of the narrative stream of happenings, events, and episodes in the case, rationalists locate separable interactions: collective action and collective choice situations. Each case thus consists of a set of chronologically linked strategic situations. These are episodic crises, recurring problems, periodic challenges, or key turning points in the case's history. Weingast (1998) shows how the pre–Civil War equilibrium was punctuated by a series of crises. Bates (1998) focuses on critical events in the formation, operation, transformation, and ultimately termination of the Colombian coffee cartel. Levi (1998) studies a series of legislative actions in France from 1793 through 1872, each of which altered conscription laws. Greif (1998) explains stylized factors about "the nature of Genoa's economy and its inter-clan relations before 1154" (p. 22), the transition from pirates to traders from 1154 to 1164, the civil wars from 1164 to 1194, and the institutionalization of the *podesteria* organization after 1194.

3. Each historical episode is probed with rationalist nuts and bolts. Analytically, one can do equilibrium analyses and comparative statics to explain why some interactions turn out one way and others, another.

4. More generally, one can derive many observable implications about the recurring pattern of politics (i.e., strategizing) manifested in the case's particular events, individuals, issues, groups, conflicts, regions, or time

periods. Weingast (1998), for example, tells us about the political use of slavery (the Riker Thesis), the political difficulties of pure majority rule, the implications of institutional compromises supporting the balance rule, and the North's tenuous commitment to property rights in slaves. Levi (1998) uses the comparative statics of her model to arbitrate among a set of exogenous forces thought to cause change in conscription policy: war-induced changes in government demand for troops, experience with past conscription policies, democratization of political institutions, nation building, and state building (especially of repressive capacity). Rosenthal (1998) matches his model against stylized facts about the goals and strategies of various actors and the resulting possible and actual institutional changes. He claims that "the model is therefore consistent with much of the public finance of Early Modern France" (p. 9). Although the overall historical narrative of sequential situations is interspersed with these sorts of models and data, an overall thesis, or metanarrative, illuminates the general pattern or overall stylized facts of the case. A protest cycle, the interrelationship of politics and institutions underlying democratic stability, the political foundations of economic development, or state (institution) building thus molds diverse strategic situations into an overarching narrative structure. And the short-run equilibria compound to produce a long-run equilibrium as the series of within-case studies compounds to produce the overall case study.

5. Significant foils are investigated. What would historians of Italy make of Greif's explanation of Italian trade and development? Does Rosenthal engage the historiography of old-regime France in a way that demonstrates the superiority of his model? How is Weingast's explanation of the U.S. Civil War different from and better than other accounts? Has Levi explained conscription in France differently and better than alternative explanations? Is there reason to think that Bates explains the Colombian coffee cartel better than the culturalists and the structuralists?

6. One draws conclusions about the conditions under which thin and thick versions of the theory's assumptions apply. Lichbach (1995) thus argues that collective action theory consists of theoretical possibilities or possibility claims: nothing in the theory says that people facing a collective action problem will always find it in their interest to use the collective action solution under investigation. The presence of solutions, that is, does not guarantee that they will be used. To find out whether they will be used and the consequences that arise, one must examine concrete strategic situations in specific historical contexts.

In sum, a modest rationalist narrative explains the historical sequence of major decision-making situations, as well as many general aspects of the historical record. There are variations of this strategy: Rosenthal (1998) structures his narratives of France and England with a single integrated model of the division of institutional control over taxation and policy control over war making between an elite and a crown. Greif (1998) develops a single model and one variation for one time period. Levi (1998) looks at a single model but in multiple cases (i.e., in this important variation, she produces a set of comparative case studies of the historical sequences of strategic situations in each nation case). Weingast (1998) proposes two integrated models—a spatial model and two interrelated sequential game models, but of one case. Bates (1998) uses a battery of different types of rationalist models in a single case. Hence, there are many ways in which a narrative "seeks to use history to construct the theory and to flesh out its implications" (Rosenthal 1998, 2).

## Conclusion

Assume a mechanism. Assume a second mechanism. Then assume a third. Stinchcombe's challenge to beginning graduate students thereby produces the top ten reasons why repression or accommodation fails or succeeds. The postpositivist search for mechanisms turns out no better than the positivist search for hypotheses: both yield long lists.

Unless mechanisms derive from research programs, they will not lead scientists to the important tasks of explaining stylized facts and developing historical narratives.

Research Programs → Combinations of Mechanisms → Stylized Facts + Historical Narratives

The only good set of mechanisms is therefore an organized set of mechanisms, an organization that is both logical (research programs) and empirical (stylized facts and historical narratives).

Indeed, social order can only be comprehended through research programs. And the mechanisms behind the conflict and cooperation between regimes and dissidents—the repression–dissent nexus and the accommodation–dissent nexus—can only be evaluated through statistical and historical studies.

## Works Cited

Aminzade, Ronald. 1992. "Historical Sociology and Time." *Sociological Methods and Research* 20 (May): 456–80.

Bates, Robert H. 1989. *Beyond the Miracle of the Market: The Political Economy of Agrarian Development in Kenya*. Cambridge: Cambridge University Press.

———. 1998. "The International Coffee Organization: An International Institution." In Robert H. Bates, Avner Greif, Margaret Levi, Jean-Laurent

Rosenthal, and Barry R. Weingast, eds., *Analytic Narratives,* 194–230. Princeton, NJ: Princeton University Press.

Bates, Robert H., Avner Greif, Margaret Levi, Jean-Laurent Rosenthal, and Barry R. Weingast. 1998. *Analytic Narratives.* Princeton, NJ: Princeton University Press.

Bhaskar, Roy. 1997. *A Realist Theory of Science.* 2d ed. London: Verso.

Cartwright, Nancy. 1999. *The Dappled World: A Study of the Boundaries of Science.* Cambridge: Cambridge University Press.

Elster, Jon. 1989. *Nuts and Bolts for the Social Sciences.* Cambridge: Cambridge University Press.

———. 1999. *Alchemies of the Mind: Rationality and the Emotions.* Cambridge: Cambridge University Press.

Greif, Avner. 1998. "Self-Enforcing Political Systems and Economic Growth: Late Medieval Genoa." In Robert H. Bates, Avner Greif, Margaret Levi, Jean-Laurent Rosenthal, and Barry R. Weingast, eds. *Analytic Narratives,* 23–63. Princeton, NJ: Princeton University Press.

Hartmann, Stephan. 1999. "Models and Stories in Hadron Physics." In Mary S. Morgan and Margaret Morrison, eds., *Models as Mediators: Perspectives on Natural and Social Science,* 326–46. Cambridge: Cambridge University Press.

Kitcher, Philip. 1993. *The Advancement of Science: Science without Legend, Objectivity without Illusions.* Oxford: Oxford University Press.

Kuhn, Thomas S. 1970. *The Structure of Scientific Revolutions.* 2d ed., enlarged. Chicago: University of Chicago Press.

Lakatos, Imre. 1970. "Falsification and the Methodology of Scientific Research Programs." In Imre Lakatos and Alan Musgrave, eds., *Criticism and the Growth of Knowledge,* 91–196. Cambridge: Cambridge University Press.

Lawson, Tony. 1994. "A Realist Theory for Economics." In Roger E. Blackhouse, ed., *New Directions in Economic Methodology,* 257–85. London: Routledge.

Levi, Margaret. 1998. "Conscription: The Price of Citizenship." In Robert H. Bates, Avner Greif, Margaret Levi, Jean-Laurent Rosenthal, and Barry R. Weingast, eds., *Analytic Narratives,* 109–47. Princeton, NJ: Princeton University Press.

Lichbach, Mark Irving. 1987. "Deterrence or Escalation? The Puzzle of Aggregate Studies of Repression and Dissent." *Journal of Conflict Resolution* 31 (June): 266–97.

———. 1995. *The Rebel's Dilemma.* Ann Arbor: University of Michigan Press.

———. 2003. *Is Rational Choice Theory All of Social Science?* Ann Arbor: University of Michigan Press.

McAdam, Doug, Sidney G. Tarrow, and Charles Tilly. 2002. *Dynamics of Contention.* Cambridge: Cambridge University Press.

Merton, Robert K. 1959. "Notes on Problem-Finding in Sociology." In Robert K. Merton, Leonard Broom, and Leonard S. Cottrell Jr., eds., *Sociology Today: Problems and Prospects,* vol. 1, ix–xxxiv. New York: Harper Torchbooks.

———. 1968. *Social Theory and Social Structure.* New York: Free Press.

Miller, Richard W. 1987. *Fact and Method: Explanation, Confirmation, and Reality in the Natural and Social Sciences.* Princeton, NJ: Princeton University Press.

Miller, Roger Leroy, Daniel K. Benjamin, and Douglass Cecil North. 1998. *The Economics of Public Issues.* 11th ed. New York: Addison-Wesley.

Moore, Barrington. 1966. *Social Origins of Dictatorship and Democracy: Lord and Peasant in the Making of the Modern World.* Boston: Beacon Press.

Robinson, Joan. 1933. *Economics of Imperfect Competition.* London: Macmillan.

Rosenthal, Jean-Laurent. 1998. "The Political Economy of Absolutism Reconsidered." In Robert H. Bates, Avner Greif, Margaret Levi, Jean-Laurent Rosenthal, and Barry R. Weingast, eds. *Analytic Narratives,* 64–108. Princeton, NJ: Princeton University Press.

Salmon, Merrilee H., et al. 1992. *Introduction to the Philosophy of Science.* Englewood Cliffs, NJ: Prentice Hall.

Schumpeter, Joseph A. 1954. *History of Economic Analysis.* New York: Oxford University Press.

Scott, James C. 1985. *Weapons of the Weak: Everyday Forms of Peasant Resistance.* New Haven: Yale University Press.

Skocpol, Theda. 1979. *States and Social Revolutions: A Comparative Analysis of France, Russia and China.* Cambridge: Cambridge University Press.

Stinchcombe, Arthur L. 1968. *Constructing Social Theories.* New York: Harcourt, Brace & World.

Swidler, Ann. 1973. "The Concept of Rationality in the Work of Max Weber." *Sociological Inquiry* 43, no. 1: 35–42.

Weingast, Barry. 1998. "Political Stability and Civil War: Institutions, Commitment, and American Democracy." In Robert H. Bates, Avner Greif, Margaret Levi, Jean-Laurent Rosenthal, and Barry R. Weingast, eds., *Analytic Narratives,* 148–93. Princeton, NJ: Princeton University Press.

# Contributors

**Patrick Ball** is director of Human Rights Programs at the Benetech Initiative. Since 1991, he has designed information management systems and conducted quantitative analysis for large-scale human rights data projects for truth commissions, nongovernmental organizations, tribunals, and United Nations missions in El Salvador, Ethiopia, Guatemala, Haiti, South Africa, Kosovo, Sri Lanka, Sierra Leone, and Peru. His most recent work, *Killings and Refugee Flow in Kosovo, March–June 1999,* was presented in testimony in the trial of Slobodan Milosevic at the International Criminal Tribunal for Former Yugoslovia.

**Vince Boudreau** is associate professor of political science at the City College of New York. His published works include pieces about protest and repression in Southeast Asia, with particular emphasis on Philippine, Indonesian, and Burmese politics.

**Christian Davenport** is associate professor of political science at the University of Maryland, College Park, as well as director of the Radical Information Project. Primary research interests include human rights violations, social movements, measurement, and racism. He is the author of articles appearing in *American Political Science Review, American Journal of Political Science, Journal of Politics, Journal of Conflict Resolution, Political Science Quarterly, Mobilization, Comparative Political Studies,* and *Monthly Review.* He is the editor of *Paths to State Repression: Human Rights Violations and Contentious Politics,* and he is currently completing two books, *Ballots and*

*Bullets: State Repression and the Promise of Democratic Peace* and *Killing the Afro, Killing the Fist: State Repression and the Black Power Movement.*

**Myra Marx Ferree** is professor of sociology at the University of Wisconsin. Her work focuses on feminism and women's movements, particularly in the United States and Germany, and on the emergence of transnational feminist networks. One of her specific interests is on discourses and how they construct realities for social movement actors.

**Ronald A. Francisco** is professor of political science at the University of Kansas. He works on the relationship between protest and repression and codes of interval data on both protest and repression.

**Hank Johnston** is editor of *Mobilization: An International Journal* and assistant professor of social psychology and social theory at San Diego State University. He is the author of *Tales of Nationalism: Catalonia, 1939–1979* as well as numerous research articles about protest in repressive states. Also, he has edited several collections of social movement research: *Social Movements and Culture* (with Bert Klandermans), *New Social Movements* (with Enrique Laraña and Joseph Gusfield), *Globalization and Resistance* (with Jackie Smith), and *Social Movement Frames* (with John Noakes).

**Ruud Koopmans** is professor of sociology at the Free University Amsterdam. Previously, he was senior researcher and codirector of the Research Group Political Communication and Mobilization at the Wissenschaftszentrum Berlin für Sozialforschung (WZB). He does research on immigration politics, European integration, and social movements. In the latter field, he has particularly worked on political and discursive opportunity structures, as well as on protest waves, with an empirical focus on cross-national comparative analyses. His publications include *Challenging Immigration and Ethnic Relations Politics* and articles in journals such as *American Journal of Sociology, American Sociological Review, European Journal of Political Science,* and *Revue Européenne des Migrations Internationales.*

**Mark Lichbach** is professor and chair of government and politics at the University of Maryland. A theorist interested in social choice and a comparativist interested in globalization, he explores the connections between collective action theories and political conflict, as well as the connections between collective choice theories and democratic institutions. He is the author or editor of many books, including *The Rebel's Dilemma,* and author of numerous articles that have appeared in scholarly journals in political science, economics, and sociology. His work has been supported by NSF and private foundations. He edits the University of Michigan's series on Interests, Identities, and Institutions in Comparative Politics.

**John D. McCarthy** is professor of sociology and director of the graduate program at Pennsylvania State University. His research interests include social movements and collective action, the sociology of protest, the policing of protest, and the sociology of organizations. Currently he is at work with Andrew Martin and Clark McPhail on a study of campus community public-order disturbances.

**Clark McPhail** is professor emeritus of sociology at the University of Illinois, Urbana-Champaign, where he continues to do research, write, and teach a seminar each year. He is the author of *The Myth of the Madding Crowd* and numerous journal articles and book chapters on the assembling processes that create temporary gatherings, the dispersing processes that terminate them, and the variety of individual and collective actions that compose the gatherings themselves. He was the Fulbright Senior Research Fellow to Great Britain in 1999–2000, where he developed criteria and procedures for analyzing videotapes of police and protester interaction.

**Carol Mueller** is professor of sociology in the Department of Social and Behavioral Sciences at Arizona State University West. She has also taught at Wellesley College, Brandeis, Tufts, and Harvard University. Her previous publications include *Frontiers in Social Movement Theory* (with Aldon Marvis), *The Women's Movements of the United States and Western Europe* (with Mary Katzenstein), and *Politics of the Gender Gap*. She publishes in the *American Sociological Review,* the *American Journal of Sociology, Social Problems, Social Forces, Mobilization, Public Opinion Quarterly,* and other social-science journals.

**Patricia Steinhoff** is professor of sociology at the University of Hawaii. Her most recent books are *Shie no Ideorogii* and *Doing Fieldwork in Japan,* which she coedited with Ted and Vicky Bestor. She is currently working on a book about how Japanese radical groups sustain and adapt their resistance to the state under varying forms of expression.

**Charles Tilly** teaches social sciences at Columbia University. His recent books include *Stories, Identities, and Political Change, The Politics of Collec-*

*tive Violence, Contention and Democracy in Europe, 1650–2000,* and *Social Movements, 1768–2004.*

**Gilda Zwerman** is professor of sociology at the State University of New York, Old Westbury. She writes about social movements and political violence in the 1960s and 1970s.

# Index

Khawaja, Marwan, viii
King, Dwight, 51
King, Jophm, xi
Kitcher, Philip, 228
Klandermans, Bert, 151
Koopmans, Ruud, ix, x
Kosovo, 189, 198
Krain, Mathew, xi
Kriesi, Hanspeter, x
Kuhn, Thomas, 227
Ku Klux Klan, 141
Kuran, Tumur, 70, 71

Labeling, 143, 146
Lafay, Marilyn, 154
Lakatos, Imre, 227
Laswell, Harold, xv
Law collectives, 97
Lawson, Tony, 237
Legitimacy, 160, 161, 164–67, 171–73,
    177–82, 184
Levi, Margaret, 239, 240, 241
Lewis, J., 87
Lichbach, Mark Irving, viii, xx, 65, 71,
    60, 65, 67, 70, 75, 76, 78, 229, 235,
    238, 240
Lichterman, Paul, 151
Linguistic resistance, 143, 144, 153
Lohmann, Susanne, 70
Lopes, Carlos, 61, 62, 63, 69
Los Angeles Police Department
    (LAPD), 28
Los Macheteros, 101
Loveman, Mara, 86
Lysistrata, 140

Malaysia, 38
Mandela, Nelson, 61, 64
Maney, Gregory, 154
Mao Zedong, 91

Marks, Gary, 36
Mass media, 9–10, 159, 160, 163, 182;
    and bias, 148, 154, 191, 203, 204;
    and censorship, 147–50, 155; cover-
    age, 148, 189, 194–97, 204; and
    mobilization, 10; and women, 147,
    154. *See also* Newspapers
May 19th Communist Organization,
    103
McAdam, Doug, xx, xiii, 87, 152, 228,
    235
McCann, Eamonn, 68
McCarthy, John, ix, xi, xvi, 151
McNeal, Robert, 66
McPhail, Clark, 151
Media. *See* Mass media
Meredith, Martin, 61, 64
Merton, Robert, 228
Miami Field Force (MFF), 7–8
Micro-cohorts, 89–94
Middle East, 102
Miethe, Ingrid, 154
Migdal, Joel, 38, 42
Miller, Richard, 227
Miller, Roger Leroy, 235
Milosevic, Slobodan, 189
Minsk (Belarus), 24
Mitchell, Neil, xi
Mobilization, 9–13, 213; and Internet,
    10–11; and mass media, 9–10,
    148–50; soft, xxiii; symbolic, 128;
    and technology, 12
Modular repertoires, 223
Montt, General Efrain Rios, 193
Moore, Barrington, 235
Moore, Will, viii, ix, xi
Morris, Aldon, 152
Movement for Independence (Movi-
    miento por Independencia), 103
Mueller, Carol, viii, ix, xi, xxvi